9XR2

11163   27

12111

D1569523

THE CRISIS OF MODERN ISLAM

THE CRISIS OF MODERN ISLAM

A Preindustrial Culture
In the Scientific-Technological Age

by
Bassam Tibi

Translated by

Judith von Sivers
Foreword by
Peter von Sivers

University of Utah Press
Salt Lake City
1988

Originally published as *Die Krise des modernen Islams:*
Eine vorindustrielle Kultur im wissenschaftlich-technischen
Zeitalter,
© C. H. Beck'sche Verlagsbuchhandlung, Munich 1981

Translation funded by Inter Nationes, Bonn, West Germany

Library of Congress Cataloging-in-Publication Data

Tibi, Bassam.
    [Krise des modernen Islams. English]
    The crisis of modern Islam : a preindustrial culture in the
scientific-technological age / by Bassam Tibi ; translated by Judith
von Sivers ; foreword by Peter von Sivers.
        p.   cm.
    Translation of: Die Krise des modernen Islams.
    Bibliography: p.
    Includes index.
    ISBN 0-87480-299-7
    1. Islam—20th century.   I. Title.
BP163.T5313   1988
297'.197—dc19   88-21934

CONTENTS

FOREWORD

Cultural pluralism is now firmly ingrained in the contemporary academic credo. Therefore, as Professor Bassam Tibi convincingly argues in this book, Orientalism can no longer be tolerantly regarded as the pardonable sin it was until a generation ago in Middle East studies. The West's alleged cultural-intellectual superiority can no longer be maintained. What was once considered an essential inferiority of Islamic culture is now, in the words of Tibi, at best a temporary technological "disadvantage." A healthy deflation of past displays of Western solipsism is the result, and there is little question that cultural pluralism has been most beneficial to the academic debate

Unfortunately, cultural pluralism does not merely ground unwarranted flights of hauteur; it also tends to encourage intellectual pedestrianism. If one is to be pluralistic, controversies are to be avoided rather than resolved. Immanentism becomes the only safe form of analysis; comparatism is too risky since, as the cultural-pluralist credo has convinced us, any claim for standards of comparison is merely a mask for ethnocentric prejudices. The credo of cultural pluralism appears to rest on two contradictory articles of faith: on the one hand it recognizes and respects pluralism of cultures and on the other hand it discourages systematic and substantive cultural comparisons.

One mark of distinction in Tibi's book is that it holds firmly to the first article of faith: there is nothing essentially lacking in Islamic culture preventing the Middle East and North Africa from achieving parity with the West. The current inequality is the product of specific adverse historical circumstances which, once redressed, will give way to a status of equality. The redressing is not easy since the effects of colonialism—the chief factor in the list of hobbling circumstances—are still strongly with us today. Nevertheless, since culture once was more advanced in the Middle East and North Africa than in the West, there is no inherent reason why it should not once again, given favorable historical circumstances, rise to at least a level of equality.

Another distinction of Tibi's book is that in it the second of the cultural-pluralist articles of faith is rejected out of hand. For Tibi it is obvious that the same intellectual tradition from which the contemporary

cultural-pluralist credo of the equality of cultures stems also provides us
with standards to compare the different cultures to each other. Although
this tradition, going back to the Enlightenment, is specific to Western
culture, Tibi rejects the notion that it cannot be used to measure other
cultures. In his view there is nothing insurmountably ethnocentric about
the core ideas of the Enlightenment.

Tibi's reasoning is on firm ground: the Enlightenment tradition of
equality is indeed indivisible. Once an inherent equality of cultures is
admitted, their visible differences cannot be relativized at liberty. Granted,
in the theory of cultural pluralism, differences lose the essentialized status
they possess in Orientalism, where they are assumed to be ineradicably
engraved in the "Oriental Mind." They become accidental differences prone
to change under different historical circumstances, as mentioned above.
But at the same time they still remain real differences which cannot be
relativized merely by reference to some immanent cultural logic. They
must be kept in the larger context of cultural pluralism, where they are
measured against the standard of equality. In other words, a reduction of
pluralism to relativism, as is the case in the second cultural-pluralist article
of faith mentioned above, destroys the cultural-pluralist context. Tibi op-
poses this reduction and presents himself as a spirited defender of the
Enlightenment tradition.

By being rooted in this tradition, the standard of equality in its
modern form has, admittedly, an ethnic origin. Yet in its original religious
expression this standard is shared by many cultures, and is the foundation
underlying the equality of all believers under God, and therefore is not
merely a culture-bound but also a general intellectual-spiritual dimension.
If it is outlawed as an unwarranted Western intrusion inimical to the
reestablishment of cultural authenticity, as is currently the case in Iran, not
only is a foreign import barred but also an indigenous intellectual-spiritual
dimension is suppressed. Conversely, if Western scholars in the name of
relativism content themselves with an immanentist analysis of the Middle
Eastern quest for cultural authenticity and refrain from measuring this
quest against the standard of equality, they miss the decisive point: the
tension between the intellectual limitations of authenticity movements and
the suppressed intellectual-spiritual dimensions such movements drive
underground.

The tendency toward cultural relativism is currently more pronounced
in Anglo-American than Continental-European scholarship. In the Anglo-
American context Enlightenment traditions are so far beyond contention

that they are often no longer remembered, even in academia. On the Continent, particularly in Germany, where Professor Tibi teaches, the Enlightenment is still a matter of public debate and its defenders therefore need to articulate it with great care. Among these defenders the so-called Frankfurt School, founded by Max Horkheimer and Theodor Adorno, is perhaps most prominent. As a scholar coming out of this school Tibi is strongly committed to a cultural-pluralist analysis within the Continental tradition. His application of this form of analysis to the contemporary Middle East and North Africa stands alone in the field as far as I know and should prove edifying to English-speaking readers who deserve to have an alternative to the cultural relativism prevalent in Anglo-American thought.

Tibi's analysis stands out for its different approach to the American debate on Middle Eastern and North African culture. Perhaps not all die-hard cultural relativists will be converted to Tibi's conclusions, but readers open to alternative views of the cultural process will certainly find his background in Continental cultural analysis stimulating. Since he adopted this analysis not by osmosis but by conscious choice, coming as he does from a Middle Eastern background, he is above any reproach of Western ethnocentrism. As a professor of international relations at the Georg-August University of Göttingen, with frequent teaching or research visits at Middle Eastern, African, and American universities, he is well-positioned to see both motes and beams, whether in Islamic or Western culture. Tibi's cosmopolitan experience provides him with excellent credentials to undertake a pluralist as well as substantive study of contemporary Middle Eastern and North African culture.

His book is a passionate plea for the transformation of what he describes as a preindustrial culture into a new culture more adequate to the demands of the "scientific-technological age." It is a plea for the secularization of Islamic religion, theology, and culture into what I would call a Middle Eastern/North African civil theology. I find his book fascinating because it is not merely an investigation of the contemporary cultural process in the Middle East and North Africa but also a guide by an avowedly secular scholar for contemporaries perplexed by the upsurge of Islamic fundamentalism and in search of a forceful expression of secular convictions.

As is well known, urbanization, mass education, and industrialization tend to both attenuate the grip of formal religion over some people and strengthen it over others in the Middle East and North Africa at the expense of the seminary-trained religious scholars who used to monopolize formal religion in the shape of clerical theology during the preindustrial period. Only Iran has sought to reverse the trend so far, although even there the theological debate is no longer the monopoly of the mullahs. In the majority of Middle Eastern and North African countries, secularists emancipated from the grip of formal religion generally look for a civil theology, whereas born-again believers, in the grip of a formal religion without trained scholars, look for a personal theology as an ethical base to provide the new rules of life demanded in crowded, desegregated, and youthful cities.

What is currently taking place in the Middle East and North Africa is that only scholarly theology and law are falling victim to secularization and in the process are being progressively superseded by civil or personal theologies vying with each other for cultural predominance. The uneasy coexistence of civil and personal theology is not only characteristic of the Middle East and North Africa but also increasingly of North America. Thus, Tibi's reflections are of great importance for the understanding of the fate of religion and culture in several parts of the world at the end of the twentieth century.

Culture and religion are too important at the end of this century to be left to the fundamentalist seekers of personal theologies who, in their pursuit of a perverse reverse Orientalism, re-essentialize culture in the Middle East and North Africa, thereby riding roughshod over the conventions of academic cultural relativism. Engaged scholars like Tibi, familiar with the full range of Continental and Anglo-American intellectual traditions, are needed to express what many academic Westerners dare not say about contemporary Islamic religion and culture.

Peter von Sivers

Department of History
University of Utah
1988

PREFACE TO THE ENGLISH TRANSLATION

This book, first published in German in 1981, is the result of an endeavor to approach modern Islam conceptually within the framework of contemporary social science. I am aware that some Muslims and scholars of Oriental studies alike may contest such an approach as being strange to Islam. I recall the comments of an American scholar about one of my papers on modern Islam offering the judgment that my social science approach hinders me from understanding the metaphysical and metahistorical meaning of Khomeini's concept of revolution. This has, however, never been a concern of mine nor of any serious social scientist. Along the line of the pathfinding sociology of religion of Emile Durkheim, I aim at understanding religion in the social process as it is incorporated into reality as a *fait social*—that is, a social fact. I, however, reject any reduction of religion to reality. Being committed to the philosophy of Ernst Bloch, I try to grasp the interplay between religion as the hub of human dreams and projections and the reality in which each religion is incorporated. This book has a larger story related to its content and, thus, goes far beyond a merely personal account of the author.

During the last years of the 1960s I had not yet made the decision to become a German citizen and, thus, belonged among the active post-1967 Arab authors who committed themselves to the option once articulated by Sadiq Jalal al-ʿAzm in his provocative book *Al-naqd al-dhati baʿd al-hazima*, first published in Beirut in 1968. Al-ʿAzm is a descendant of a prominent Damascene family. He completed his Ph.D. degree at Yale and was teaching at the American University of Beirut when he published the above-cited book, in which he argues that Arabs should ultimately learn to face the realities as they are, beyond the distractions of Arabic poetry. The point of departure of this anguished self-criticism was the crushing defeat of the June War of 1967. The years 1967–70 marked the hopes of enlightened Arabs, documented in a great literary production, of moving away from self-congratulatory attitudes and even more from "self-glorification to self-criticism." I belong to the group of authors active during that period, and published numerous articles in *Dirasat ʿArabiyya*, *Al-Adab*, *Al-ʿUlum*, *Al-Taliʿa* as well as in *Mawaqif*. In my own study of the literary Arabic debates of the *Nahda*, that is, from the 1850s on, I have never witnessed greater debates either in terms of the number of publications (books and articles) or in the degree of intensity as those that took place in the years 1967–70. However, the hopes of those years soon faded. Instead of the anticipated unfolding and spread of self-critical awareness, a neo-Islamic fundamentalism took over. The reappraisal of political Islam contributed to preaching the millenarian dream of *al-ḥal al-islami* ("the Islamic solution"). The crisis of the present could have been met by looking realistically and creatively to a feasible and better future; instead, a utopia retreating back to the seventh century has been installed. Backward-oriented dreams replaced the creative imagination of the hoped-for future. One of the pioneer propounders of *al-ḥal al-islami* employed this formula as the title of a widely read two-volume publication in which he dismissed our options as "imported solutions" (*ḥulul mustawrada*). This author, Yusuf al-Qurdawi, declared the restoration of the Islamic order of the seventh century to be the way out of the crisis. Qurdawi's book was to be followed by dozens of publications yearning for the same millenarian dream.

While the Middle East was experiencing the ordeals of the repercussions of the June War, which the Moroccan historian Abdallah Laroui accurately called the "epoch of crisis," I disassociated myself from active political writing and committed myself to scholarship in the German academic community. From the point of view of the intellectual enlightenment of the Frankfurt School of Social Science (Theodor Adorno and Max Horkheimer) in which I had my academic training, the Middle East has been hopelessly lost to the millenarian dreamers. It was within this context of choices that I acquired German citizenship and became a German university professor. However, the drive to understand why Arabs decided to adopt the millenarian dream as well as why they preferred the option of the "return of the sacred" never deserted me. I devoted my work to studying the role of religion in the process of development and began to realize that our generation has underestimated this role and failed to grasp its significance accurately. The second provocative book of al-ᶜAzm's, *Naqd al-fikr al-dini* ("Critique of Religious Thought," first published in 1969), is imaginative, but it revealed the failure of the critical political literature of the years 1967–70 to grasp the role of religion in its societal context. This assessment does not imply turning one's back on the Enlightenment, to which I was and still am committed. Wishful thinking should, however, be kept apart from the analysis of the real. This is the imperative to which I have subjected my thought ever since I disassociated myself from political commitments in the Middle East as well as in Germany. I refer to this context because it provides the background of the story of this book. These remarks also make clear that it was the June War and not the so-called Iranian Revolution that smoothed the way to political Islam. The Iranian case is a case of its own, which is not to say that this political event did not also have its effect on the Arab Middle East. Nevertheless, the idea of writing this book came to mind in 1977 before the Iranian Revolution took place. My personal background produced an identity crisis, bringing up a clash between the Islamic norms and values I had internalized in the course of my upbringing in my birthplace and home city of Damascus, on the one hand, and the intellectual approach of the Frankfurt School of Adorno and Horkheimer in which I had my academic training, on the other. The result of this identity crisis was an increased desire to grasp religion all the more firmly, without, however, being committed to it as a faith. The unshaken commitment to scholarship in the European sense of a straightforward pursuit of truth has been more meaningful to me than any faith, secular and religious alike. I have never given up my conviction that every human condition, including religion, can be subjected to scrutiny.

From the beginning it was clear in my mind that I would not be able adequately to come to grips with the object of my inquiry—modern Islam—within the confines of scripturalism, be it the convictional one of the Muslims themselves or the scholarly one of Oriental studies. Belief in Islam is not merely belief in a "text"—that is, in scripture (Qur'an and Hadith)—but rather a social fact, a *fait social* in the Durkheimian sense. Thus, the methodology of sociology of religion has been an essential part of my referential framework for the study of Islam. Being a scholar of international relations, I have always been aware of the fact that since the incorporation of the "abode of Islam" (*dar al-Islam*) into the modern international system a "world of Islam" of its own no longer exists, if it ever had existed before. The continuing widespread use of this term is indicative of an inaccurate perception of our world order by the scholars who use it. As a professor of international relations it has been part of my job for years to teach my students that the first international system of sovereign states in world history came about after the Peace of Westphalia (1648). One of the leading scholars in this field, Charles Tilly, discusses in his book *The Formation of Nation States in Western Europe* the historical process of the globalization of this international system: "The Europeans and their descendants managed to impose that state system on the entire world. The recent wave of decolonization has almost completed the mapping of the globe into that system." The "abode of Islam" is no exception. Most Muslims still perceive this system as a threat and fail to recognize that they have already become part of it. In this sense, modern Islam cannot simply be examined and conceptualized within the confines of the sociology of religion. International relations is the other discipline needed to help us understand the environment of "Islam" and the constraints, both internal and external, generated upon it.

The preceding comments make clear that this book is the result of an endeavor to study Islam in an interdisciplinary way, employing the research tools of social science with a focus on sociology of religion, developmental studies, as well as international relations. I am aware that I am breaking new ground in combining the study of culture (Islam as a cultural system) with the analysis of the structure of international relations and thus conscious of the potential for scholarly risks as well as of my own limitations. The majority of the students of international relations care little about "culture," viewing it as the terrain of anthropology. Anthropologists, for their part, view culture as if it were an island; only a few go beyond these confines in an attempt to grasp the specific environment which is today the international system. In combining the *Anthropologie Politique* of Georges Balandier with Norbert Elias's reconstruction of the worldwide historical *Prozess der Zivilisation* in this book I have tried to establish some preliminary conceptual ground on which to base my analysis of modern Islam. I have continued the work done in this book in the years since its publication in German in 1981. The result is my monograph *Der Islam und das Problem der kulturellen Bewältigung sozialen Wandels* (1985) which I hope will be available soon in translation.

From among my five monographs published in German in the course of the last two decades, this book has been the most difficult to write; and without the emotional support of my wife, Ursula, who created the necessary environment, this book could never have been completed. The scholarly response to this book since its first publication in German has been most encouraging. I would like to single out Barbara Stowasser's review in the *Middle East Journal*, not only because of the reviewer's generous assessment but also because this review contributed to drawing the attention of my American colleagues to this book, which might not have occurred given certain language barriers. I'm indebted to Barbara Stowasser for having done this job. The numerous reviews of the German version of this book strengthened my conviction that I have been on the scholarly "right path" (*sirat al-mustaqim*)—an Islamic term with a specific religious connotation that I am employing here in a secular scholarly sense.

A German reviewer coming from Oriental studies, who was among the very few contesting my approach, advanced the criticism that I, being a Muslim and writing in German on Islam, am addressing the wrong audience. Notwithstanding the fact that I do not have the least inclination to be involved in such polemics, I refer here to this attitude to emphasize the view shared even by Islam that scholarship has no cultural boundaries. The Islamic precept *utlubu al-ʿilm wa law fi al-sin* ("search for scholarship even in China") might have a different connotation from the European notion of *science and man*. Nevertheless, it indicates that scholarship as a human inquiry has no confines. Leaving this aside, I should mention that I have always included the issues addressed in this book in the numerous lectures I have delivered throughout the Middle East over the past years. The most controversial idea in this book, namely that the argument of secularization can be articulated in Islamic terms, was the major content of a paper I delivered at the First Islamic Conference on Islam and Civilization held at the ʿAyn Shams University in Cairo in November 1979. The paper was published in Arabic in Beirut (in *Qadaya ʿArabiyya*, 1980) as well as in English in Cairo in the proceedings of that conference (Cairo 1982, edited by Mourad Wahba). The major arguments of chapter six on Islam and social change were also published in Arabic in Beirut in issue number 2 of the journal *Al-Waqiʿ*. In other words, I have never avoided confronting a Muslim audience, readers and listeners alike, with the provocative, although scholarly, ideas presented in this book. Truth is always provocative and can only be evaded at the expense of truth itself.

A wide range of friends and colleagues in Europe and the Middle East, and in the United States as well, have supported my work. I feel obliged to omit the mention of any name since I cannot possibly mention them all.

As regarding this English publication I have to express my great gratitude to Peter von Sivers. He is among the colleagues interested in my work, and he invited me to deliver a lecture at his university in November 1984. In the audience was Norma Mikkelsen, an editor of the University of Utah Press, who later contracted to publish this book although other presses had been interested in it. My commitment to Peter von Sivers has been extended to Norma Mikkelsen and to the University of Utah Press.

The greatest credit goes to Judith von Sivers, who admirably translated the German text into accurate and sophisticated English. I am greatly indebted to all three, Peter and Judith von Sivers and Norma Mikkelsen, who jointly facilitated making *Die Krise des modernen Islam* available to a much broader, English-speaking readership.

The translation of the book from German was funded by a generous grant from *Inter Nationes*, Bonn, which I would like to acknowledge here with great gratitude. I am writing this preface at the University of Michigan Center for Near Eastern and North African Studies, where I am currently working to advance my expertise on modern Islam with a grant from the Rockefeller Foundation. My study of the political literature of Islamic revivalism (1970–85) within the framework of the University of Michigan Rockefeller Fellowship supports all the conclusions present in this book and even compels me to stregthen the emphasis of my finding. I am particularly grateful to Ernest McCarus, the director of the center, for providing me with the best possible working environment in Ann Arbor and for allowing me to be a guest in his own office and most of all for having discussed with me this Preface, notwithstanding his very busy schedule.

This is the second of my five German books which has become accessible in an English translation. I hope that it will be as well received as was the first translated book, *Arab Nationalism: A Critical Inquiry*, among readers and reviewers.

BASSAM TIBI

University of Michigan
Center for Near Eastern and
     North African Studies
Ann Arbor
February 1988

INTRODUCTION

ISLAM AS A DEFENSIVE CULTURE IN A
SCIENTIFIC-TECHNOLOGICAL AGE

The nature of a particular society is determined by its socioeconomic structure. But this structure is itself only a component of the social whole and, therefore, a society cannot be understood through socioeconomic analysis alone. Since societies are also sociocultural systems, both socioeconomic and sociocultural analyses are required if existing structures of domination are to be adequately explained. The wholeness of a given society is the creation of the intimate intertwining of economics, culture, and politics; and any attempt to divide it schematically into a socioeconomic base and a political or ideological-cultural superstructure, as is the wont of most marxisant writers, is a violation of its natural integrity. Economics, culture, and politics are the social structures which, taken together, constitute the totality of a society and must be understood in terms of their specific origins and their validating forms. Of course, there are always human beings operating within these structures, and although one would not want to assert that human actions are merely derived from social structures, nonetheless they need to be examined and analyzed if one is intent on making human action at least partially explicable. But, again, this is not to say that an interpretation of these structures can provide any sure footing for determining the nature of the human beings who live and act within them. What is necessary is a rigorous theory of society capable of providing both a nonschematic structural analysis and an adequate theory of action.

In this rather succinct way I have presented the methodological core of my analysis of Islam as a defensive culture in contemporary World Society. As Ernst Bloch warns us in his study on Hegel: "Feeble, insignificant thinking is seldom concise. It is wordy . . . [and] endlessly circles around a subject because it cannot seem to touch, perhaps does not really want to touch, the subject it has condemned itself to express. The more protracted the babble, the thinner the meaning and the more treacherous its condensation."[1] I have tried, not always successfully, to keep this caveat in

1

mind while writing this book and have abjured both shortcuts and detours on the path leading to my subject. The problem at hand cannot be dealt with properly either through a narrow politicoeconomic theory or through normative and subjectivist, sociocultural or anthropological procedures and *particularly* not through the exegetical and philological methods espoused by German Orientalists and other Islamic scholars of this persuasion.

The basic thesis of this book, compactly stated, is that, in the process of its colonial penetration of non-Occidental societies, European bourgeois industrial culture was transmogrified into what can only be called today's "World Society."[2] Europe was able to conquer and reorganize a large portion of the non-Western world with the power provided by a culture based on science and technology. To reduce this World Society (which is relentlessly shaping itself toward uniformity) to a world market dominated and explained by the movement of capital is a rather violent reduction, to my mind, of the actual processes underway today.[3] The convulsive events in Iran and throughout the Islamic world serve to reconfirm Max Weber's observations on the social power of religious convictions. A system of religious ethics, as Bloch insists, can have a peculiar historical power "in such a manner that economic structures are themselves eventually infused by a superstructure which acts autonomously to prepare the way for the entrance of cultural and religious elements. It cannot, however, create these elements by itself."[4]

Struggles and conflicts in our World Society take the shape of regional formations on all levels—economic, political, and cultural—of a given society. The central concern of this study is the worldwide conflict between the dominant scientific-technological Western European culture and the preindustrial non-Western cultures which enjoy only a very low degree of mastery over nature. World Society is not egalitarian because its structures are asymmetrical; or, as the Norwegian peace researcher Johan Galtung puts it, we live in a feudal world order.[5] There is no single, shared world culture relative to which European, African, or Oriental/Islamic variants could be recognized as distinct but equal. There is rather a dominant Western European culture whose superiority lies in its scientific-technological development and its high degree of mastery over nature.[6] Being predominantly preindustrial, non-Occidental cultures find resistance to Western domination difficult.

Furthermore, the economic, cultural, and political structures of non-Occidental societies were severely shaken by Western colonial penetration, and the process of ineluctable structural disintegration continues even today. Old structures have crumbled and no new ones have appeared to take their place. Students of social development call this situation "structural heterogeneity" and point out in their (unfortunately, too narrowly economic) analyses the parallelism which exists between modern and traditional economic structures.[7] Structural heterogeneity, however, is a far-reaching concept and can be observed in all spheres of society. Scholars encounter preindustrial cultural elements coexisting with phenomena of Westernization in every region of the Third World. A rather extreme example of this can be seen in the case of a Malaysian science student who calls on the help of a magician in order to pass his university exams.[8] Heterogeneity clearly exists in people as well as in structures.

The methodological starting point sketched earlier demands that an adequate theory of society take into account the identity of the human beings acting within social structures. The process of Westernization with its attendant disintegration of preindustrial social structures, when not accompanied simultaneously by a process of industrialization, produces people with damaged identities.[9] The family remains the primary source of socialization in all preindustrial societies. It is within the family that normative systems are internalized and a corresponding development of ego identification takes place. In school, and especially at the university, a secondary socialization process occurs. Modern educational institutions in the Third World contribute to the diffusion of Western scientific-technological culture but in a form shorn of its Western roots, as we shall see in this study. Unfortunately, the pernicious delusion that this education fosters social mobility and that it alone contributes to the modernization of society still reigns.[10]

The gap between the North (industrial) and the South (preindustrial) deepened during the 1970s. In almost all non-Western societies there was a turning away by the educated elites from the very Western European culture they had once so eagerly respected and internalized. Today even members of this Westernized educated elite regard Western culture in the same light—as ensnaring and threatening—as does the bulk of the non-Westernized population. In a situation such as this, people return to their autochthonous culture, reactivate it as the source of a social identity, and arm themselves with it against the menacing dominant culture. This reaction is hardly new or encountered for the first time in the 1970s; it is, in fact, as old as the first contact of non-Westerners with Western European culture in the framework of the emerging World Society. The only new element here is that the turning away from the dominant culture has become a mass phenomenon and, consequently, a political force. In this study I shall use the case of Islam to illustrate this process.

In the course of his investigation of fanatical behavior in mass movements Eric Hoffer found that his basic frame of reference was corroborated by movements in the Third World:

> The discontent generated in backward countries by their contact with Western civilization is . . . the result of a crumbling or weakening of tribal solidarity and communal life.
> The ideal of self-advancement which the civilizing West offers to backward populations brings with it the plague of individual frustration. All the advantages brought by the West are ineffectual substitutes for the sheltering and soothing anonymity of a communal existence.[11]

A mass movement arising out of an historical situation such as this cannot be understood unless it is recognized what "a refuge it offers from the anxieties, barrenness and meaninglessness of an individual existence."[12] The events in Iran are merely the latest confirmation of this. The modernization of Iranian society was despotically dictated from above and consequently produced a paroxysm of social change which counted among its excesses rapid urbanization (e.g., the transformation of Tehran into a metropolis of millions within a decade), the deracination of small farmers through migration, a corresponding deterioration of cities into slums, and so forth. Nikki Keddie has discussed how the two cultures—that of the Westernized elite and that of the Shi⁽i Islamic masses—coexisted, privileged and underprivileged, side by side.[13]

In Islamic societies Islam itself is the substance of an autochthonous culture, even though there is no uniform Islam. One of the central theses of this book is that Islam was originally an Arab religion which was adopted and assimilated by non-Arab peoples. Thus, there are, for example, distinctly Iranian, African, and Indonesian variations of Islam, each variant representing an autonomous cultural dimension. I shall rather mulishly insist on this despite the obstinate, even propagandistic, insistence of some Muslim scholars on the "unity of Islam,"[14] not to mention those official spokesmen who want to hold imperialism responsible for any internal Islamic discord.[15]

The revitalization of autochthonous cultures provides a defense against the threatening dominant culture. Anthony F. C. Wallace has demonstrated how religion can be simultaneously a cultural dimension, a political ideology, and a ritual of revitalization.[16] Political movements organized around resistance against a dominant foreign culture can be defined as revitalization movements. Just such a revitalization movement provided the impetus for and carried along the uprising against the Shah of Iran. Bryce Ryan has observed that revitalization movements are

expressive collective actions which aim at a comprehensive social reconstruction, often of a Utopian nature. Their central function in developing countries is to provide the organizing medium through which the general dissatisfaction with the status quo can be expressed and the mobilization of energy facilitated in order to make vast changes in the social order possible. . . . Such movements arise out of a diffused discontent [created by] oppression, discrimination, and prejudice. In most Third World countries these conditions were aggravated by [an] acculturative thrust to traditional institutions.[17]

A preindustrial culture which positions itself at the center of the resistance against penetration by a scientific-technological culture is a defensive-culture. In its current historical state, Islam is still a preindustrial culture. But one must bear in mind that Islam developed from its seventh-century religious founding into a sophisticated imperial civilization. Following the collapse of the Arab Islamic Empire, and the destruction of a nascent industrial revolution by Mongol military invasions in the thirteenth century, *the once highly developed Middle East* stagnated for centuries and today is considered a *backward region* in World Society.[18] Even Westernized Islamic scholars have adopted a defensive posture vis-à-vis the menacing dominant culture they reluctantly confront. Seyyed Hosein Nasr summarizes his reflections on this problem in the following way:

To conclude, it must be asserted categorically once again that to preserve Islam and Islamic civilization, a conscious and intellectual defence must be made of the Islamic tradition. . . . Muslims cannot hope to follow the same path as the West without reaching the same *impasse* or an even worse one. . . . The Muslim intelligentsia must face all the challenges mentioned here. . . . They must cease to live in the state of a psychological and cultural sense of inferiority.[19]

Another Islamic scholar, Muhammad El-Bahey, takes a similar position in order to emphasize that

since the beginning of the Western colonial penetration of Asian and African Islamic countries Islam has been confronted with a crusader mentality. This mentality is not identical with crusading Christianity but rather documents an attitude of revenge vis-à-vis Islam. . . . In addition to this confrontation Islam now finds itself in a struggle against an invasion of crusading intellectual currents, especially those of an atheistic Marxism.[20]

The passages quoted here are typical; defensive-cultural thinking is religiously dogmatic and makes no attempt to analyze the situation which engendered it. This defensive-cultural and religious dogmatism will be of particular concern in this study because it dominates the developmental process (see chapter 6). Although I do not share René König's ideas on developmental theory, nevertheless, his definition of "defensive-culture" strikes me as helpful:

> What was described as a counter- or contra-acculturation is clearly one of the most crucial consequences of cultural defense mechanisms; that is, a defensive-culture proper is produced, in which one's own and the foreign elements interpenetrate in an almost indissoluble way. . . . This defensive-culture always seems to become operative during times when an impasse looms and only redemption or destruction seem possible.[21]

Defensive-cultural mechanisms are a reversion to the autochthonous but are never free of the foreign influences against which they are in reality directed. The concept of an "Islamic Republic" is an excellent example of this. It was formulated by the Iranian Shi‘i clergy as a mobilizing political ideology for generating mass outrage against the despotic domination of the Shah; but the concept cannot be found in the dogmatic Islamic sources. A "republic" is a European form of government and is identical neither to the Sunni Islamic caliphate nor to the Shi‘i Islamic imamate.[22] The very term "Islamic Republic" betrays the character of contemporary Islam: it is a defensive-culture.

All versions of modern Islam are understandable only in the context of their confrontation with Western European culture as the masters and purveyors of the modern technological-scientific age. This confrontation has both political/economic and cultural/civilizational aspects. The fact that Muslims are condemned to being included among the peoples of under-developed regions of World Society has sunk deeply and bitterly into their consciousness since the nineteenth century. The bitterness is compounded by the recognition that Europeans are the people from whom technological-scientific culture has sprung.[23] Economic penetration of the non-European world during the age of colonialism was thus accompanied by cultural penetration. Non-European peoples have responded to the European challenge through defense, imitation, or integration of the new culture into their own heritage. Their own culture, although influenced by Europe (the concept of an "Islamic Republic" being an example of this influence), is mobilized for the purpose of self-affirmation vis-à-vis the dominant culture. In this sense the form taken by cultural retrospection in the Third World also must be seen as an expression of a defensive-culture.

After their conversion the Arab bedouins supplied the support and passion required for the expansion of the Islamic Empire, whereas Islam provided the religious foundation for the creation of a new high culture.[24] As the French Islamist Maxime Rodinson writes:

> A century after an obscure camel-driver named Mohammad had begun collecting a few poor Meccans round him in his house, his successors were ruling from the bank of the Loire to beyond the Indus, from Poitiers to Samarkand.[25]

Although the Arabs may have been culturally inferior to the peoples they conquered and Islamized, they should not be considered merely as invaders but rather as conquerors bearing a new religious message. Moreover, early Islamic culture "absorbed a rich measure of Greek thought, took over methods from Indian medicine, appropriated principles of administration . . . without . . . experiencing any uneasiness over the assumption of non-Arab or non-Islamic cultural elements."[26] The cultures of Byzantium and the Persian Sassanids were similarly incorporated into Islamic culture without friction. And here the question arises whether this phenomenon could reoccur today; could modern technological-scientific culture also be incorporated into Islam without friction? Arnold Hottinger, the leading German-language journalist currently reporting on the Middle East, has written: "A constructive mastery of modern life, founded on the basis of Islamic tradition, and developed further in a creative fashion—that is the task facing the Islamic world."[27] But modern Islam is a defensive-culture; nearly all literary products of Islamic thought in modern times have taken the form of an apologia and are devoid of creativity, a fact which cannot be attributed to any alleged deficiencies of the Muslim mind. European culture dominates World Society because it arose out of the Industrial Revolution. Johan Galtung suggests that the decisive point to note about the dependent relationship existing between center and periphery during the technological-scientific age is "the gap between two nations in terms of the level of their industrial manufacturing capabilities."[28] What is thus decisive is the composition of a specific culture and not so much the efforts of its individual members to be creative. The central question is whether Islam can be adapted to the exigencies of the industrial age without losing its original substance. Von Grunebaum, to my mind, seized on the essential point when he compared the possibilities of today's modernization, which he equated with "Westernization," to the assimilation and adaptation of early Islam to the "high cultures" that preceded it (for instance, the "Hellenization" of Islam) and came to the conclusion that "the imprint of Westernization which the last 150 years bear is completely different. . . . The aim behind the admission of Western influence was not the perfection of one's own possibilities, but rather the removal of a condition one perceived as backwardness."[29]

Western European culture is dominant because it has a technological-scientific base. The explanation for the backwardness of Islam can be reduced to the absence of this technological-scientific dimension. Given these rather simplified explanations the question must now read: in what way can a nonindustrialized culture be modernized without sacrificing its own character? Von Grunebaum remarks in his study on modern Islam that "the greatest difficulty the Muslim world has encountered in its struggle against Westernization can be found in the contradiction between the successful acceptance of a foreign goal and the inability to abandon the traditional point of departure."[30] The question of the compatibility of Islam and technological-scientific culture should be at the center of any religio-sociological investigation of Islam. The discussion of the connection between culture and religion in our time and of the reception of this epochal problem by Islamic scholars is intended to be part of the answer to this question.

PART ONE

INTERNATIONAL CULTURAL COMMUNICATION
IN WORLD SOCIETY AND ISLAM

The developmental gradient between the industrialized Northern Hemisphere and the underdeveloped Southern Hemisphere is an issue in the North-South conflict which cannot be reduced to an economic dimension alone because the conflict is also an intercultural affair. The structure of communication in World Society exhibits considerable inequalities (asymmetries). Modern Islam cannot really be understood without the background of World Society.

In this first section I shall discuss my conceptual approach to modern Islam and develop some of my central theses.

In chapter 1 I demonstrate how the type of cultural interaction usually described as acculturation determines the entire North-South gradient. In the course of colonial penetration, preindustrial, non-Western cultures slowly lose their autonomy and disintegrate. Modern Islam cannot be interpreted adequately unless the effects of Westernization, analyzed at length in chapter 1, are taken into account. In conjunction with the problem of "Orientalism and Occidentalism" the possibility of a world culture informed by technology and science will be discussed. This prospective world culture would be based on cultural pluralism and free from control by any dominating authority and thus could offer symmetrical intercultural communications.

In chapter 2 I work from the assumption that religions are also political ideologies in the process of social change in order to pose the question of which intellectual instruments should be used for the analysis of extra-Occidental ideologies to which Islam belongs. These ideologies can be understood only within an international intercultural framework.

In chapter 3 I analyze the acculturation process using the example of the modern Islamic Middle East and develop a three-phase periodic scheme in order to systematize the course of this process and explain why the present-day repoliticization of Islam must be seen as a form of counter-acculturation.

9

CHAPTER 1

ACCULTURATION, WESTERNIZATION, AND INTERCULTURAL COMMUNICATION IN WORLD SOCIETY

In the Introduction I emphasized that we live today in a World Society which not only bears the imprint of Western industrial nations but is also dominated by them. My plea for equality in World Society should not be viewed as morally exhortative since I am investigating existing structures of domination critically and trying to indicate how equality might be realized. As mentioned earlier, Europeans were able to conquer the world with the help of a culture based on their technological and scientific achievements. Culture is to be understood here not in a literary, but in a material way as a specific historical form of social reproduction. The elimination of hegemonial structures in World Society and their replacement by democratic structures are goals that cannot be achieved until the chasm separating industrial and preindustrial cultures is eliminated. This does not mean that European industrial culture should be proclaimed as *the* world culture but, rather, that technological-scientific culture should become a shared component of all cultures so that a technological-scientific world culture could develop. European achievements could thus be integrated into other cultures without cultural individuality being maimed or choked off altogether. The concept of culture is not instrumental. The question is whether the processes of acculturation occurring now in present-day World Society and the forms of Westernization proceeding from this acculturation can contribute to the goal set here. We know that the asymmetry dominant in all spheres determines the processes of intercultural communication. But it is nevertheless necessary to ask whether the existing structures of communication can effect positive changes.

This chapter contains the initial conceptual formulations to be used in this study of Islam as a preindustrial culture. The analysis will be carried out in three steps. First, the concept of acculturation will be considered in order to ease us into the second section in which I shall present a critical analysis of all those things usually associated with *Westernization*. The third section is devoted to the central thesis of this study: to explain industrial culture as a scientifically and technologically based culture.

By way of introduction it should be noted that "acculturation" is a loanword for "cultural contact." It has its own, quite specific meaning which cannot be easily or accurately rendered through this formulation. Cultural contact is a constant in human history (for example, the Hellenization of Islam). Acculturation, however, is a modern phenomenon. The concept describes the expansion of Western European culture into the entire world and its superimposition on non-European cultures.[1] This dominant culture has an industrial and technological-scientific base, whereas the dominated extra-Occidental cultures are preindustrial. The original acculturation process was, of course, an aspect of European colonial penetration of the non-European world.[2] The emergence of Westernized elites from the Westernized educational systems of the Third World was also a product of this process.[3] That an industrial culture is "superior" whereas preindustrial cultures occupy an "inferior" position in the intercultural process of communication in contemporary World Society is, needless to say, not a value judgment but a simple statement of fact. It merely confirms that Westernization occurs within the framework of an asymmetrical structure of interaction; that is, the international system is characterized not only by a socioeconomic asymmetry but also by a cultural asymmetry. However, to conclude from this that *every* Westernization is an act of cultural imperialism[4] seems to me to be quite problematical and ignores, among other things, the universal historical character of the contemporary intercultural process of communication as determined by World Society.

When the concept "technological-scientific culture" is used in this context the question arises of whether one should not simply strike the appellation "Western European" and speak only of technological-scientific culture, as Darcy Ribeiro has done.[5] Although I often refer in my work to a potentially universal technological-scientific culture, I must part company with Ribeiro when he uses the concept of culture instrumentally in order to filter it out from Eurocentric arrogance. Western European development brought forth not only modern science and technology but also a tradition of enlightenment and a specifically Western democracy. This component will be at the center of the discussion in the concluding chapter on "Orientalism and Occidentalism."

Processes of Acculturation in World Society

It was emphasized above that acculturation is not a traditional form of cultural contact in that the corresponding cultural framework exhibits a completely new quality: the new process takes place in a World Society unknown and unimagined in classical history. The Industrial Revolution thrust Europe into a heady position of dominance from which it could conquer and mold the entire world in its own image. Europe and, later, America constitute the center of this international system, whereas the nonindustrialized countries huddle on the periphery. Johan Galtung has observed of the World Society based on this asymmetrical system that "opportunities in the world are distributed extremely unevenly. Up until now this problem has been expressed through the concept of *under-development*."[6] This unequal distribution of opportunities has deep roots in the structure of world economy. Galtung calls the organization of this world "feudalistic" because it is a system which "rests on the combination of a concordance between [social] ranks and an interaction pattern which [in turn] is largely dependent on those of the highest rank."[7] With "concordance between ranks" Galtung means the existence of a system in which two kinds of agents act: the privileged (those in the highest rank) and the underprivileged (those in the lowest ranks). By "interaction pattern" Galtung seems to mean something existing between the two agents. "Interaction, both good and bad, is monopolized to an extent by those who occupy the highest rank in every respect." North-South affairs can be characterized by this interaction pattern. In peace research one calls individuals on the highest rank "top dogs," those on the lowest rank, "underdogs."

We can observe today a tendency toward increasing self-awareness on the part of representatives of the developing countries in international organizations. This state of affairs is connected with the fact that a certain portion of the underdogs have entered into the joy of being able to partake of top-dog privileges, especially in the area of education, as a result of the global systems of communication and the means of transportation available in contemporary World Society. These enlightened underdogs are always recruited from the Westernized elites. Galtung calls this interweaving within the structure of World Society, "equilibrium of ranks." The self-aware representatives of the developing countries are those underdogs who have enjoyed access to the education of the top dogs. In the course of their education they have encountered the universal ideal of the equality of man. This ideal, however, "is so fundamentally contradictory to the established feudal order that its days are now numbered."[8] Should the feudal order crumble, however, this should not be taken as evidence of the ruin of European Western culture, as Ribeiro suggests, but rather as the successful diffusion of this culture throughout the entire world, as we shall see in the third section of this chapter in conjunction with some of Norbert Elias's ideas. For it is precisely those Europeanized elites who, with the help of their Western education, were put into positions from which they could question the very order that produced them.

Given this, it seems useful to me to discuss the problem of acculturation using the work of a Westernized non-Occidental scholar, Samuel Kodjo, who completed his *Habilitation* at the University of Cologne. Kodjo is now a university professor in Nigeria, passing on the education he acquired at a European university to the next generation.

Kodjo uses the terms "center" and "periphery" without, apparently, knowledge of Galtung's center-periphery paradigm. For Kodjo the relationship between center and periphery is a relationship based on power. The power of the center is supported by the strength and centrality of its economy, which dominates the peripheral economy. This asymmetrical interaction can also be discerned in a cultural context: the economic center is "also a cultural and civilizational center and the economic periphery a cultural and civilizational periphery."[9] In cultural anthropology this type of cultural interaction is always described as a cultural contact with an imputed reciprocity. Kodjo suggests that expressions such as "cultural superimposition [or] planned cultural destruction"[10] be employed and notes, critically, that the aspect of domination (or asymmetry, as Galtung would say), which is included in this cultural contact under the conditions of colonialism, is shunted aside in most cultural anthropological studies.

The study of cultural contact between "inferior" and "superior" cultures is very complex and requires a multidisciplinary approach. ("Inferior" and "superior" are used in the sense of domination of one culture by another by means of the structurally acquired ability to do so.) In the first phase of cultural contact "more or less violent reactions [are] triggered," especially in the inferior culture. As is well known, the return to an autochthonous cultural heritage is one of the "violent reactions" of non-Western peoples and especially of those societies which once had produced a materially developed culture. Kodjo shows, however, that these reactions not only fluctuate but also slacken:

Then it becomes a question of gradual renunciation of the struggle for the salvation of the cultural identity which is largely identical with a psychological and cultural self-resignation. In spite of its psychological-cultural consequences for the group of individuals involved, this self-resignation, and at the same time self-projection into a foreign culture, is in all probability conditioned by the established, inflexible power system, its . . . social effects on the people of the area of contact, and, last but not least, by the duration of its effect.[11]

Westernization, however, means the "loss of culture" for the group involved "because the transfer of a culture is not usually accompanied by the transfer of its physical and economic determinants and relations. A foreign culture *intrudes practically*, however, whereas *conditions prevail that hinder the realization of its success*"[12] (that is, spread of the foreign dominating culture in the dominated culture).

These assertions of Kodjo's are in line with the attempt I made earlier to periodize the cultural history of the "underdogs" in World Society. I characterized *the first phase* of "violent reactions" as "revivalism." Anticolonial movements in this phase are movements of cultural revitalization.[13] *The second phase*, "self-resignation and self-projection into a foreign culture," is the phase of Westernization and the emergence of Europeanized elites. In the course of their Western education these elites internalize the values and norms of a highly developed society but have to live in a society lacking the "actual sociological substratum" (Mühlmann) for these norms. A normative Westernization takes place without a simultaneous structural Westernization occurring. Western education and the absence of possibilities for success produce the cultural anomie which Maria Mies[14] has investigated. Unfortunately, it seems that Kodjo has not read Mies's work. The cultural retrospection evident in the Third World today marks the *third phase*. People are in need of a cultural identity (whether a social or a group identity) which Westernization was not able to provide. "Cultural loss" (Kodjo) was a product of Westernization; and cultural retrospection, the best-known variant today being the repoliticization of Islam,[15] documents the reaction to this "loss of culture." Kodjo cites Balandier's concept of *chirurgie sociale* to express the plight of Westernized elites who are at home nowhere—neither in Europe, whose culture they have internalized, nor in Africa, from which they have been uprooted.

I concur with Kodjo in his criticism of cultural anthropologists. In my inaugural lecture at the University of Göttingen (see note 1, this chapter) I pointed out that they do not "put the factors of power and coercion decisively at the center of the discussion."[16] Furthermore, acculturation processes in the colonial context lack any reciprocity, and here again I am in agreement with Kodjo. But Kodjo limits the concept of acculturation so severely that it can only be used to express assimilation or even imitation:

Every cultural diffusion may be regarded as acculturation only if it is induced, accompanied and fortified by an unequal, one-sided power constellation; if this power . . . is an instrument of repression in the hands of a foreign group . . .; if the indigenous culture is despised by the foreigners; if the contact cultures display fundamental gradients between themselves . . .; if indigenous inhabitants feel unequal to the situations of contact and apathetically and hopelessly abandon the struggle for the preservation of their own cultural identity; and if no understanding is offered for the adoption of the foreign culture so that an enculturation [sic] which reflects the indigenous culture is made impossible, then a pure phenomenon of a mostly unreflected imitation emerges.[17]

Kodjo suggests that a differentiation should be made between the concepts *cultural diffusion* and acculturation. Although he is aware that any acculturation presupposes a cultural diffusion, according to Kodjo the concepts have to be "distinguished" from each other because cultural diffusion means that "without further specification [there is] spontaneity, freedom of choice, freedom of refusal, and feedback in the cultural contact"[18]—features he finds lacking in acculturation. Cultural enrichment cannot take place in a process of acculturation "especially since this [enrichment] can occur only if the indigenous culture is maintained and if foreign cultural characteristics are reinterpreted in a fixed and useful reference to the indigenous culture."[19] Cultural diffusion for Kodjo is always partial; it allows for selection, reinterpretation, and adaptation and thus makes it possible to transform the process of acculturation into one of assimilation. By contrast, acculturation is total: the superior foreign culture is grafted onto (*Okulation*) the ruins of the inferior indigenous culture. Kodjo emphasizes that "the colonial cultural contact, as Africa experienced it, presented a potentially whole character in the sense that almost no aspect of traditional African life remained unaffected by the phenomenon of colonialism."[20] In this quotation the clause "as Africa experienced it" has to be taken as a corrective for the entirety of Kodjo's remarks on the problem of acculturation. It was noted earlier that Kodjo views acculturation as "assimilation" and "imitation" and that he cannot conceive of any cultural enrichment through acculturation. This narrowing down of the concept of acculturation stems from Kodjo's generalization of the African case.

Uwe Simson has also done research on this problem and offers a theory for understanding the intercultural processes of communication in which the distinction between nonliterary and materially developed cultures is central. In the case of a nonliterary culture the superior culture does not

encounter elements in the inferior culture corresponding to its own; therefore, cultural penetration can be total, especially since this culture is
"confronted with cultural formations in state, economy, law, religion, etc.,
for which there [is] nothing corresponding in its own tradition."[21] By
contrast, cultural communication between the penetrating West and the
dominated but materially developed cultures, those of the Middle East, for
example, is distinguished by the fact that the dominated culture in this
case "is able, in principle, to set up in opposition to cultural elements of
the [nominal] partner corresponding elements of its own."[22] It is absolutely
essential that this differentiation be made if one is to investigate the cultural penetration of the non-Western world by the West without blunder-
ing into faulty generalizations.

Over against Kodjo's thesis of the total character of every acculturation,
another form of acculturation can be cited: that is, modern acculturated
Islam (Islamic modernism), which fulfills the criteria of voluntary decision,
selection, and reinterpretation of foreign and autochthonous cultural
elements.[23] But even for Africa the thesis of acculturation as imitation
cannot be maintained. The late developmental sociologist, Richard F.
Behrendt, distinguishes between passive-imitative and active-syncretistic
types of acculturation.[24] Many modern African ideologues point to a form
of acculturation in which elements from the foreign culture are selected and
reinterpreted within the autochthonous culture.[25] In all these acculturative
ideologies, however, the received elements remain dominant. Nevertheless,
Kodjo's contention that cultural norms are transferred but the conditions for
their success remain unrealized is correct and of central importance. The
consequence of acculturation is cultural anomie; only a normative Westernization but no corresponding social transformation has taken place.

In my inaugural lecture at Göttingen (see note 1, this chapter) as well
as in my study of the romantic developmental ideologies in West Africa
(see note 25, this chapter), I have been sharply critical, similarly to Kodjo,
of acculturation and cultural penetration in the colonial context. However,
my criticism is not aimed at European culture but at the European colonial
system. The diffusion of European culture in the non-Occidental world can
be correlated with social progress, especially considering that Europe went
through a period of enlightenment unknown in the non-Occidental world.
*But the European colonial system has never pushed for a cultural diffusion in
the sense of this enlightenment, even though the colonial ideology of a "mission
civilisatrice," together with a prohibition of the writings of Rousseau and
Montesquieu, was promulgated.*

The principles of the Enlightenment and the French Revolution, although authentically European in origin, can no longer be regarded as something peculiarly European; they are universal and no longer restricted to a specific national culture. To deny this would be tantamount to asserting that basic human rights, as developed for the first time in human history and established as supreme values during the European Enlightenment, are solely European and that advocacy of them would constitute a call to mimic Europe. Readers of newspapers will remember how the Islamic clergy in Iran denounced those who demanded a constitutionally anchored freedom of the individual vis-à-vis the state as imitators of Europe and enemies of Islam. Unreflected criticism of Europe, and of acculturation, as often exercised by Westernized non-Occidental intellectuals in their search for identity, can lead to great suffering. Westernization is by no means synonymous with "cultural loss" or even "cultural death," as the Westernized intellectual Kodjo[26] emotionally insists.

The Form and Content of Contemporary Westernization

Non-Western people became acquainted with Western European culture through the agency of colonial penetration; thus it appeared to them as the culture of the rulers. As colonizers, the Europeans represented the world's "upper stratum" (to use Norbert Elias's term), and they remain the "upper stratum" even today. If a Westernized African intellectual pillories Western European culture through the medium of that culture (that is, using the scholarly methods acquired from a European education and his European *Habilitation* as a platform), this is perfectly understandable given the "international system of stratification."[27]

In order to give a just answer to whether *every* Westernization is culturally imperialistic we first have to explicate the thesis implicit in the question: there is probably no *Westernization* as such, but rather different forms with correspondingly different contents. The task, therefore, is to demonstrate that talking in general terms about the phenomenon of Westernization as an intellectual, psychological phenomenon, without classifying it within the structure of World Society, betrays an undiscriminating mind. If the proper methodological consequences are drawn from this postulate, Westernization can be classified in three historical forms:

Colonization and Westernization. Galtung is justified in criticizing the analytical confinement of Marxist theory, which collapses all spheres of life to a one-dimensional, economically determined perspective. In his theory of imperialism Galtung distinguishes structurally among several equally important types of imperialism, cultural imperialism being but one among five.[28]

Galtung's categorization can help us understand that colonial penetration was not only a socioeconomic but also a cultural phenomenon. Colonization was in its time described as an acculturation;[29] the missionizing of Africa may also be classified under this rubric. The German missionary and theologian Gustav Warneck was decisive in setting the direction to be taken by those carrying the colonial, mission-supported cultural message: "wherever the Christian mission is taken, it opens a new epoch of spiritual life."[30] The goal of this patriotic missionizing is both clear and unconcealed: if it "contributes to a reconciliation of the indigenous people with the foreign regime so that they eventually submit to it voluntarily, then a great service has been rendered to the Fatherland."[31] Johanna Eggert, who has dealt with mission schools in Africa, comes to the conclusion that these schools had the function of guaranteeing "the procurement of labor outside the mission areas."[32] Eggert is of the opinion that "without the mission schools . . . the solidification of European-oriented economic and political structures between the two world wars would have been delayed considerably."[33]

According to Galtung's typology cited above, one has to differentiate among five types of imperialism (economic, political, cultural, military, and communication). Each type is convertible into another, with a "spill-over" effect. For example, cultural imperialism can be transformed into economic imperialism: "The advantages which can be derived from one type of imperialism must be convertible at any time into the other types."[34] We have seen with the example of cultural missionary work how the advantages of cultural penetration (Westernization) can be transformed into economic ones.

In this regard we can also point to the findings of the French anthropologist Gérard Leclerc, which demonstrate that acculturation in the colonial age was a part of modern colonialism:

Whoever refuses to recognize the concrete characteristics of this acculturation, that is, its colonial traits as well as the specificity of acculturation and modern "change," will also be blind toward the specificity of modern colonialism. Whoever judges colonialism in the sense of change or a phase of industrialization . . . misjudges and "banalizes" the aspect of deculturation and destruction of national cultural characteristics which is so apparent to those colonized.[35]

Certainly colonial penetration has contributed to the diffusion of technological-scientific culture, albeit unintentionally and indirectly, so that preindustrial cultures were either convulsed or dissolved by this diffusion, as we shall see below. A qualification should be mentioned here, however: Westernization, as goaded forward by colonization, has to be regarded as historically retarding.

Westernization through the Education of "Bridgehead Elites." Johan Galtung coined the term "bridgehead elites" in order to indicate how structural dependence can be maintained today without a military presence. The elites characterized by this term are those who have interiorized, in the course of their Westernization, the norms and values of the dominant nations and who defend the interests of the foreign culture rather than those of their own society. Galtung stresses that "the center of the principal nation has a bridgehead in the periphery and it is, to be sure, a well-chosen one: namely, in the center of the peripheral nation. This bridgehead is established in such a way that the center of the periphery is bound to the center of the center; the bond being a harmony of interests."[36]

In this context Westernization is functionally employed to produce bridgehead elites. An advocate of this strategy, Dieter Oberndörfer, explains it thusly: "An increasing renunciation of the deployment of armed force at the present time is, for instance, balanced by the requisitioning of cultural and political means in order to enforce foreign policy ideas."[37] To be sure, Western European culture has given birth to the first genuinely democratic culture in the history of the world, but a Westernization that is only supposed to replace the deployment of military force can never have as its final objective an expansion of the European democratic tradition.

A former student of Oberndörfer's who has an insider's familiarity with this study of the system-conforming elite describes it thus:

If it is possible to successfully influence the norms of the elites, control of social change is virtually secured. The promotion of the educational system furthered by the principal centers has this motivation: to the degree that they have interiorized "modern" . . . values the satellites will obey. The adaptation of the elites is followed by the disciplining of the masses, consequently by the peaceful integration . . . into the structure of the needs of the principal centers.[38]

Westernization as Propaganda for the Center's Export Industry. Foreign cultural policy financed through public means could make a contribution to the diffusion of Western European culture in non-European areas of the world by facilitating fruitful intercultural communication. Unfortunately, as Maria Mies discovered in the course of her research work in India, foreign cultural policy is generally employed functionally as a pillar of foreign policy and instrumentally for the export of industry from the industrial nations. From discussions with those cultural functionaries responsible for implementing this policy, she came to understand their attitudes, which can be summarized as follows: "At some time the work abroad has to pay off concretely; at some time and in some way it has to benefit our economy."[39] This declaration gave rise to Mies's observation that "as during the period of early colonialism the missionary always followed on the heels of the conqueror, so German cultural institutions follow German business as it expands into the countries of the Third World."[40] This is not a polemical sentence but a conclusion drawn from empirical field research.

As Mies expresses it:

The results of my investigation have . . . demonstrated that the teaching of the German language has contributed toward directing the attention of a portion of the urban middle stratum to the products of German industry and thereby to the increase of market chances for German products in India. On the other hand, the teaching of German has [also] assisted in the distribution of German technology and German know-how in India.[41]

Mies confirms that Indians develop certain aspirations, especially consumer demands, in the course of learning the German language. She notes critically that "the teaching of German has done its share in strengthening the seductive [lure] of the Western land of milk and honey and has thereby diverted the attention of the educated groups from the problems of their own country."[42] That the relationship of Indians to the German language is a materialistic one is due to the social milieu in which they learn German; therefore, Mies proceeds with more leniency than do some authors in their attempts to come to terms with German cultural activities abroad. Instead of demanding an abolition of the teaching of German altogether, she pleads for a modification of the current social milieu in which German is taught. For, as she says, "the learning of a new foreign language can certainly play a fruitful role in that it can provide an impetus for new ways of thinking and set in motion a critical discussion with a foreign social reality." But this is possible only "if a language is no longer seen as part of the economic and cultural export of a central power or as a means for enlarging and securing its own economic and political sphere of influence."[43] It is not only in India that this penetration remains the highest guiding principle for Western cultural policies abroad, in spite of promises to build up "partnership relations," but also in most of the Third World as well.

The Process of Civilization and the
Future Scientific-Technological World Culture

In the preceding remarks I have attempted to elucidate how acculturation is to be distinguished from previous forms of cultural contact in terms of its global character: acculturation now takes place within a World Society which encompasses the entirety of humankind. This World Society represents a social formation characterized by domination and asymmetry. The inhabitants of the Western Hemisphere constitute the upper stratum of World Society and dominate non-Westerners through their scientific-technological culture. Equality and democracy can be achieved in World Society only through an elimination of this asymmetry: that is, through the dissemination of scientific-technological culture throughout the entire world. The so-called North-South gradient can be placed within this framework. The significance of the North-South dialogue, which aims at leveling this gradient through peaceful means, can be interpreted within the same framework; a fact of which many politicians of the Third World are unaware, otherwise they would not plead simultaneously for the North-South gradient to be removed but for their preindustrial culture and social structures to be preserved.

The process of civilization is as old as human history and is not confined to a specific continent. However, if the concept is applied specifically only to modern world historical development, then it must be conceded that the process of civilization achieved a historically unique zenith only in Europe. This process has been extended from the Western Hemisphere into a worldwide process of civilization.

Norbert Elias's outline of a theory of civilization stands out as the most coherent of the numerous attempts to explain this process. For Elias, the process of civilization means "the transformation of human behavior and perception in a very definite direction."[44] Although it is true that this process is not unilinear or determined, neither is it diffuse nor without structure. Modern, differentiated society, in which the process of civilization is admittedly still awkward, has nevertheless reached a climax of sorts and is distinguished from a self-sufficient warrior society by the fact that it exhibits a regulative principle interiorized by its members; in the latter "the principle of warlike or predatory attack" prevails.[45] Behavior exhibited in the dense traffic of a modern metropolis illustrates this system of self-regulation. External restraints are translated into self-restraints and the entire sphere of instincts and emotions is regulated by self-control. The prerequisite for such a development is the emergence of a central authority possessing a monopoly on power. This is not peculiarly European; the phenomenon of the emergence of a central power controlling larger regions is attested to in the history of Asia. It is, however, specifically European that this central power is not despotic but is itself curbed by being tied to "legal norms" (*gesatzte Regeln*), as Max Weber would say. The process of civilization is an historical process and it is within this framework and particularly through competitive pressure that a differentiation of social functions comes about. The legalization of power as a factor in the process of civilization is a purely Western European phenomenon, the advantages of which, unfortunately, are enjoyed only by the people of the Western Hemisphere. [46]

Although Norbert Elias interprets civilization as an alteration of human behavior, he also emphasizes that this transformation is conditioned by social development and is not a simple subjective change. The transformation of behavior

in the sense of an ever more differentiated regulation of the entire psychological apparatus is determined by the course of social differentiation, by the progressive division of function and by the expansion of the chains of interdependence, into which, directly or indirectly, every regulation, every expression of the individual is inevitably incorporated. [47]

This *social differentiation* and the *division of function* connected with it are the result of the development toward a modern industrial society which has taken place in Europe, where "the individual is largely protected from sudden attack, from the shocking invasion of physical violence into his life. But at the same time he is himself forced to repress his own passionate outbursts which might impel him toward bodily attack on others." [48] According to Elias it is also peculiarly European that this "metamorphosis of external social restraints into internal self-restraints into an automatic regulation of instincts and an emotional control which have now become habitual . . . in the West is now occurring with ever-growing frequency among the masses." [49] Although it is true that stratification exists in contemporary society, it is nonetheless egalitarian in that even as the *contrasts decrease, the variations simultaneously increase.* [50]

Civilizational processes have taken place, as I have intimated above, not only in Europe but also elsewhere:

What makes the process of civilization in the Occident a special and unique phenomenon is the fact that in the West certain things were established, such as complex functional divisions, stable power and tax monopolies, interdependencies and competitions extending over such vast expanses and among such large human masses *as had never before been seen in the history of mankind.*[51]

Without industrialization and the technology spawned by it, this civilizational mobility would be unthinkable. Modern Western European culture is a scientifically and technologically based industrial culture.

This process of civilization began and reached its zenith in Europe, and takes place today within a global framework. Europe extended itself through colonial penetration and became the center of the emerging World Society. The European colonialists pursued their own economic advantage, of course, in their exploitation of non-Western peoples, but "they strove, for the most part, *without desiring it*, toward a reduction of the discrepancies in social power as well as in behavior between colonizers and colonized."[52]

As we have seen earlier in this chapter, World Society is characterized by global systems of communication and transportation which permit people in the periphery both to hear and to experience tangibly how people in the center live. The Westernized elites in non-Western societies are a product of a dense world-societal communications network. Norbert Elias also emphasizes this development in his theory of civilization:

Today, from Western society, as a kind of upper stratum, Western "civilized" modes of behavior are widely spread into areas outside the Occident. As was the case inside the Occident itself, models of behavior spread from this or that elevated stratum, from certain courtly or commercial centers.[53]

Elias is right in describing modern industrial civilization as "the distinguishing characteristic which marks Occidental superiority,"[54] which becomes in the course of intense competition between non-Occidental countries a *universal sign of superiority.* Just as the disparities between the upper and lower strata within Europe have been reduced in the process of civilization, so today the distance between the Western European upper strata (top dogs) and the non-Western lower strata (underdogs) is shrinking as the process of civilization in World Society moves ineluctably on. "This incipient recasting of Oriental and African attitudes in the direction of European standards of behavior, *represents the most recent discernible surge of civilization.*"[55]

However, the question arises here whether the future world culture will indeed be only a technological-scientific one; that is, must modernization be necessarily equated with Westernization as Norbert Elias suggests? At the beginning of this chapter I quoted from Darcy Ribeiro, who also

proposes a hypothesis. Ribeiro reduces civilizational processes to technological revolutions and thus regards modern culture as the technologically most
developed because it arose out of the Industrial Revolution. According to
Ribeiro this industrial, technological development is more a question of a

natural and necessary phase of human progress which would have arisen inevitably
somewhere, perhaps in the Islamic, Chinese or Indian milieu. That it spread first
in the West permitted the Europeans to Europeanize a large portion of the rest of
mankind.[56]

Thus, for Ribeiro this development is not a specifically European one
and to insist that it is constitutes an "ideological mystification," since it
is only a "fortuitous" development.[57] Ribeiro's position can be understood as a legitimate emotional reaction to what is clearly an intolerable
European civilizational arrogance. However, it is historically incorrect,
because Western European culture cannot be mechanically reduced to a
technological, industrial revolution, as we shall see in the concluding section of this chapter.

Even though Ribeiro's argument contains reactive elements, he never
succumbs entirely to the Third World romanticism (*tiers-mondisme*) so con-
spicuous among Third World intellectuals. Ribeiro envisages a future
scientific-technological world culture on the point of unfolding, which will
"unify all of mankind into a single system of interaction" and which
will be devoid of any content that can be solely associated with Europe. The
evolution, he says, will

homogenize all the peoples of the world and finally bring them together in one
civilization embracing all mankind. It will no longer be possible to identify this
civilization with one specific race or cultural tradition. For the first time mankind
will be in a position to control and direct the evolutionary process itself.[58]

"Orientalism" and "Occidentalism"

Up to now we have been considering *acculturation* as a modern and, in terms
of world history, a unique form of cultural contact. It is a concept which
expresses the penetration of the entire world by a single culture. As I have
repeatedly emphasized, Western European culture is dominant because it is
industrial; other cultures are dominated because they are still preindustrial. It has been argued that this fissure in World Society can be
conquered if non-Western peoples integrate the new culture into their own.
The form and content of the Westernization of non-Occidental areas have

been analyzed and it has been established that they by no means contribute in any vital way either to overcoming underdevelopment or to democratizing World Society. The analysis of the civilizational process by Norbert Elias has shown us that the upper stratum of this World Society has no desire to bridge the existing chasm, even though this stratum contributes to the beginning of "the same transformation of social functions and thereby the behavior, the whole psychological apparatus, of the non-European countries grafted onto extant civilizations forms."[59] It is inevitable that the ruse of reason (*List der Vernunft*) produces a critique of domination when Western European culture comes to non-European regions of the world.

Seen from historical and philosophical perspectives, European expansion into the entire world may appear as a global process of civilization. For those non-Western peoples directly concerned, however, this inevitable expansion means the eruption of a new form of violence, modern technology, into their lives and the violent dissolution of their former way of life. Westernized non-Occidental intellectuals, who learn in Paris or London that *humanitarianism* is the principal content of European Western culture, but who later observe how the European colonizers establish their domination outside Europe at the point of a bayonet, find it impossible to take European culture as a model for their own societies.

The knowledge which helped Europe conquer the world includes more than just the disciplines of the natural sciences and technology, of course. During colonization, for example, the anthropological concept of the "savage" played an important role. Furthermore, in the Islamic Orient a fully developed colonial tradition of scholarship exists which the American literary critic Edward Said calls "Orientalism." "The Orient was created— or, as I prefer to express it, orientalized. . . . The relationship between Occident and Orient rests on power, on dominance and on varying degrees of a complex hegemony."[60] Western Orientalist scholarship remains rooted even today in this tradition. European scholars of Islam regard themselves as the masters of Oriental studies: they alone are in a position to attain a scholarly understanding of Islam. I am quite well acquainted with the Orientalism which Said defines as a "Western style of domination, intended to restructure and acquire authority over the Middle East,"[61] not only from literary sources but also personally through acquaintance with the older "Orientalist" scholars in the Federal Republic of Germany. In order to be just I have to mention that some younger colleagues are visibly endeavoring to liberate themselves from this Orientalist tradition.

Islamic reactions to the scholarly despotism of the West have been disparate and contradictory. Unfortunately, even Arab intellectuals, such as Said, are not immune from these ambiguous responses. At the end of his book Said states unequivocally: "I have hoped that I could show my readers that the answer to Orientalism cannot be Occidentalism."[62] Among most Islamic scholars reactions take on a decidedly culturally defensive form, whereas Said draws deliberately on "emancipatory" European scholarship (for example, Michel Foucault, Antonio Gramsci, among others), in order to understand "Orientalism." Despite this, Said has a distinct tendency to stretch the argument too far. The Damascene critic of Said, Professor Sadiq Jalal al-ʿAzm, suggests that the work of Said be called "Orientalism in reverse."

Two professors at the University of Medina, ʿAli M. Garisha and Muhammed S. Zaybaq, simply call the twentieth century the Age of Ignorance (*jahiliyya*)—a term generally used in Islamic historiography for pre-Islamic history. At the center of their criticism is not European domination as such but rather industrialization:

The civilizations of the twentieth century, or more precisely, the "cultures of ignorance," are constructed upon machine and industry, and regard man as being of secondary significance. Islamic civilization, however, puts man in first place; for Islam, man is the producer.[63]

The answer to the question of why the Muslims belong today to the backward peoples of the world lies, for these two Muslim scholars, in the fact that the Islamic community "has strayed away from the Holy Scriptures and the orthodox tradition (*Sunna*) of their Prophet."[64]

During my stay in Cairo for the First Conference of Islamic Philosophy on Islam and Civilization in 1979, I observed that "the Islamic solution" is regarded as the only way out of the crisis. It has not yet been recognized that the lack of a scientific-technological culture and the attendant structures of underdevelopment are problems which must somehow be surmounted. The book series by Yusuf al-Qurdawi, *Al-Hal al-Islami (The Islamic Solution)* typifies this situation. In the second volume of this series it is emphasized that

the Islamic solution means that Islam is both the orienting maxim and the guide for the community in all areas of life, material as well as intellectual. The Islamic solution means that the entirety of life is molded into a fundamentally Islamic form and character.[65]

The Islamic solution is developed further in the course of the argument and because of their authenticity I shall quote his arguments verbatim:

The Islamic solution means the establishment of a totally Islamic society. The first prerequisite for this is the establishment of a totally Islamic form of government. . . . In order to build this Islamic form of government or state we must . . . bring society back under Islamic protection (*hazdira*) . . . and cleanse it of all foreign bodies and secret germs which have penetrated it. . . . An Islamic society can only be governed islamically. To accept secular, nationalist, socialist or liberal democratic forms of government in Islamic society is a serious mistake because to do so is to overlook the fact that the union of religion and state is one of the characteristic features of Islam. . . . This is especially important in this age in which modern technology and the apparatus established with the help of science provide the state with enormous energy.[66]

If we disregard the culturally defensive features of these passages it can be stated again that Islam remains a preindustrial culture. We shall see in chapter 6 that preindustrial societies which can display only a modest mastery over nature rely heavily on a correspondence between the sacred and the political. In the passage quoted above the fear expressed of the "enormous energy" possessed by science and technology goes hand in hand with the emphasis on the necessary correlation between the sacred and the political.

In spite of my complete sympathy for, and concurrence with, Said's criticism of Orientalism, I cannot share his anti-Western perspective. The future of the Middle East cannot be borne by a preindustrial culture. Neither Europe nor the European traditions of enlightenment and democracy are to be condemned but rather those European hegemonial powers which have promulgated, in the past as in the present, a Europeanization of the non-Western world in words while preventing it in deeds. Modernization is not merely a transformation of norms. It means nothing less than the industrialization and democratization of the Third World.

Max Horkheimer, one of the most rigorous critics of bourgeois society in Europe, nevertheless feels compelled to defend it. For

in spite of its ominous potential, in spite of all its internal and external injustices, it still constitutes an island in time and space, the end of which in the ocean of tyranny would also signify the *end of culture*—the island to which critical theory still belongs.[67]

For Horkheimer it is

the right and duty of every reflective individual to measure [European Western culture] according to its own concept of itself, to take a critical attitude toward it yet remain faithful to its ideas, to defend it against the fascism of the Hitlerian, Stalinist or any other kind.[68]

Setting Horkheimer's arguments up against Ribeiro's here, we must agree with the former that the aspired-to world culture of the future cannot be defined in merely instrumental terms as a technical-scientific culture. An industrial society is not a value in and of itself and should not be set up as an abstract goal. The industrial societies of the West suffer today under the social manifestations of overindustrialization: environmental destruction and alienation of the individual. We need to be careful not to allow this criticism to deteriorate into an anti-industrial romanticism which can be found today not only in the Third World (see note 25, this chapter) but also in the youth movements of industrialized societies under the guise of pseudopolitics. Our criticism should rather be concentrated on the fact that the scientific-technological component of contemporary "industrial culture" has become detached from the genuinely European, historically democratic tradition. The intercultural, pluralistic, and technical-scientific world culture envisaged for the future should not be defined instrumentally as Ribeiro has done, but rather humanistically, along the lines of Barrington Moore, within the tradition of the history of democracy which, at this point in the history of humankind, has reached its unique climax in Europe.

If we follow the lead of Moore, who has investigated the forms of government of different models of social development in Europe, America, and Asia, it becomes clear that Western feudalism produced institutions which lent themselves to the possibility of a democratic development, contrary to other non-European social structures. The most important aspect in this development

was the growth of the notion of immunity of certain groups and persons from the power of the ruler, along with the conception of the right of resistance to unjust authority. Together with the conception of contract as a mutual engagement freely undertaken by free persons . . . this complex of ideas and practices constitutes a crucial legacy from European medieval society to modern Western conceptions of a free society.[69]

Such a protection of the individual from the arbitrariness of state authority is, according to my own research, unknown in any culture other than the European. Islam, for example, knows neither a tradition of the right to resist state arbitrariness nor an institutionally controlled obligation to observe legal norms[70] (Max Weber: "*gesatzte Regeln*"), although Islam belongs among the few non-Western cultures which have at their disposal a highly developed legal tradition.[71]

In order to prevent misunderstandings, I would like emphatically to repeat my thesis: I am not pleading in the abstract for the future history of the world to take the form of a technologically and scientifically based culture in industrial society. The totalitarian system of the Soviet Union is, for example, technical-scientific but it denies the individual any personal liberty outside the confines of the state. The process of civilization has to be understood, in Norbert Elias's sense, as a Europeanization of the world. *This means a reduction of contrasts and a simultaneous augmentation of uniqueness, and thus not an "aping" of Europe,* as Frantz Fanon assumed. Herder once envisaged a free World Society in which asymmetries could be overcome and different but equally entitled cultures would live together within the framework of a cultural pluralism. But these cultures would all possess in common the technical-scientific dimension and perhaps the Western European democratic tradition as well, institutionalized on a world-wide scale.

However, neither the United States nor the Western European countries are contributing in any way to the realization of such a free World Society. They continue as they always have to interpret Westernization as the establishment of bridgehead elites in the periphery and not the humanizing of the Third World through industrialization and democratization. In order to buttress the above quote from Horkheimer, that one must measure Western culture according to its concept of itself and at the same time stand behind it, I want to quote the Westdeutscher Rundfunk reporter Ansgar Skriver who, after his return from the United Nations Conference on Trade and Development in Manila, described the behavior of the Western countries there in these words:

The Western industrial countries, in spite of their obvious intellectual as well as material superiority, have still not been able to devise a long-term policy of development oriented toward the future and peace. . . . The self-assured and often paternalistic bearing of the rich touches upon fears born of too many colonial experiences.[72]

It is not Westernization that has to be criticized but the policies of the Western industrial nations which have not only *not* contributed to Westernization (in the sense developed here of a process of civilization) but also have actually undermined this process. The United States as well as

Western Europe are only rhetorically committed to the modernization of the Middle East, which for them is, in reality, merely a reservoir of petroleum—that is, a vast "gas station"—while at the same time being unstinting in their efforts to support and strengthen the most archaic form of government in the entire region, that of Saudi Arabia, where the congruence of the sacred and the political exists in its purest form.[73]

CHAPTER 2

ACCULTURATION AND NON-WESTERN IDEOLOGIES.
MODERN ISLAM AS A POLITICAL IDEOLOGY

In the Introduction I cited the anthropologist and scholar of religion
Anthony F. C. Wallace, who contends that religions are political ideologies.
Wallace's interpretation deals with

rituals intended to control, in a conservative way, the behavior, the mood, the
sentiments and values for the sake of the community as a whole. . . . Ideological
rituals may be said to have as their aim social control . . . ; they intend to instruct,
to direct, and to program. . . . And we should note that much of what is written
about "religion" deals almost entirely with its ideological rituals and their
functions.[1]

Islam as a cultural system satisfies the conditions of these religious
rituals. Ideologies are certainly capable of making themselves independent,
but can be understood adequately only within their actual social context.
Religion as political ideology is also subject to change and is not a uniform,
immutable system of norms. Contemporary Islam, for example, is a different social phenomenon from early or medieval Islam,[2] although Muslims
reject this historical differentiation of their religion. A Muslim scholar of
religion who, in his dissertation written in 1947, dared to offer an historical interpretation of Islamic religious truths ended up having his work
rejected and his future destroyed. He was censured by Muslim scholars for
having behaved in a "clearly criminal" way in the writing of his thesis.[3]

As a political ideology modern Islam must be seen in the context of the
acculturation processes described in chapter 1. Even though one might
argue with Herbert Schnädelbach that "there are as many different notions
of ideology as there are social science chairs,"[4] one cannot help but acknowledge that the numerous points of departure toward the "scholarly
approach of *Ideologiekritik*" (critique of ideology) share a localization of their
ideologies within a shared social framework. Non-Western ideologies, however, are moored in a world historical context and cannot be located within
one particular society. I have attempted to show earlier, through the example
of West African romantic developmental ideologies, how West African

village tradition has been synthesized with modern European thought on the critique of civilization. An examination of both these sources is absolutely essential for the understanding of these ideologies.[5] Moreover, the critique of modern Islamic ideological thought also demands that attention be paid to European influences. These altered conditions, unknown to the traditional critique of ideology, and unrecognized even in more recent scholarship, cannot be explained through using scholarly points of departure previously employed. Peter Christian Ludz, who, although quite justly critical of the blurred use of the notion of ideology in the social sciences (pleading for a "concept close to the materials"[6]), nevertheless leaves one with the impression that research on ideologies is a Western European problem. He ignores the 76 percent of humanity living outside the industrialized world—an offense of omission committed by many of his colleagues. This faulting of earlier points of departure in the critique of ideology concedes, however, that the criticism of non-Western ideologies which we are dealing with here can be linked up with the existing research on ideologies and needn't begin at zero.

Ideology and the Critique of Ideology: An Attempt at Conceptual Determination

As early as 1941 Max Horkheimer complained in his contribution to the festschrift for Leopold von Wiese about the way the notion of ideology was being handled and gave this description of the unhappy situation:

Under the appellation of "ideology" today it is rare for any precise concept to be discerned. The word, like many others . . . originated in philosophical and scholarly literature and eventually entered common daily use. One could say that its theoretical profile was lost: behind the general idea there remains only the vaguely remembered resonance of the theoretical constructs in which the currently eviscerated notion [once] had its meaning. With ideology one usually means nothing more than any kind of mental connection, a theory, an idea in particular or something intellectual in general."[7]

Indeed, even in the scholarly literature this eviscerated notion of ideology has prevailed. For example, if there is talk of ideology in the Middle East then one can assume that the local intellectual tradition is meant.

The concept of ideology goes back to the end of the eighteenth century when the origin of ideas became a subject of philosophical discourse. An attempt was undertaken to discover the dependence of ideas on each other and to search for the origin of this complex in the human body and its physiological processes. From its inception this tradition insisted upon the dependence of the mind on the material body (understood here as physis). Because ideology delineates the dependence of the mind on basic material processes in this tradition it is commonly known as "physiological materialism."

In modern ideologies a new emphasis has been given to this conceptual definition. According to Marx, consciousness is "not merely . . . dependent on the bodily processes in the individual human being but also on the basic structure of society."[8] Thus the conception of the superstructure which divides society within the framework of a superstructure-base scheme was born: individual thought exists only in the context of the entire cultural sphere from out of which the superstructure is constituted. Although Marx himself never postulated such a scheme, post-Marxian Marxism has reduced the critique of ideology to a materialistic superstructure conception.

Nevertheless, Marx's notion of ideology did acknowledge the philosophical distinction between the true and the false, insofar as ideology was conceived of as "appearance" and therefore as something spurious, even if socially necessary. This differentiation is often lost in the concept of absolute ideology contained in the sociology of knowledge which, even when attempting to confront Marxism, adopted the superstructure conception fully in its unsophisticated form. All thought becomes superstructure: that is, ideology. Every idea in the sociology of knowledge is attributed to a social stratum. "Every world view, so it teaches, is conditioned by the perspective provided by a socially determinative point of view,"[9] says Horkheimer. All thought in the anti-Marxist sociology of knowledge, as well as in the currently widespread popularized Marxism, becomes thinking chained to a particular point of view or, as Helmuth Plessner says,"a 'tension between superstructure and base,' leveled to a general form of human being."[10]

For sociologists of knowledge and for doctrinaire Marxists all thinking is "ideological." The sociologist of knowledge proceeds from the total concept of ideology; the Marxist from his conception of superstructure in which even Marxism itself becomes the "ideology of the proletariat" (although for Marx the theory remained a critique of ideology). Scientists, for whom science stands in contrast to ideology, rail against both positions. As a consequence of this imprecise handling of concepts, ideology, once a sovereign philosophical category, has been reduced to the level of an invective used by politicians to characterize and disparage an opponent's thinking. Intellectuals have also joined the ranks of those exercising their distrust of ideology not as an analytical tool but rather as a weapon against those who think differently from themselves.

I am of the same mind as Helmuth Plessner, who insisted as long ago as 1953 that one must

finally form a front . . . against such a dissociation of the concept of ideology from its original association of ideas and against its technical reinterpretation, as it were, for the purpose of a nonobligatory use in empirical research."[11]

A return to idealism, however, cannot be regarded as an alternative to the concept of superstructure. Reductionism is inherent in both. Whereas the idea of superstructure reduces mind to matter and interprets it as a social structure, society is viewed in idealism as a product of mind. This was so not only in terms of the history of ideas in classical idealism but also in a sanitized form in which idealism dominates contemporary American social sciences. Mind molds society through a system of norms and values. Modernization theory, as established in the American social sciences, was "molded by a pronounced normative, subjectivist prejudice, just as is the more recent action theory, which in itself refers back to modernization theory."[12]

It is not only unsophisticated Marxists who interpret ideology as a form of superstructure to be derived from the base. More sophisticated Marxist authors, thinking in more differentiated terms (for example, those from the Berlin ProKla school, who are contemptuously but correctly called "derivationists"), also regard all social phenomena as local manifestations of a logically determined "core structure," or, the "movement of capital."[13]

Ideologies neither fall from the sky nor represent autonomous entities. Nor are they reflecting automata possessing no independent "imaginary power" with which to determine history. They belong within "the context of society and [are] at the same time autonomous."[14] The critique of ideology pursued by the Frankfurt School under the formulation, "critique of dominance,"[15] seems to me still to contain some useful points of departure. Herbert Schnädelbach, a representative of the group, writes: "Detached from the theory of society . . . ideology becomes merely a theme of research in the humanities. The relationship between being and consciousness can then be presented simply as a causal relationship."[16] In the critical theory of society such a causal relationship, whether idealistic or coarsely materialistic, must be rejected. Consciousness means conscious existence. Thought is mediated socially, but is neither bound by being nor an expression of class interests, as sociologists of knowledge and Marxists in spite of their mutual opposition assume in common. Such an interpretation of ideology "leads to a general relativism which categorically excludes emancipation of thought from positions conditioned from one moment to the next by [class] interests."[17]

Ideology is always situated within the context of social evolution without, however, being reduced to it. I reject the reductionism inherent in both the concept of superstructure and in the "normative, subjectionist prejudice" of modernization theory. Ideology is an ingredient of society which cannot be subdivided into a base-superstructure scheme: ideology and social structure are in a dialectical not a schematic causal relationship.

The Problem of Ideology in Non-Western Societies

My assertion that ideology is always found in the context of social evolution applies to an endogenous social constellation with its own social dynamics. European history illustrates this relationship. But most non-Occidental societies, whose history has been determined by foreigners since the inception of colonialism, no longer possess endogenous social formations generated out of their own social dynamics, to which ideology could belong as a natural component. This realization has far-reaching consequences for the study of ideology in non-Western societies.

The social structures of non-Western societies were deformed by colonial penetration and were forcibly integrated into the emerging world market. The social structures of Third World countries cannot be understood unless one recognizes how profoundly autochthonous cultures were shaken. Colonized people are, of course, acutely conscious of the questions posed for their own way of life by colonialism. If one wants to investigate ideology in non-Occidental societies the concept of ideology must itself be put into a different context.

The division of the social sciences into a Marxist view, based on the superstructure-base scheme and objectification on the one hand and the "normative, subjectivist prejudice" on the other, is encountered once again when one looks at ideologies in non-Occidental societies. Most Western Marxists, who usually work deductively, concentrate on analyses of social structures and neglect the study of non-Western cultures. They justify this through vague references to the relationship of these cultures to the superstructure which could allegedly be derived from the base. Doctrinaire Marxists reduce Marxist theory to a five-stage model—the famous modes-of-production sequence. Thus, the non-Occidental regions of the world find themselves in the feudal phase according to Marxist scholars and are permitted to leap over the capitalist to a noncapitalist path of fulfillment. According to this view ideologies can be divided into reactionary systems intent on preserving the feudal structure and progressive systems which are committed to a noncapitalist path of development.[18]

Set against this simplistic interpretation of ideology, sociological, cultural anthropological, and political science interpretations seem both more differentiated and more appetizing. Extensive research on non-Occidental cultures and the ideological phenomena inherent in them has been done in these disciplines. But even this research has been unable to provide convincing explanations for non-Occidental ideologies.

The American sociologist Daniel Bell announced in 1960 "the end of ideology," at least in those Western societies which could demonstrate consensus on the welfare state, federal power structures, political pluralism, and a system of mixed economy. "In this sense the ideological age has ended."[19] One could interpret this statement as meaning that ideologies can still exist only in non-Western societies. Although Bell's ideas have not always been embraced by his colleagues, it is interesting that American scholarly research on ideology in the 1960s and 1970s was concentrated on non-Occidental ideologies. However, Ludz is correct in noting that Bell has contributed to transforming the notion of ideology into an empty formula. Even such a prominent American social scientist as David Apter, who points to the fact that only the "common" traits of ideology have disappeared from Western societies and that the new ideologies are "more sophisticated," fails to grasp the essential point in his comparison between ideologies in industrial and preindustrial societies.[20]

Those social scientists who conjure up an "Age of Ideology" in underdeveloped societies speak of modernization ideologies as engines of social change. These ideologies contribute to development and industrialization and "are based on a national culture and refer to local conditions,"[21] as Paul S. Sigmund recognizes. Sigmund has also observed how insidiously Western influences enter into "ideologies of modernization" without the supporters of a given ideology renouncing either an emphasis on the autochthonous elements in their ideas or the rejection of Western culture.[22] But Sigmund is ensnared by the very error he exposes. In his work, too, the notion of ideology is interpreted in terms of modernization theory. Underdevelopment is reduced to cultural traditionalism and social evolution to a change of value and norm systems.[23]

The Political Ideology of Islam and the Secular Ideologies

One finds documented in the political history of the modern Islamic Middle East a series of religious and secular ideologies (pan-Islamism, pan-Arabism, socialism, and so forth). Compared to Westernized ideologies Islam has the advantage of possessing a solid social mooring, while the secular ideologies are carried along by influential but "socially marginal ideology-producing groups."[24] Modern Islam is, however, not a pure autochthonous entity. It is itself an expression of the continuing argument with the penetrating colonial, industrial West.

The history of the modern Islamic Middle East began, as did that of what remains of the non-Occidental world, with the encounter with Europe in the colonial context. Historians are justified in having this history begin with Napoleon's expedition to Egypt in 1798.[25]

European authors always trace the ideologies which originated in these past two centuries to the influence of Europe. In an important study the Berlin Orientalist Walther Braune made his ironic opinion of such authors clear by writing that the explanation which holds that Arab nationalism

has to be traced back to European influence is tantamount to carrying dates to Basra. Obviously the Arab Orient has been touched in this as in almost any other modern respect by Occidental thought. All influences become effective only when the conditions for their reception and transformation are provided.[26]

If one recognizes on the one hand Eurocentric authors who attempt to exculpate European colonial penetration by deeming it a cultural mission and who attribute all non-Western ideologies to European influence, one also has to recognize on the other hand the nationalistic or religiously clothed resistance of the colonized who dispute the putative European influence on their ideologies. In West Africa the ideology of *négritude*, contrived to prove both "africanicity" and authenticity, is quite clearly a product of acculturation, although not in the sense meant by Eurocentric cultural anthropologists.[27] Modern Islam in the Arab Middle East, in spite of shrill accusations against European hegemony, is unthinkable without European colonialism. Nikki Keddie has perspicaciously entitled her book on the leading Islamic modernist, Jamal al-Din al-Afghani, *An Islamic Response to Imperialism*.[28] Keddie suggests a connection between Afghani's reading of Francois Guizot's *Histoire de la civilisation en Europe* and of Ibn Khaldun's *Muqaddima* (Prolegomena to his *Kitab al-ʿibar*): that is, a commingling of European and classical Arabic influences. Afghani appropriates Guizot's idea that the moral condition of people is decisive for the development of all civilizations and connects this idea with Ibn Khaldun's notion of *ʿasabiyya*[29] on group solidarity as providing an explanatory pattern for the rise and decline of cultures. According to Afghani the struggle facing Islamic modernism is the need to create a sense of group solidarity in order to strengthen the moral constitution of Muslims. Reinforced by this group solidarity Muslims can respond effectively to the colonial challenge and can emerge from it with strength.

This ideology of Islamic modernism bears witness in equal measure to elements of both modern European and classical Arab culture. Islamic apologists resolutely take the position that Islam is an unvaryingly constant culture. However, as with any other ideology, Islam exists within the context of social evolution and is, consequently, variable over time. Even original Islam can be understood only within the context of its historical period, as we shall see in chapter 4.

Certainly Islamic modernism was a progressive ideology, in that it mobilized the Arab Middle East by infusing it with an anticolonial purpose; but it had to give way to another ideology more adequate to the latter part of the nineteenth century: intent on liberating themselves from Ottoman rule, the Arabs aspired to national autonomy. However, the ideological legitimacy of the Ottoman Empire was itself based on the ideology of Islam and, therefore, its use in the struggle against the empire by the Arabs was precluded. This situation explains the adoption of an ideology which originated in Europe: nationalism. The conditions necessary for the adoption of this new ideology existed in World Society given the nature of nation-states as well as those regions striving for nation-state autonomy (Walther Braune).

Arab nationalism was a progressive ideology similar to Islamic modernism seen in its historical context in that it was directed against a religious, despotic, Oriental empire. Since early Arab nationalism was promoted by Westernized intellectuals who had graduated from English and French educational institutions and were strongly influenced by the European Enlightenment, it was usually quite liberal and anglofrancophile. When England and France colonized the Arab Middle East, these early liberal Arab nationalists suffered a severe shock which led them to turn to the popular nationalism espoused in the writings of Satiʿ al-Husri, who was celebrated until his death in 1968 as "the theoretician of Arab nationalism." His voluminous *oeuvre* is still considered to be the most comprehensive literary source for Arab nationalism.[30]

Although this secularized Arab nationalism and the later versions of non-Marxist Arab socialism which are partially based on it[31] served as legitimizing ideologies for military regimes,[32] they could not prevent the rebirth of political Islam or, for that matter, the repoliticization of Islam as we shall see in chapter 3.

Maxime Rodinson, expanding upon Karl Mannheim, distinguishes between "ideological" and "utopian" ideas. If utopian ideas include a program, or a resolve, to overcome an existing situation, they will be able to become politically effective if they appear to correspond to given conditions.[33] Rodinson calls these utopian ideas "mobilizing," in contrast to "nonmobilizing" ideas, such as artistic, philosophical, or scientific conceptions.[34] This distinction seems to me to be a fertile point of departure for studying ideologies in non-Western societies.

Ideologies in these societies have their social roots as well, of course, but untangling what comes from the national society itself from what has been assimilated from Europe within the colonial context is a complicated business and makes one rather envy those who study the simpler question of European ideologies. Cultural anthropologists call this process of assimilation an exogenously induced cultural change (that is, acculturation), signifying with these terms the strong colonial, Eurocentric influence on the context of change. The term "acculturation," around which the discussion of chapter 1 was centered, can be usefully employed in critical analyses (1) if it is successfully liberated from this colonial European influence and (2) if it is recognized that the term indicates the existence of elements from two cultures in one and the same non-Western ideology.

Since ideologies exercised in the developmental process of non-Western societies have, in Rodinson's sense, a mobilizing effect, the study of these societies' ideologies must be a central constituent of developmental sociology. Insofar as the origin as well as the mobilizing effect of these ideologies can no longer be tamed and confined on the national level but are seen to be embedded in World Society, the critique of ideology should also assume a central place in the discipline of "international relations."[35]

CHAPTER 3

THE REPOLITICIZATION OF ISLAM AS CULTURAL RETROSPECTION AND COUNTER-ACCULTURATION

In the framework of the general conceptual discussion of chapter 1 I tried to make clear that the forms of Westernization produced in the process of acculturation bring about the transfer of a culture without its anchoring itself sufficiently for structural success. Only a normative Westernization of society, not a structural transformation in the sense of industrialization, has taken place. Precolonial, traditional social structures no longer exist but have been dissolved and disfigured into structurally deformed social constructions, which in the disciplines of international relations and sociology of development are termed "structures of underdevelopment."[1]

In the critical analysis of ideology in chapter 2, I intimated that Westernized ideologies, such as secular nationalism and variations of socialism, have been thrust aside and replaced by political Islam as the substance of an autochthonous culture. These ideologies were, as Wilhelm E. Mühlmann early on evaluated them, "superstructures . . . without an actual sociological substratum."[2] They could not offer Westernized intellectuals any stable identity, whereas autochthonously anchored Islam could.

Sociologist of religion Niklas Luhmann has put forward the thesis according to which, religion is no longer required for identity except in traditional societies undergoing a process of dissolution. Modern societies have functional equivalents for religion which they relegate to the private sphere.[3] The French anthropologist Georges Balandier has also pointed to the correspondence existing between the sacred and political realms in those societies which have not attained the stage of dominion-over-nature and thus remain "traditional" societies.[4] If partisans of a particular political system in such societies succeed in sacralizing politics, they achieve a guarantee of stability for their system. It seems appropriate to point out here the timeliness of Samuel Huntington's assertion that political development has to be interpreted as a type of institutionalization.[5] If we follow Huntington's line we must regard most societies in the Third World as political systems with a low degree of institutionalization. Sacralization, as shown by Balandier, is a substitute for institutionalization.

The fall of the Pahlavi dynasty in Iran was hastened by, among other things, the Shah's attempt to impose modernization on Iranian society from above and by fiat; the principal consequence was the annihilation of small farmers' and bazaar merchants' livelihoods.[6] The Shah's modernization policy did little toward transforming the existing structures of underdevelopment and, thus, the secularizing measures of this modernizing Oriental despot lacked the requisite social base. If one compares Iran with Saudi Arabia, whose monarchy bears witness to a stable political system,[7] it becomes clear that political systems in underdeveloped, weakly institutionalized societies forfeit their stability if the dominant elites are secularized without a sociostructural transformation being attempted at the same time (a transformation which should not be equated with any superficial modernization, such as an Americanization of life-styles).

In Saudi Arabia the Islamic clergy (*ulama*), together with the army and the royal family, are the sustainers of the political system.[8] By contrast, in Iran under the Shah the clergy belonged to the opposition. Had the Shah not been so intent on secularization and had he attempted instead to woo the clergy into some kind of engagement with his efforts, it seems quite certain that his powerful political opponents would have had great difficulty in toppling his regime.

The phenomenon of Islamic repoliticization is not confined to Iran, however, but can be found in the entire Islamic Middle East, where an intense need for religiosity may be observed. In this chapter I want to formulate a number of religiosociological ideas concerning this repoliticization of Islam and introduce the hypothesis that this repoliticization documents both a cultural retrospection and a search for identity: in short, a counter-acculturation.

Underdevelopment, Crisis, and The Repoliticization of Islam

In the social sciences as practiced by German-speaking scholars, two antithetical positions predominate among those dealing with non-Western societies. One position takes as its starting point a political-economic analysis of underdevelopment, asserting that this phenomenon is a creation of the world market; sociocultural problems are regarded as meaningless. In contrast to this position René König proposes the idea that

economic problems play . . . a part, but only a secondary one; rather, what is
primary is the . . . identification and recognition of indigenous value traditions
after a long period of . . . a loss of self . . . [as] conditioned by colonialism.[9]

Today one can observe in the Third World a turning toward cultural
retrospection as a reaction to the crisis. In the Islamic Middle East this
movement has taken the form of a repoliticization of Islamic society. This
phenomenon cannot be explained either through references to the world
market or through technocratic input/output analyses. But König's opinion
of the secondary role played by economic problems is also untenable if one
reminds oneself that famine, sickness, and general physical misery *cannot* be
overcome through cultural retrospection. Nevertheless, people are not
merely mechanical bodies; they require an identity which cannot be acquired by either physical satiation or convalescence. The repoliticization of
Islam is a sociocultural, ethnopsychological phenomenon which, however,
cannot be adequately understood if the problem of material pauperization
and the socioeconomic structures of underdevelopment are ignored.

But the question arises of why secularism was unable to succeed in the
modern Middle East. Many observers were surprised by the repoliticization
of Islam because they had assumed secularism to be a reality.

When ʿAli ʿAbd al-Raziq, Egyptian religious teacher, published what
was, in 1925, his politically and religiously pathbreaking study, *Islam and
the Forms of Government (Al-islam wa usul al-hukm),* [10] and aggressively championed the view that Islam was a religion and neither a political ideology
nor even a species of state, it was thought that the conflict between a
fundamentalism striving for political power and secularism had been con-
clusively decided in favor of the latter. Before the publication of his study
ʿAbd al-Raziq had been active as an Islamic judge and had been working
since his student years at the Islamic Al-Azhar University on Islamic law
(*Shariʿa*). He argued that the Prophet of Islam, Muhammad, had been a
religious and not a political leader and contended that the forms of government that had been developed in Islam, that is, the caliphate for the
Sunni Muslims and the imamate for the Shiʿi-Persian Muslims, possessed
no legitimation in the Qur'an or the *Sunna.*

In all the other Arab as well as non-Arab Islamic countries in the
Middle East, Islam was relegated to the background, giving place to a
triumphant nationalism. This was a secular nationalism which held that
membership in the nation constituted the primary bond of the larger
group. The spiritual father of Arab nationalism, Satiʿ al-Husri, adopted the

German version of nationalism from Herder and Fichte, who maintained that each nation was a cultural community bound together by a common language but not, for example, by a common religion. I have demonstrated in my book *Arab Nationalism: A Critical Inquiry*[11] that Islam has been reduced by Arab nationalists to a cultural quantity. Arab Christians and Arab Muslims are bound together by their common language and therefore form one nation; whereas Persians and Turks, for example, who have only Islam in common with the Arabs, are foreign peoples. The result of the secularization demanded by Arab nationalists in the Middle East was not only the separation of state and religion but also a rupture of the Islamic community (the *Umma*) in many countries. Under these conditions even such Islamic scholars as ʿAbd al-Raziq came to interpret Islam in a secular way, that is, only as a religious bond, so as to salvage it. Since that time, it has generally been believed that Islam is no longer a political factor in the Middle East, assuming of course, that one disregards fanatical sects, such as the Muslim Brothers,[12] and archaic political systems, such as Saudi Arabia. And yet, strangely enough, since the beginning of the 1970s we have witnessed a rejuvenation of Islam, the revitalization of a religion.

The Islamic peoples suffer today under both an economic pauperization and a profound identity crisis requiring an ethnopsychological interpretation. Islamic political leaders believe that cultural retrospection on the autochthonous Islamic past is in itself sufficient to overcome these problems.European politicians and developmental experts became aware of the repoliticization of Islam only through events in Iran, although the repoliticization process was already under way at the beginning of the 1970s and Iran only its climax. The reaching back to an autochthonous culture is characteristic not only of the Islamic Middle East but is also a general Third World phenomenon; "the ideology of authenticity" in Zaire comes to mind as an example and, more generally, the clinging to indigenous cultures in Asia and Africa. These are reactions to the crisis which is now so troubling to the Third World.

A look back over the history of colonization and decolonization makes clear that the relationship of non-European peoples to both their own and to European culture can be divided into *three phases*:

1. Early colonial ideology denied the intrinsic value of non-European cultures. Nineteenth- and twentieth-century colonialism, supported by European culture, was considered superior on the grounds of its scientifically based character and, as a consequence, was regarded as a "cultural message," or a *mission civilisatrice*—in short, as the "burden of the white

man."[13] Anticolonial resistance took the form of a rejection of the dominant culture and a determined clinging to one's own. An emphasis on the autochthonous vis-à-vis the foreign is a form of self-assertion, hence a defensive-culture.[14] I call this first phase *the revitalization of autochthonous culture*.

2. Colonialism was not only an economic but also a cultural system. As Johan Galtung has shown, economic penetration was accompanied by a cultural penetration. Cultural Westernization could be brought about through the dissolution of the traditional, precolonial system of education (for example, the prohibition of Qur'an schools in colonial Algeria) and the establishment of Western educational institutions. Cultural Westernization entailed an acceptance and interiorization of European value and norm systems within the framework of the educational system. But Westernization also meant the acceptance of the actual structures of a developed society as they existed throughout Europe; Westernization is not merely formal intellectual acquiescence.[15] If the Westernization of education is to become relevant in terms of development, it has to be accompanied by the industrialization and modernization of the society in question, as I shall discuss in chapter 7.

However, the second phase in the history of colonization and decolonization being periodized here did not fulfill this precondition. The Westernization of education produced not modernization but alienation. Sociologists of development coined the term "cultural anomie" in order to describe the consequences of a merely cultural Westernization. The state of anomie is a deviant state. Thus, the condition of an Islamic society influenced by Western norms is one of anomie. The suffering generated by Westernization can be diagnosed as the sorrows attendant on cultural anomie. The decolonization ideologies advocated by Westernized intellectuals document an attempt to deal with the loss of identity suffered, to overcome it, and to find a new identity, neither autochthonous nor derivative. Nationalism, as well as the various forms of Third World socialism (Arab, African socialism, and others) belong here, and all have to be labeled "acculturative ideologies." Although not novel, I shall characterize this second phase with the term *Westernization*.

3. What might be called the "pure" Westernized ideologies (e.g., liberalism in Egypt, parliamentarianism in India and Nigeria) as well as the Western-influenced Third World ideologies (Nasserism, Nkrumaism) have proved to be failures and, as a result, it would seem that the only alternative remaining is that of autochthonous, precolonial culture. The

third phase of the process described here is the *crisis* phase. In Iran the forced modernization of social structures miscarried. Urbanization, for example, resulted in the conversion of Tehran into a massive slum.[16] The regime of the Shah erred in not offering the pauperized masses of Iran even an ersatz identity to replace Islam. However, things were no different for the Egyptians to whom Nasser appeared to offer just such a replacement identity in the form of his "Arab socialism." The Sadat regime almost effortlessly swept away Nasser's heritage under the slogan of "de-Nasserization."[17] Nationalism, socialism, and other forms of Westernization have not conquered underdevelopment nor even delayed the process of impoverishment. Islam, on the other hand, was once able not only to provide a secure identity but also to transform the Middle East from a primitive bedouin society into an Islamic world empire with a highly developed culture of its own. Even though today Islam is the culture of a backward region, the vision of a powerful, sovereign Islam persists in the consciousness of Muslims. This third phase can be described as one of *cultural retrospection*.

In the following section I shall explain further the three-phase, periodic scheme sketched here and attempt to provide a religiosociological interpretation of the repoliticization of Islam in the concluding section.

The Place of Islam during the Three Phases of Social Development in the Modern Middle East

The first phase began with the European colonization of the Muslim Middle East. Islam was mobilized as an assertion of identity. It is important to show historically in what way Islam assumed its role as an identity. I am an advocate of the thesis that Islam, since its inception, has been an Arab religion for the Arabs and that it therefore provides the religious substance of a cultural identity. The pre-Islamic Arabs were uncivilized bedouins lacking a materially developed culture. Islam was the turning point, as I shall explain at length in chapter 4 and shall only sketch broadly here.

Muhammad first founded a small sect of his adherents in Mecca, but was forced to emigrate to the nearby city of Medina in 622 (the first year of the Islamic calendar). Muhammad founded a city-state, theocratic in nature and organization, with its legal system firmly based on the Qur'an, the revealed sayings of the Prophet which are today known to us as Tradition (*Hadith*). In the course of the expansion of Islam, the theocratic city-state of Medina produced a world empire, and a world religion grew out of the small sect surrounding Muhammad. By the end of the thirteenth century the Arab Islamic Empire was the abode of one of the greatest world civilizations and cultures. The Ottoman Empire, established in the four-teenth century, also developed into a powerful Islamic world empire, but in this case we have a feudal, military empire which proved incapable of producing a high culture.[18] In this respect the Ottoman Empire was inferior to the efflorescent, bourgeois, democratic culture of Europe; it disintegrated and was finally dissolved in the year 1924.

What once had been a highly developed Islamic culture degenerated under the Ottomans. Neither science nor literature nor architecture could flourish as they had during the period from its origins in a primitive bedouin society in the seventh century to its destruction in the thirteenth century under the onslaught of the Mongols.[19]

This history of grandeur and disintegration has been deeply impressed onto modern Islam. The confrontation with Europe in the course of colonial penetration, the process of disintegration in the Islamic Ottoman Empire, and the eventual expansion of the dominant European culture throughout the entire world appeared acutely menacing to the Muslim peoples of this period. The mobilization of Islam (first phase) was the initial response. The leading Islamic intellectual of the nineteenth century, Jamal al-Din al-Afghani, understood the value of using Islam as a weapon against Europe. Afghani's American editor and biographer, Nikki Keddie, entitled her text selection from Afghani *An Islamic Response to Imperialism.*[20] Modern Islam, I must emphasize again, is a defensive-culture and cannot be understood without this, admittedly, quite simplified historical sketch. Scholars spe-cializing in Islam who have complete mastery of it as a religion inevitably fail when they attempt to interpret the reactions of contemporary Muslims in the Middle East because they base their conclusions on Islamic doctrine and not on the historical process. The rise and decline of Islam can never be deduced from its doctrines. Maxime Rodinson has persuasively shown that there is no *Homo islamicus* and no specific Islamic path of development.

In the periodization I have suggested here for understanding the mod-ern history of the relationship between European and Islamic cultures I have called the first phase the *revitalization* of Islam. This Islamic revital-ization assumed two forms which I shall explain below. The *Westernization* of Arab Islamic intellectuals (the second phase), however, led to a normative secularization and thus only ostensibly to a privatization of Islam and its reduction to a mere cultural quantity.

In the eighteenth century there was an answer to the crisis of Islam: a return to the Ur-Islam of the Prophet. The call arose out of the desert of the Arabian peninsula where an Arab named Muhammad Ibn ʿAbd al-Wahhab called for the struggle against the foreign domination of the Ottomans.[21] The Ottomans succeeded in suppressing the uprisings fanned by the Wahhabi movement until the princes of the Banu Saud appropriated Wahhabi Islam and, under the banner of this ideology, founded what is today the kingdom of Saudi Arabia.[22]

Al-Wahhab called for a return to the bedouin society of the Prophet. His adherents destroyed all manifestations of a material culture, which they contemptuously called "innovations" (bidʿa), in the cities they conquered. In nineteenth-century Egypt the reanimation of Islam took a completely different direction. The two most important reformers, al-Afghani and his disciple Muhammad ʿAbduh, the fathers of Islamic modernism,[23] were forced into exile as a result of their resistance to British hegemony. In France they published the Arabic language journal Al-ʿUrwa al-Wuthqa (The Unbreakable Bond) in which they pleaded for a reawakening of Islam but not in the sense of a romantic return to the Ur-Islam of the Prophet. They pressed instead for the acceptance of European scientific culture and all achievements of bourgeois democratic Europe, insofar as they could be integrated into Islam.

The archaic direction taken by the Wahhabi version of modern Islam contributed to the formation of the Saudi Arabian state. In Libya, the archaic Sanusiyya movement also led to the foundation of a state.[24] The second direction, Islamic modernism, could not be developed in an effective political direction. In general, however, secular nationalism and, later, secular socialism prevailed.[25] The Westernization of education produced Arab intellectuals whose Westernized secular norms and values were no longer Islamic. Today these secular ideologies, unable to fulfill their visionary promises, are suffering an acute crisis. And it is out of this crisis, when both social and political legitimacy have been cast in doubt, that the repoliticization of Islam has sprung.[26]

I think there are two causes underlying this repoliticization: first, the identity crisis under which the Islamic people are suffering, and second, the socioeconomic crisis and its attendant ineluctable pauperization which provide a fertile soil for religious ideologies of salvation. Islam offers itself as salvation in the form of an identity and promise of future prosperity.

The processes of Westernization were already under way in non-European societies in the nineteenth century. But the cultural identity of the Westernized elites had a fragile base, since their acquired cultural and educational values and ideas had no counterpart in the social structures of their indigenous societies. Consequently, the forms of Westernized consciousness they advocated had no substance or meaning within the existing social structures of their communities. The search for one's own identity seemed to offer a remedy for a forlorn estrangement, and Islam became the ideological substance of such an autochthonous identity. To this sociopsychological background of the repoliticization of Islam must be added the socioeconomic framework of Third World societies which are becoming increasingly poorer and which find themselves in an inexorable process of pauperization. One need only mention here the increasing indebtedness of the developing countries to the rich countries to illustrate this process.

Which Islam provides the spiritual, ideological substance for its repoliticization? This question is deliberately and rightly posed here, for one must always bear in mind that a uniform, indivisible Islam exists only in the dogma but not at all in the reality. Islam, as is well known, was assimilated into the cultures of the various peoples who were Islamized. This is one of the central theses of this volume and will be elaborated upon further in chapter 5. Thus, Persian Islam is not Arab Islam and the latter is not African Islam. In addition to these national differentiations a distinction has to be made between popular, mystical Islam (*Tariqa* Islam) and legal Islam (*Shari'a* Islam). Detlev Khalid imputes revolutionary, even secularist traits to popular Islam and holds it to be perfectly compatible with Marxist currents.[27] However, the actual history of Islam refuses to support this view. Islamic scholars (*ulama*) have historically functioned as spokesmen of Islam.[28] The source of their authority has always been Islamic law, the *Shari'a*, and not any popular religious tradition: popular Islam[29] has always been relentlessly condemned by representatives of official Islam. Islamic scholars continue even today to be champions of repoliticization. Thus, it is clear that *Shari'a* Islam is the bedrock of the contemporary revitalization of Islam. In terms of the politics of development the repoliticization of Islam ranks as nothing more than an expression of a defensive-culture; it is an expression of the identity crisis and material misery of the Islamic peoples.

Does repoliticization offer a real alternative and escape from this crisis? In order to answer this question a religiosociological interpretation of the role played by Islam in the process of development is necessary. And this I discuss next.

The Repoliticization of Islam

In the Introduction I designated the "international system" as World Society: that is, as the product of European penetration of the world in the colonial period. The European market became the world market and European bourgeois society became World Society. This is not to say, however, that the national societies of the Third World became bourgeois societies. Only portions of Third World societies were modernized and integrated socioeconomically, culturally, and politically into a metropolitan center. In the theory of underdevelopment this state of affairs is described by the concept of "structural heterogeneity." I would prefer not to take up the theoretical discussion of development here.[30] In this context it is only necessary to emphasize that a bourgeois society does not necessarily emerge in non-Occidental societies through socioeconomic penetration. At best, a modern sector which can be integrated into the economy of the metropolitan center emerges. Cultural penetration—that is, the transfer of education—runs parallel to this socioeconomic penetration and creates a Westernized elite with interiorized European norms. But, as mentioned above, these interiorized norms lack corresponding social structures and the elites are left adrift. Maria Mies took up the concept of anomie[31] from Emile Durkheim and Robert Merton and derived from it the concept of cultural anomie in order to describe this unsettling situation. Durkheim means with anomie that disintegration of norm and value systems in the wake of which a condition lacking all regulation emerges. Anomic behavior for Durkheim is deviant behavior; anomie conditions phenomena of social pathology. Mies transfers this condition to intercultural situations which arise between a dominant culture and a subordinate one, referring back to Bronislaw Malinowski's dynamics of cultural change. Internalization of the norms of the dominant culture by members of the subordinate culture is inextricably bound up with seductive promises. In actual fact, however, the expectations raised are never fulfilled and feelings of betrayal and repulsion necessarily arise. "Allurement and repulsion remain the mechanisms which lead to anomic phenomena when the 'primary culture' [Western industrial society] comes into contact with the 'subcultures' of the Third World."[32] Mies introduces the concept of cultural anomie in order to describe the consequences of asymmetrical processes of interaction in the cultural sphere of World Society. Her attempt at cultural definition is as follows:

Cultural anomie comes into being when two cultural systems collide in international contact. When one system puts forward a claim to dominance and is capable of maintaining it materially and permanently, the people of the subordinate system acknowledge this claim and are enticed into attempting to rise into the dominant system, but are structurally restrained from rising.[33]

With this frame of reference we can understand better the general process of a cultural retrospection which is taking place today in the Third World. Repoliticization is the Islamic variant of this process of reflection on the past. I have discussed above the three-phase periodization of the asymmetrical processes of interaction between the center of World Society and non-Western cultures, in this case, more specifically, Islam. To repeat, there is, first, the revitalization of one's own culture in reaction to the penetration by the dominant culture; second, the adoption of the penetrating culture with all its alluring promises and great expectations; third, the defensive return to one's own culture takes place in which a corresponding retrospection provides solace for the nonappearance of the anticipated fruits of Westernization together with rejection of the anomic behavior of those Westernized by their own societies. According to this periodization the repoliticization of Islam is the third phase.

Finally, I would like to discuss two questions: first, the religio-theoretical meaning of Islamic repoliticization and, second, its social function, in the sense intended by the French sociologist of religion, Henri Desroches.[34]

According to Niklas Luhmann, religion "function[s] within the social system to transform the indeterminable world into a determinable world."[35] This function of religion is particularly strong in those societies experiencing a transition period. According to Luhmann this transition period cannot be regulated "because identity has to be maintained in the course of change."[36] Reflection on the religion of the past is a form of seeking and finding identity. "The individual undergoing transition is 'not-only-but-also' or 'neither-nor' simultaneously! His identity becomes murky and indeterminable. This situation makes the problem of determining the indeterminate acute."[37] Luhmann also calls this "determining the indeterminate," *"the bridging of change"* in which religion assists. A further partial function of religion is the *tangible absorption of disillusion.* According to Luhmann it is important for an adequate theory of religion "that neither of these two partial functions . . . is alone sufficient to characterize the function of religion and that neither of these partial functions can be reduced to the other."[38] It is instructive to connect this theory of religion with the theory of cultural anomie when attempting to interpret the repoliticization of Islam. As mentioned earlier, Islamic societies are in a process of rapid social change: that is, in a "transitional situation." The concept of cultural anomie describes the disillusionment resulting from unfulfilled expectations invested in Westernization. Repoliticization represents the operation of the two partial functions of religion described by Luhmann: the bridging over of change and the absorption of disappointment in a state of cultural anomie. Luhmann continually points to the waning importance of religion in complex societies capable of offering functional equivalents for religion.

This raises the question of whether repoliticization plays a promoting or inhibiting role in the noncomplex societies in which it occurs.[39] The central task of these societies is the overcoming of underdevelopment. The positive interpretation of the repoliticization of Islam includes its usefulness in bridging change and absorbing disappointment. By contrast, its negative aspect lies in its utter inability to contribute to the conquest of underdevelopment. Repoliticization is no alternative.

PART TWO

ISLAM AS AN ARAB MONOTHEISM
AND ITS NON-ARAB VARIANTS

The position of Islam in World Society since the nineteenth century has been at the center of our analysis so far. World Society is characterized not only by extensive and dense transportation and communication networks but also, and primarily, by a socioeconomic and sociocultural asymmetry and a corresponding structure of domination. In the asymmetrical structure of World Society, modern Islam belongs among the dominated pre-industrial cultures. In my analysis of the intercultural processes of communication I attempted to explain the mechanisms of acculturation and counter-acculturation.

Whether currently dominated or not, Islam nevertheless belongs among the high cultures of world history. The origins of Islam and its contributions to the "process of civilization" are at the center of this second section. Pre-Islamic Arabia, known today as the Arabian peninsula, had neither an institutional center nor a developed material culture. Islam originated and grew in the two relatively developed, socioeconomically speaking, cities of Mecca and Medina and pacified the bellicose rival bedouin tribes of the entire peninsula. This internal pacification could have been accomplished initially only through an external expansion, as I shall show in detail in chapter 4. Nevertheless, in my opinion it is incorrect to describe Islam as a "warrior religion" (Elias Canetti), because following the military phase of expansion which created the borders of the new Arab Islamic Empire, a high culture flourished, representing an important advance in the "process of civilization."

My central thesis in chapter 4 is that Islam was originally, and continues today to be, an Arab monotheism, in spite of the fact that it has made a claim to universalism since its inception in the seventh century. I shall illustrate this contention using the example of the conflict between the Arabs and the Islamized non-Arabs (*mawali*).

It can justifiably be set against my thesis of an Arab Islam that the number of non-Arabs in the Islamic populations of the world is, proportionally, far larger than that of Arabs. This fact provides the starting point for a further thesis which I shall develop in chapter 5 apropos the West African example. There is no unified Islam either in reality or in religious doctrine. What was initially an Arab Islam was assimilated into the cultures of Islamized non-Arab populations and thus de-Arabized. West African Islam, for example, has been fully integrated into the West African animistic cultures, even though in its original Arab version it was rigorously monotheistic. Today there is an orthodox Arab Islam and a multitude of non-Arab variants of Islam.

Islam was able both to disseminate an urban culture within a nomadic environment and to establish it as the dominant culture within the *pax islamica* (W. Montgomery Watt). In West Africa, too, Islam was the vehicle for the spread of "state rule in an urban culture," as Gerd Spittler has pointed out for the case of Gobir. Even though the Islamization of West Africa was well under way before European colonial penetration began, it may safely be asserted that the spread of Islam occurred only parallel to colonial penetration. Islamization coincided with colonial penetration; two urban cultures found themselves in an accidental historical alliance. This may be one of the reasons behind the fact that the Islamization of West Africa qua establishment of an urban culture primarily served to further the ends of domination and was unable to produce a materially developed culture comparable to that of early Arab Islam.

CHAPTER 4

THE RELIGIOUS FOUNDATION OF ISLAM:
ISLAM AS AN ARAB IDEOLOGY AND CULTURE

Islam asserts a universal claim and is not confined to any particular ethnic or national group. I have already mentioned that after the establishment of a *pax islamica* in the Arabian peninsula, Islam spread to the far parts of the earth and became a world religion. Nevertheless, it cannot be disputed that Islam was originally an "Arab religion for Arabs" (Maxime Rodinson), a characterization still generally accepted today. At a conference in Cairo in 1979 I was allowed to follow the extremely interesting controversy between Mukti Ali, an Indonesian scholar of religion who presented a paper entitled "Islam and Indonesian culture," and Arab scholars from Al-Azhar University.[1] For Ali there was no inherent contradiction involved in holding fast to Islam as a religion and to Indonesian culture as his national and cultural frame of reference, whereas the Arab Muslims uncompromisingly insisted on the essentially Arab character of Islam.

In literature, too, this controversy continues. For the Pakistani Islamic scholar Fazlur Rahman, the thesis which maintains that Islam is a national religion of the Arabs is totally unacceptable since Islam, in his opinion, has a universal claim.[2] This is correct, of course, but does not alter the fact (emphasized by Carl Heinrich Becker among others) that Islam "in its inception was internally and externally bound to Arabdom."[3]

The researcher can detect even in very early Islam the seeds for potential conflict between non-Arab Muslims, who measured Islam against its claim to universality, and the Arabs, who regarded Islam as their own religion, fashioned for and by themselves. The eminent scholar of Islam H. A. R. Gibb has also drawn attention to the fact that

here and there voices might be raised against the Arabs, but in the field of religious thought they were ineffective against the weight of Araberthum, the Arab idea. The inner history of the Islamic civilization cannot be understood unless that fact is fully realized and given its due place.[4]

Islam originated as a political ideology which became "mobilizing" (Rodinson) and was thus able to produce a highly developed material culture. In chapter 1 the process of civilization was discussed along the lines proposed by Norbert Elias, and the emergence of an institutionalized center was identified as an important element in this process, one that had already taken place in Asia during the Imperial Age. In recent history this process has thus far been limited, unfortunately, to Europe and America, where the entire society displays a high degree of industrially conditioned differentiation and division of function. In the Muslim Middle East there were beginnings of such a development, particularly during the period of the ʿAbbasids (750–1258), which was brought to an end with the invasion of the Mongol barbarians.[5] That Islam is today a preindustrial, backward culture should not lead to the rash Eurocentric conclusion that this betrays the fundamental nature of Islam. As is the case with all cultures, Islam is only understandable from an historical perspective. I shall now discuss how it came about that Islam once was able to manifest a high culture. I trust that its present position has become clear from the detailed presentation of the structure of World Society presented in chapter 1.

The Historical Context for the Rise of an Arab Islamic Culture

In the debate on the origins of state and civilization there is general agreement that religious change precedes the rise of central state institutions. As this institutionalized center is being generated, it "creates a religious overlay above the familistic and local segmental cult levels that is society-wide, encompassing all activities. This religion worships true gods, not just vaguely defined spirits. The public monuments and temples where the ceremonies take place pertain to the society as a whole, and are built by society-wide corvée labor,"[6] as the anthropologist Elman Service stresses. These assertions refer, however, only to polytheistic religions. According to the logic of cultural evolution, if a monotheistic religion becomes political it should produce a far more powerful central institution. This is indeed the case with Islam, as we shall see below in greater detail.

But first we need to deal with the historical framework and sociocultural milieu from which Islam originated. The pre-Islamic Arabs were polytheists, lived in segmented tribal units, and possessed no institutionalized center. Two forms of social structure existed side by side. In Mecca a mercantile center developed within which the ethnic group of the Quraysh formed a stratum of wealthy merchants. By contrast, the primitive bedouins living in the desert maintained themselves materially by robbing trading caravans. The Quraysh of Mecca worshipped two main female goddesses, Allat and al-Uzza (the goddess Manat should be added).[7]

In the sixth century the civilized world was dominated by two world empires, the Roman Byzantine and the Persian Sassanid. The Arabs of this period, who were predominantly bedouins, were called Saracens because they lived in tents (Greek: *skene*). B. T. Sprenger characterized them as "parasites of the camel," by which he intended to describe their desert existence. As already mentioned, they lived primarily from the spoils taken in the plundering of merchant caravans, which was a form of acquisition and conquest called *ghazu* but which, however, prohibited the killing of human beings.

The bedouins possessed neither legal norms nor a central state power. Human lives were protected, as it were, through the institution of the vendetta. A bedouin avoided killing in order to avoid jeopardizing his and his family's lives by acts of blood vengeance. The harsh life of these people precluded the rise of indigenous art. Poetry, for example, was considered propaganda. The poet acted as the bard of his ethnic group and not as an independent artist. Thus, the bedouins had a low level of aesthetic development. Perhaps the institution of the vendetta best explains the morality of the bedouins, which Rodinson calls "tribal humanism." All ideals and vitality culminated for them "with man. Man was the highest value for man. But one is dealing here with social man, man within the context of his clan, his tribe." The bedouin is unfamiliar with abstract thinking. "He is a realist and the hard life of the desert has given him little preparation for reflection on the infinite."[8] In order to avoid becoming a victim of *ghazu*, merchant caravans paid off the bedouins, and only a strong state could neutralize danger from *ghazu*.

In order to gain greater control over the Arab regions the two world empires cultivated their own Arab vassals. Byzantium had its Ghassanid dynasty and Sassanid Persia had its Lakhmids. Both Arab dynasties also fought against each other in the name of the warring Byzantines and Sassanids. "As mercenaries or as auxiliary troops the Arabs were indispensable pillars of the two great empires."[9] These serviceable Arabs had no existence of their own. Jews and Christians had their Divine Being, whom the Arabs also knew under the name of "Allah" but whom they venerated along with other gods, such as the two mentioned above. The Christian and Jewish monotheists despised the Arabs. "For them they were a type of savage who were not even in possession of an organized church as all civilized peoples are."[10] For the Arabs, however, Judaism and Christianity were "foreign ideologies, bound to the powers who were quarreling over domination of the Arab peninsula."[11] The sociostructural changes produced by the mercantile economy which developed in the Arab interstice between the Byzantine and Sassanid empires, and particularly in Mecca, were critical for the foundation of the Islamic religion. The period can be defined by its acute need for an Arab ideology. "Men like Mohammed, Arabs, heard these stories . . . that the Jews and Christians were supported by world empires, that they were embraced by powerful and rich organizations. Their claims rested on sacred texts."[12] The Arabs, however, possessed neither a separate empire nor a separate sacred scripture. The "realms" of the Ghassanids and Lakhmids were nothing more than vassal states of Byzantium and Persia.

Muhammad's revelations, which began in the year 610 and lasted until his death in 632, began to be collected and systematized under the first caliphs and have come down to us today in their unchanged form as the Qur'an, or, "recitation."[13] I do not want to discuss here the myriad different interpretations of this revelation, one among many of which is my own modest contribution,[14] so for the purposes of this study I will simply repeat C. H. Becker's contention that the Arabs entered the ranks of the older "peoples of the book" (ahl al-kitab) with the Qur'an and thus acquired history, as we shall see further below.

For Rodinson, Muhammad was the founder of a new ideology which was able to function as a "mobilizing" force because it corresponded to the demands of the period for a uniquely Arab, monotheistic ideology. According to Rodinson, an understanding of ideologies presupposes that the historical period, the subjects of ideology, and ideology itself are comprehended immanently. An appreciation of Islam as an ideology requires that "the conditions under which [this ideology] could arise in the man Mohammed, in his personal history within the framework of a given society, be shown."[15] Rodinson, as sociologist and historian, rejects schematic, objective interpretations of history which leave no latitude to living, acting human beings.[16]

Islamic ideology flourished and spread not only because it satisfied the requirements of the time but also because its founder was a combination of the religious visionary, the prudent politician, and the shrewd military strategist. "He united in one single being Jesus and Charlemagne."[17] The resonance of Muhammad's message can be attributed to the fact that Islamic ideology was "an Arab religion for the Arabs."[18]

The reaction of the ruling elites to the new ideology also contributed to its rapid expansion. Stable social systems with a central state power have the capacity to integrate the novel, but Meccan society lacked both stability and centralization. It also lacked an institutionalized ecclesiastical structure which could have absorbed spiritually the ideological revolt of Muhammad. In the beginning Muhammad had few disciples and those he had were eager for compromise with the dominant Quraysh. But the "conservative Quraysh were angry. . . . They attempted to exert a general pressure on the entire clan of Hashim, in order to get them to remove their protection from the scabby sheep."[19] Through means such as these the Quraysh not only helped to create a firm solidarity among the fledgling Muslims, but they also engendered through their repression an even greater degree of cohesion in the small but steadily growing sect.

When the persecution of Muhammad's sect by the Quraysh in Mecca grew intolerably intense, its members began to emigrate discretely and after careful preparation in the year 622 (the beginning of the Muslim calendar) to the neighboring city of Medina, where they were received by other adherents of their sect. Medina became a theocratic city-state governed by Muhammad. In the military altercations between Mecca and Medina, God's Messenger proved himself to be both a clear-sighted politician and a capable military strategist. Seen psychoanalytically, the orphaned Muhammad's deprived childhood produced his strong attraction to women, which led to the instrumentalization of his passion for the new ideology in multiple marriages to daughters of influential bedouins, thus compelling the loyalty of their ethnic groups to his cause. It seems clear that "these marriages were not affairs of the heart but merely political expediencies."[20] However, these political matings of Muhammad could not by themselves eliminate the segmentalized partition of the peninsula by rival tribes. The establishment of a source of authority, recognized and submitted to by all the tribes, was crucially important. Monotheistic Islam mediated the "religious overlay" (E. Service) which transformed the tribe (*qawm*) at the microlevel of segmentalized Arab bedouin society into the Islamic society (*Umma*), encompassing all Arabs. The renowned historian of Islamic religion W. Montgomery Watt cites the "unifying of the Arabs"[21] as the most important historical achievement of Muhammad. In this sense Muhammad's work was also to create a cultural foundation inasmuch as it is, according to Freud's theory of culture, "one of the primary achievements of culture to agglomerate people into large units."[22]

The Theocratic City-State of Medina as the Omphalos of the Pax Islamica: Islam as an Arab Religion

In the sociology of religion, monotheism signifies the proclamation of a comprehensive and unique source of authority. In the Qur'an this is formulated as "Obey God and His Messenger and never let your labors go in vain" (47:33),[23] followed by the warning, "Indeed, God does not need you, but you need him. If you give no heed, He will replace you by others different from you" (47:38). Since God revealed the Qur'an in the Arabic language, He thereby gave the Arabs a special position. The pertinent verses of the Qur'an attesting to this are numerous. God has sent down the Qur'an "in the Arabic tongue" (12:2). The unbelievers speak a "non-Arab" language, the scripture revealed by God through Muhammad speaks in "eloquent Arabic language" (16:103). Finally, the Qur'an was revealed "in plain Arabic speech" (26:195). Watt belongs to the group of prominent scholars of Islam who have emphasized the essentially Arab character of Islam: "The religion founded on the base of the Qur'an is an alternative to the other religions of the foreigners" he writes in his important book *Muhammad at Medina*.[24] In his chapter on Muhammad in *The Cambridge History of Islam* he writes: "The Qur'an offers the Arabs a monotheism comparable to Judaism and Christianity but without their political ties. This may be described as the external political relevance of Muhammad's claim to be the Messenger of God."[25] The internal significance is documented in the *pax islamica* of the city-state of Medina, which Watt calls "the federation of the Arab tribes" and which encompassed all the rival bedouin tribes of the Arabian peninsula. Monotheistic authority served as the internal legitimacy for this federation, while military expansion held it together externally:

Thus internal peace and external expansion were complementary. Internal peace gave the Arabs a unified army and unified command needed for effective expansion, while the expansion was required in order to maintain internal peace.[26]

This description, however, is true only for the founding phase of the *pax islamica* when the distinction between *dar al-Islam* (domain of Islam) and *dar al-harb* (domain of war), between an internal peace and an external state of war, was still central. The *pax islamica* lost its original meaning during the period of high Islam; it is incorrect to assert, as Elias Canetti has, that Islam "displays the unmistakable traits of a martial religion,"[27] without distinguishing between different time periods.

The Qur'an contains the ideological legitimation for this *pax islamica* of Medina. Muhammad, the head of state, is the messenger of God: "And I have chosen you. Therefore listen to what shall be revealed" (20:13). "I am God. There is no God but Me. Serve Me, and recite your prayers in My remembrance" (20:15). The Islamic theory of revelation is presented most clearly in *sura* 53, "The Star," verses 1–18.

He who believes in this revelation and follows it will be rewarded in heaven, and he had best be obedient if he wants to avoid punishment for contumacious behavior. "He that obeys God and His Messenger shall be admitted to gardens watered by running streams; but he that turns and flees shall be sternly punished" (48:17).

Although Islam bears testimony to the far-reaching influence of Jewish[28] and Christian monotheism[29] and accepts both Jews and Christians as *ahl al-kitab* (people of the book), it nonetheless leaves no doubt but that God "has sent forth His Messenger with guidance and the true faith" (48:28). In Medina no opposition to the *pax islamica* of the Prophet was permitted: "It is not for true believers—men or women—to take their choice in the affairs if God and His Messenger decree otherwise. He that disobeys God and His Messenger strays far indeed" (33:36).

When reflecting on this legitimacy, one must always bear in mind the relations of rivalry and bellicosity in which the segmentalized Arab bedouin societies existed prior to the coming of Muhammad in the seventh century in order fully to understand and appreciate Muhammad's work, the establishment of his *pax islamica*, for the splendid historical achievement that it was. Solidarity and loyalty were, of course, important pre-Islamic values, but for the bedouins they were restricted to members of one's own ethnic group (*qawm*). In Muhammad's *pax islamica* this sense of solidarity and loyalty was enlarged to include the entire Islamic community (*Umma*). Watt emphasizes in his analysis of Islamic political philosophy that from its inception Islam has demonstrated the unifying power of loyalty and solidarity in the political and social organization of the community.[30] Marshall G. S. Hodgson describes Muhammad's historical achievement in these terms:

The political structure which Muhammad built was by now clearly a state structure like the states in the nations round about Arabia with an increasingly authoritative government, which could no longer be ignored with impunity. Muhammad sent out envoys who taught the Qur'an and the principles of Islam, collected the *zakāt*, and presumably arbitrated disputes so as to keep the peace and prevent feuding.[31]

Watt, too, regards Muhammad's labor as laying the religious foundation for a political, social, and economic system.[32]

After Muhammad's death his successors extended the political, social, and economic system of Medina (the *pax islamica*) through military expansion, which conjointly included Islamization and Arabization. From the original Islamic city-state of Medina an "international political order" emerged (Hodgson), and a "world civilization" was spawned.[33] The two world empires, the Byzantine and the Persian-Sassanid, which had bred and groomed Arabs as mercenaries and had nourished the Arab satellite states of the Ghassanids and Lakhmids, capitulated under the Islamic onslaught: "Within ten years the Persian world power was extinguished and 'Rome,' that is, Byzantium, had lost all its Eastern provinces."[34]

Helmut Böhme has studied the Islamic subjugation of the two world empires and the resulting worldwide Islamization and, speculating on the origins of this new historical force, adduces three central features which help to explain this new phenomenon: "1. The impetus of the new faith . . . ; 2. the exhaustion and erosion of the old power systems; 3. the rigorous adoption, renewal and further development of the economic, administrative and social traditions of the Roman and later of the Persian empires."[35] The mature Islamic civilization was no longer purely Arab, of course, nor was Islam merely a religion for a specific ethnic group as it was originally. One observes here an intercultural synthesis documenting a brilliant period in the cultural history of humankind.[36] This extraordinary world civilization, further enriched in high Islam by Hellenization,[37] should be remembered today by those superficial observers who hold Islam responsible for the underdevelopment of the Islamic regions of contemporary World Society. Of course, the reflective brooding on the glories of this lost high culture does nothing to help in solving the problems of the present; although as I have discussed at length in chapter 3 regarding the repoliticization of Islam, this cultural retrospection does solace modern Muslims by offering them an identity.

Islamic world civilization was an intercultural synthesis, although, to repeat, Islam was originally an "Arab religion for the Arabs" (Rodinson). Over time other peoples adopted and assimilated it and today's Islam exhibits rich cultural variations. French scholar-author Pierre Rondot, for example, has emphasized the specifically Persian national character of Twelver Shi'i Islam, evident in practices such as the holy 'Ashura ritual: "The traditional scenes of the Persian theater present the drama and evoke an astonishing paroxysm of popular excitement."[38] Rondot explains this further in another passage: "However, in Iran with its 83% Shi^{c}as this particularly subtle and fertile aspect of Islam is expressed best. Here, the popular consciousness identifies its belief in the imamate with the Iranian nation."[39] The Shi^{c}i ritual of self-flagellation during the *muharram* processions is clearly Persian, but it also appeared at a later date in the non-Persian Shi^{c}i communities of the Arab Middle East (Lebanon and Iraq), as Werner Ende has shown.[40] However, the fact that the Twelver Shi^{c}a[41] has taken on a peculiarly Iranian character since the Persian Safavid dynasty (founded 1502) does not necessarily lead to the conclusion, too often encountered in Sunni Islamic literature (which even I at one time erroneously advocated[42]), that Shi^{c}i Islam is simply a Persian national religion.[43] Ende has established through his research that the classical conflict between Muslim Arabs and non-Arabs (*mawali*), which I discussed earlier in this chapter with reference to Gibb and which is quite alive even today (witness the quarrel over the character of Islam), cannot be identified with the fundamental schism of Islam which occurred in the seventh century and produced orthodox Sunni and Shi^{c}i sectarianism.[44]

In the Arab Sunni literature Shi^{c}i Islam is associated with the attacks by non-Arabs on Islam. The attitude of the non-Arab Muslims is characterized in these writings by the term *Shu^{c}ubiyya* (ethnic pride). In a rather well-known publication by the Iraqi jurist ^{c}Abd al-Hadi Fakiki the *mawali* attitude is excoriated in these terms:

the serpents of the Shu^{c}ubiyya expand and spit out their venom. Those who affect foreign ways (the Shu^{c}ubiyya) and seethe with hatred against the Arabs . . . secretly retain the religion of their ancestors. . . . The Zoroastrian influences in Iran are a proof of this. . . . Heresy (*zandaqa*) is indeed the goal aspired to by the Shu^{c}ubiyya . . . in order to destroy Arab essence.[45]

A prominent Arab economic historian, ^{c}Abd al-^{c}Aziz al-Duri, in a 1960 publication identified Islam with "arabness" (*^{c}uruba*) and defined the Shu^{c}ubiyya in the following way:

The Shu^{c}ubiyya movement is the expression of a non-Arab consciousness, especially among the Persians. The Shu^{c}ubiyya represent the attempt to nullify Arab existence and annihilate Arab predominance. It is identical with heresy (*zandaqa*) because [it] attacks the very basis of Arab predominance, that is, Islam itself. For the non-Arab, Islam and Arabness are synonymous."[46]

I must once again quote Werner Ende, who states that the assertion according to which there is "a close relationship between the national consciousness of the non-Arabs and the heretical movements . . . by no means appeared for the first time with the rise of Arab nationalism, but . . . can be found in the Sunni authors of the Middle Ages."[47] Ende points to many Arab writings in which the "promoted association between Shiᶜa, Shuᶜu-biyya and heresy"[48] is documented.

These examples illustrate the thesis that Islam is an "Arab religion for the Arabs" and document the abhorrence felt by Arabs at the idea of Islam being assimilated by other cultures. They oppose this assimilation on grounds that it is "heresy" (*zandaqa*) and equate it with non-Arab national pride. If viewed in this light the assimilation of Islam by non-Arab cultures has to be interpreted as a de-Arabization of Islam, which is in itself quite legitimate of course, especially if considered from the norm of cultural pluralism.

In chapter 5 I shall analyze this de-Arabization of Islam using West Africa as an example and shall try to show that West African Islam is a nearly new, albeit clearly West African, religion.

The West African variant of non-Arab Islam and orthodox Islam share, however, a common element: they are both variants of a preindustrial culture, as I shall explain.

CHAPTER 5

THE UNIVERSALIZATION OF ISLAM: THE CASE OF THE ISLAMIZATION OF THE NON-ARAB PEOPLES OF WEST AFRICA

The establishment of the *pax Islamica* chronicles a higher stage in the process of evolution; it represents the conquest of the segmentary tribal organization of the pre-Islamic Arabian peninsula through a new central institution. The transition from polytheism to monotheism is a religio-historical component of this developmental process. Freud sketched this development in his interpretation of monotheism:

With the merger of the tribes and peoples into larger units the gods, too, organize themselves into families, into hierarchies. One among them is usually elevated to the position of sovereign over [both] gods and men. Hesitantly, then, the further step is taken to render what is due to only one god; and finally the decision comes about to grant all power to one single god and to tolerate no other gods beside him.[1]

The pre-Islamic Arabs, despised by the monotheistic Jews and Christians as pagans, could step forth as equals after the foundation of Islam. As Freud expressed it: "The reclamation of one almighty Ur-father produced an extraordinary augmentation of self-confidence in the Arabs and this in turn led to great temporal triumphs."[2] And here the question immediately arises whether the adoption of Islamic monotheism by other peoples was able to generate a similar development. Islam is understood by Muslims as being both universal and uniform, even though, as I have repeatedly stressed, its Arab character is always emphasized. I am putting forward the thesis here, however, that the adoption of Islam by non-Arab peoples meant its assimilation into their respective cultures. The Africanization of Islam is at the center of this chapter.

Islam is not only a religion, of course. The very fact that in the year 622, only twelve years after its proclamation, the political system of the *pax Islamica* was securely established in Medina demonstrates the power of Islam as a system of order. The substance of Islamic doctrine is found in the *Shari'a*.[3] The *Shari'a* is a complex system of law with corresponding jurisdiction regulating, or better, inflicting discipline on all areas of life.

Ernst Bloch, rejecting the economic explanation of religion, suggested that "the original essential element" in the phenomenon of religion should be considered and understood as "the intimacy of the oldest dream, as the broadest eruption of the history of heresy, as the ecstasy of walking upright, and as the chafing, rebellious, most ardent will to paradise."[4] Unfortunately *Shari'a* Islam is as secular as any legal code and cannot fulfill such spiritual needs. During the ʿAbbasid period (750–1258), when Islamic civilization was at its zenith, the secularization of Islam went on at an alarming pace. A. J. Arberry interprets the blossoming of Islamic mysticism (Sufi Islam)[5] during this period as a "reaction to the wealth and luxury which flooded the Islamic world after the conquest of Byzantium and the Persian Empire destroyed the former simple ways of life. Other forms of worldliness also conditioned the rise of Islamic mysticism."[6]

From Sufi Islam *Tariqa* Islam issued. *Tariqa*, translated literally, means "way" and in this context signifies a personal form of practising Islam, freed from the strict prescriptions found in the *Shari'a*. *Tariqa* Islam became the mode of religious expression first of the Arabized peoples, such as the Berbers of North Africa, and then of the non-Arab Islamized peoples who found in *Tariqa* Islam what was denied them in *Shari'a* Islam: a means of assimilating Islam into their own culture. West African Islam is a variant of *Tariqa* Islam.

The Islamization of West Africa: Characteristics of African Islam

It is not possible within the framework of this study to deal with all forms of African Islam. I shall discuss here West African Islam as being both representative as well as one of the most important variants of Islam.[7]

The Islamization of West Africa took place between the eleventh and sixteenth centuries through the agency of, first, the military conquests of the North African Almoravids who were ravaging West Africa in the search for gold and slaves and, second, through the more benign conduit of long-distance trade with North Africa. Thus, Maghrebi merchants contributed their share to the Islamization of West Africa by opening it up through their mercantile activities.

We know from the sparse ethnographic reports of this time that the West African adoption of Islam remained entangled in superficial forms. Anthropologists describe a mixture of animism and Islam in which the adopted religion is no longer recognizable.[8] Donal O'Brien concedes that even today any attempt to make a sharp division between animism and Islam should be undertaken with great caution:

Many elements of Wolof religion were absorbed into Islamic belief and practice. Present-day anthropologists who have studied religion among the Wolof have identified many features of local Islam which can be traced to pre-existent local beliefs.[9]

Thus the *Tariqa* Islam which was disseminated in West Africa during the end of the eighteenth and the beginning of the nineteenth centuries contained such substantial traits of animist African culture that true Islamization cannot be attributed to this historical period. A new phase, however, was introduced by new social emissaries, members of the Islamic brotherhoods (*khouan*).

The brotherhoods grew out of Sufi Islam, which was initially cultivated only by ecstatic, ascetic Muslim believers on an individual basis. The great Islamic mystic, Husayn al-Hallaj (858–922), represented Islamic mysticism at its finest. Al-Hallaj paid with his life for his efforts to spiritualize Islam. According to al-Hallaj the individual participates in the Divine will through an ecstatic union with God. In this union an exchange of individuality occurs between God and man: "I saw my lord with my heart's eye and said, 'Who are you?' He answered, 'You.' "[10] For Islamic orthodoxy this is heresy. Such ecstatic practices are undertaken collectively in brotherhoods, through *dhikr*; that is, through the recitation of Qur'anic verses and religious texts and through the crying out of the various names of Allah in the course of a violently ecstatic dance which produces at its conclusion an exhausted collapse of the faithful. These practices fulfill the need for the religious, in Bloch's sense, far better than erudite treatises of the Islamic scholars on the *Shari'a* can, and it was in this form that Islam was spread, first in North Africa and later in sub-Saharan Africa.

All brotherhoods embodying Islam in West Africa today are offshoots of two major ones: the Qadiriyya, founded in twelfth-century Baghdad, and the Tijaniyya, which originated in eighteenth-century Morocco. Both brotherhoods are manifestations of *Tariqa* Islam. The most important West African brotherhood, the Mourids (aspirants), is an offshoot of the Qadiriyya and was founded by the marabout Amadu Bamba. The most important offshoot of the Tijaniyya was founded by the marabout Ibrahima Niass. The word "marabout" comes originally from the Arabic word *ribat* (fortress). The *murabits*, or faithful, originally lived in fortresses in order to defend Islam. In West Africa the marabout, as sheikh, embodies religious authority and leads the brotherhood. His knowledge of Islam is a source of power and his role as master and mediator is acknowledged by his disciples. As it evolved, however, the maraboutic institution took on completely different forms and functions. The marabout performed functions similar to those of the animistic medicine man and dominated his disciples (*talibés*) through magic. The African marabout claims to be able to speak with God and summon spirits. Through his contact with God he can procure a blessing (*baraka*) for his obedient disciples, and through his relationship with the spirits he can punish aberrant behavior. Since West African societies are not yet complex social systems possessing correspondingly complex structures of role differentiation, the marabout is not only a religious leader but often also a trader, judge, teacher, magician, and everyday preacher.[11]

The reality of African Islam described above—an Islam which perhaps shares only its name in common with the original Islamic religion—has encouraged some scholars to assume that West Africa was still animistic prior to the expansion of brotherhood Islam. In fact, the Tukulor chiefs and some members belonging to the Wolof people were already Muslim before the nineteenth century, but here one is dealing with a very lax form of Islam. O'Brien emphasizes that these people clearly "did not see themselves as non-Muslims, and would not have been considered so at an earlier stage in the diffusion of Islam."[12] After the penetration of West Africa by *Tariqa* Islam this "lax Islam" was condemned and the existing social order which was supported only by "nominal Muslims" was called into question. Colonization of West Africa by the French and British from the middle of the nineteenth century onward took place parallel to the warring between the adherents of *Tariqa* Islam and the chiefs or rural notables of the ethnic groups who still practised a discredited animism. A French colonial official, Robert Arnaud, viewed the conflict between the Wolof chiefs and the adherents of *Tariqa* Islam as a class struggle and saw in the introduction of the new Islam

a true social revolution because in reality it documents the opposition of the proletarian caste against the aristocracy: a class struggle. . . . With the help of Islam they [the lower castes—B.T.] formed a block against the aristocracy.[13]

Initially, colonial penetration contributed only indirectly to the diffusion of *Tariqa* Islam by hastening the dissolution of the inherited Wolof order and thereby weakening the Wolof chiefs in their struggle:

The Wolof social system was in severe crisis and as a result its people were groping for some kind of security. . . . Largely because of this insecurity, Islam in the form of brotherhoods took hold among the Wolof in the end of the nineteenth century. The brotherhoods offered an order of life that seemed more adequate than the old one had been.[14]

The Islamic brotherhoods therefore created a revitalization movement in West Africa because they had assailed both animistic Islam and the social order of the Wolof chiefs. After their victory things remained unchanged. The marabouts soon aligned themselves with both the Wolof chiefs and with the colonial system and through their firm internal hierarchical organizational structure contributed to the solidification of archaic structures.

O'Brien describes the new social importance of the marabouts who had inaugurated *Tariqa* Islam:

Maraboutic authority had something to offer to each of these social categories, to the ex-rulers and to the ex-subjects of the Wolof states. The slaves, low-caste clients and poor peasants found security and protection under the *marabouts*, new masters who could provide patronage and leadership although in forms adjusted to the circumstances of colonial rule. The chiefs and their high-class associates, on the other hand, recovered some of their lost prestige through marital and other alliances with maraboutic families."[15]

The revitalization movement supported by the Islamic brotherhoods did indeed lead to a more intensive Islamization of West Africa, but it did not lead to a victory over the animistic traits of the prevailing African Islam. Religious renewal exhausted itself in the social ascent of the new religious authorities, the marabouts. The new maraboutic Islam however remained profoundly African. The marabouts, who had once opposed the inadmissible mixture of Islamic monotheism and pagan animism, took over the positions of magicians and medical men themselves, a point I shall discuss in greater detail below.

This second wave of Islamization in West Africa can be seen in the perspective of social history as representing the expansion of urban influences to the countryside, especially since the Islam of the brotherhoods originated in the cities. Before I discuss Islam as an African identity I want to explain the relationship between maraboutic Islam in West Africa and the colonial penetration of this region.

Maraboutic Islam and the Colonial System

As I have emphasized, precolonial Africa was made up of segmentary societies[16] lacking, with a few exceptions, any centralized government.[17] Africa was therefore similar to pre-Islamic Arabia. Islam, however, is an urban culture with claims to universality. The ethnosociologist Gerd Spittler describes the process of West African Islamization as the extension of state domination over the peasants. Islam was spread in West Africa from the urban centers and consequently encouraged an urban orientation for the peasants. "The Muslim is expected to have a supralocal orientation. . . . A Muslim belongs to a universe which transcends the tribe."[18] In this way Spittler establishes the relationship between Islamization and the development of a supralocal market.[19] We might pursue here the two historical events mentioned above which accidentally coincided: Islamization, which spread the domination of urban centers, and European colonial penetration, which dissolved inherited rural structures. The encounter of these two historical developments helps to explain why the colonial system actually furthered Islamization. Martin Klein shows in detail that the marabouts were excellent instruments for the colonial system to use in order to integrate the rural areas into the urban market structures: "The marabouts were more in sympathy with and better able to adapt to the market economy, and were, not surprisingly, more interested in protecting commerce than the traditional pagan societies were."[20] Islamization and colonization contributed equally to the weakening and dissolution of tribal structures. Mervin Hiskett illustrates with the example of Hausaland that Islam created "cultural homogeneity" there and "to a large extent, overcame the fissiparous forces of tribalism."[21] One more aspect of the coincidence of colonial penetration and *Tariqa* Islamization still needs to be more closely considered.

At the advent of French and British colonial masters in West Africa many indigenous ruling systems such as that of the Wolofs collapsed. Those autochthonous ruling systems which were functional were kept alive by the colonial system. The British system of *indirect rule* was known for its cooperation with African Islam. It granted local autonomy to the Islamic Fulani emirates and African notables in northern Nigeria, thus enlisting them in its service and thereby sparing the cost of erecting a colonial administration. The French colonial system also mobilized the Islamic brotherhoods for assistance in its colonial penetration. The Mouridiyya Brotherhood, although initially anticolonial, played a major role in the establishment of the peanut monoculture in French West Africa. The spread of Islam in West Africa since the nineteenth century occurred with colonial approval. In *The Cambridge History of Islam* we read:

The fact that so many Muslims accommodated themselves to European rule led to new tensions within the Muslim community. In part also, and this was the greater part, the effect of European colonialism was to enlarge Islamic opportunities in three main ways: through indirect rule, direct employment of Muslims, and generally increased mobility.[22]

The French colonial system called on the Mouridiyya Brotherhood to assist in the establishment of a French form of indirect rule. And it should be remarked in this context that "the Mourids were soon in the position of producing more than half of the total peanut output for export from Senegal."[23]

The maraboutic organization of the brotherhoods was ideally suited for offering up the members of a brotherhood, the disciples of the marabout, as rural workers to the colonial system:

The *marabouts* consolidated their position both politically and economically by turning their followers to the cultivation of groundnuts, a task in which the Wolof peasants could benefit themselves and enrich their religious leaders.[24]

Carl Heinrich Becker, the leading German Orientalist of his time, Prussian Minister of Culture, and one of the fathers of German Islamic studies as a colonial discipline, emphasized in 1910 the advantages of African Islam for European colonial rule:

But Islam offers the Negro other advantages as well. It succeeds by adapting itself to native customs; it demands only a decision of the will, the pronunciation of certain formulae and the more or less obligatory execution of circumcision. The Christian missionaries on the other hand fear, for good reason, a degradation of Christianity and therefore grant baptism only after a lengthy education. Furthermore, Islam gives the Negro a higher degree of civilization and a certain inner discipline, without tearing him out of his natural milieu. The Christian Negro, by contrast, is almost always deracinated, without becoming a true member of his new environment. He simply remains the eternal "native."[25]

It would be trivial to point out the colonial ideological elements in this quotation, and the critique of ideology should not exhaust itself in "unmasking" in any case. Becker was not only a colonial ideologue but also a competent Islamic scholar. Two important points should be noted in this quotation: first, the significance of Islam as an identity for the African, since Islam, contrary to Christianity, does not deracinate the African;

second, the significance of Islam as a Puritan ethic in the Weberian sense: that is, as a work discipline. "Islam creates a spirit of discipline, an inner stability and an outer courtesy of behavior in an infinitely more expansive fashion than [Christian] missionizing could ever achieve."[26] Becker expresses the desired goal quite clearly as "the reconciliation of Islam with European rule."[27] The example of the Mouridiyya Brotherhood, which contributed politically to the establishment of French colonial rule and economically to the introduction and consolidation of a monoculture (work discipline for the African), should suffice as illustration of the political and social significance of *Tariqa* Islam.

In his field research in West Africa, Gerd Spittler concentrated on the domination of the peasants, and documents how this control was intensified through the extension of the influences of urban centers. Islam as an urban culture contributed to this process. It is useful, therefore, to look more closely into the inner structure of the Muslim brotherhoods in West Africa and the social role they played in the extension of dominance over the peasants.

The social milieu of a brotherhood (*khouan*) in West Africa is rural and its members are peasants. Their leaders, the marabouts, do not work because they are mediators between God and the believers and regard their task in life as procuring the blessing (*baraka*), for which they are rewarded with material goods (*hadaya*). Thus, the ability of the marabouts to advance to the position of large landowners becomes understandable. The marabouts accommodated themselves to the colonial system and were rewarded with privileges. Alliances with the former Wolof chiefs through marriage complete this picture.

Each brotherhood is constructed along strict hierarchical lines and is divided into lodges (*zawiyas*). The marabout himself exercises direct authority over his disciples (*talibés*) who are always subordinate to the marabout who imparts his religious instruction to them at a teaching center (*dara*). Each *khouan* is distinguished by absolute obedience to its marabout. The marabouts in turn practice a strict hierarchy among themselves and each brotherhood has more than one marabout. The authority exercised by the marabouts over the peasants rests on their knowledge of Islam, on their magical abilities and on their contacts with Allah and the spirits. Obedient *talibés* are rewarded with *baraka* and the faithless are threatened with punishments by the spirits. With this perfectly organized system of social hierarchy, maraboutism can be seen as a well-functioning contemporary example of an archaic system of dominance. We might recall here the definition of religion given by Wallace cited at the beginning of chapter 2, according to which religious systems are based on rituals which preserve and control.

Is Tariqa Islam an African Identity?

The distinction I make between *Tariqa* and *Shariʿa* Islam at the beginning of this chapter should not be interpreted as a suggestion that only *Tariqa* Islam has found an entry into Africa. *Shariʿa* Islam has also assumed an African form, as can be seen in the establishment of Islamic law in Africa.[28] The Hamburg Africanist Brun-Otto Bryde has shown in some detail that the *Shariʿa* belongs, together with African customary law and acquired European law, among the three sources which merge to make up the African legal mixture.[22] But only *Tariqa* Islam could be Africanized and therefore accepted as a way of life. Martin Klein reports that this Africanization

has, in fact, been one of the strengths of African Islam. The marabout, who in most cases was illiterate and often scorned by his more learned Catholic rivals, has been more successful because he is an African; and the Koran is all the more widely accepted by Africans because it is taught with an African accent.[30]

The Swiss ethnopsychoanalyst Paul Parin, who has done research on Dogon society, could, on the one hand, confirm that Islamization "among numerous individuals from the Dogon people . . . led to an impoverishment of certain satisfactions and to certain reductions in the efficiency of the Ego," but that, on the other hand, Islam plays a "socially unifying role . . . when a Dogon moves into Islamic foreign territory or when Islam spreads through his [own] village."[31] Parin also insists that Islamization does not create identity conflicts,[32] whereas such conflicts are produced by Westernization. I shall consider this problem further in the following section in conjunction with my controversy with the African sociologist Samuel Kodjo (see also chapter 1).

The most important source for maraboutic Islam can be found in Sufi Islam. Mystical Islam originated in the Arab Middle East. The divine qualities which the marabout claims to be endowed with are the same as those claimed by representatives of Sufi Islam. Islamic mystics maintain that they become one with God and in this unity partake of His essence and therefore, as Rodinson puts it, "feel a certain disdain for the Prophet, this species of camera, robot, loudspeaker, phonograph—if such things had existed at that time—who was used by God for the transmission of His message."[33]

Certainly, the West African marabouts are continuing in the Arab Islamic tradition of mysticism when they lay claim to the possession of divine attributes. And, as we have seen, the early Islamic mystics, together with all mystics of all religions, experienced unity with God during their ecstatic rituals. But the maraboutic Islam practiced in West Africa, especially its ubiquitously reoccurring element of magic, is a unique expression of African culture in which a degree of domination over nature is absent and this absence manifests itself in religious rites.

Now the question arises whether Islamization is not a cultural imperialism similar to Christian missionizing or whether Islam would be or could become a basis for an African identity. I cited Becker above, who stresses that the Westernized African loses the prop of his own culture but fails to find essential connections with the new culture: he remains "a native," albeit deracinated. This does not happen to the Islamized African. Islam is not a foreign ideology in Africa; it is an autochthonous one: "Certainly, many pagan superstitions and pagan practices survive in black Islam. The Mohammedan Africans who still continue to live partially according to the faith and practice of animists are numerous."[34] African Islam is thus an ideology of acculturation which reaches deep into West African society, whereas the ideologies of Westernization remain on the surface and are supported only by Westernized, deracinated intellectuals. "Certainly Islam has the great advantage of having been introduced by non-Europeans. This privilege is very valuable today and plays a major role on the level of emotions."[35] Nearly all Africanists who work on Islam have stressed that Islam respected the pre-Islamic tradition of the Islamized peoples and therefore had easier access to Africa.[36]

In the first phase of the expansion of the Islamic brotherhoods in West Africa, Islam acquired a certain anticolonial significance. O'Brien concedes that "the dignity of Islamic ritual, and pride in membership of a wider Islamic community may have offered a psychological compensation for subordination to European control, a means of preserving self-respect."[37] One does not need to be an apologist for Islam in order to defend it from the accusation of collaboration with the colonial power. Islam is not an abstract ideology. It always assumes an historical form compatible with whichever historical evolution it happens to be connected. The Islamic revitalization movement was guided by marabouts who were rooted in the West African tradition of magic and deficient in power over nature. With maraboutism, what had earlier been a system of ethnic chiefdoms was reproduced under an Islamic mantle and, consequently, any change or social uprising, such as early Islam was capable of producing under Muhammad in the seventh century, was precluded. One cannot overlook this form of maraboutic organization in African Islam if one wants to accurately estimate the political and social significance of Islam in contemporary West Africa.

Maraboutism continues to exist in the form of an African variant of Islam. After achieving independence the Westernized West African intellectuals, who had led the decolonization movement and had now advanced to positions as statesmen, took over the administrative heritage of the colonial system. Maraboutism belongs to what they inherited and was left unmolested by the new politicians, who needed the marabouts, among others, for establishing and shoring up their authority. Senegal is a prime example for this thesis. The marabouts continue today to play the role assigned them by their colonial masters for the postcolonial West African governments: consolidation and stabilization of the regime in power. In Senegal, for example, the marabouts sell the votes of their adherents to the party of choice, thereby enriching themselves from a modern source. Furthermore,

the politically "moderate" Senegalese Government can use the *marabouts* as a conservative balance to urban radical demands. . . . In circumstances of political crisis, a united Mouride brotherhood might conceivably become a means of violence . . . against revolutionary opponents of the regime.[38]

African Cultures and Islam as Preindustrial Cultures

From ethnological research we know that there is no uniform African culture, just as we know from Islamic scholarship that a uniform Islam is merely the wishful thinking of Islamic apologists. It is easy to verify the existence of many distinct African cultures and also of many rival Islamic tendencies; but a harmonious, uniform structure cannot be found, even though a central community can be identified. For in spite of the cultural differences existing between Islam and the pre-Islamic African cultures mentioned above, it is clear that Islam expanded easily in West Africa. The obvious question here is why Africans accept Islam, a culture foreign to Africa, more readily than Western European culture. Samuel Kodjo makes a distinction between "relatively equal" and "diametrically polarized cultures."[39] According to Kodjo, Islam and African culture (note that he is writing here in the singular!) are relatively equal, whereas the latter and Western European culture stand in diametrical polarization to each other.

Cultural historians do not dispute the fact that Arab Islamic culture was far superior to African animistic cultures. In spite of this, both these cultures shared certain features in common, the most important being that both were *preindustrial cultures* which could not rely on science and technology. Although they differed in the degree of domination over nature they could exercise, it can nevertheless be said of both that they cannot be described as cultures based on a mastery of nature. The correspondence of the sacred and the political is the distinguishing mark of a culture lacking domination over nature, according to the French anthropologist Georges Balandier. In both Islam and the African animistic cultures, religious and political authority coincide: religion is always political. To be sure, in high Islam a Greek-influenced, rational Islamic philosophy arose within the framework of Hellenization. This philosophy clearly recognized a subject-object relationship foreign to African cultures. But this rational philosophy could not prevail against the political theology of the Islamic scholars.[40] The animistic African looks at nature as an extension of his own subjectivity; he is embedded in it.

Nature appears as an impenetrable and inscrutable power; magic formulae substitute for missing rational explanations. The same holds true for mystical Islam. In spite of this religious affinity, because they had a more developed material culture than did the Africans, the Arabs also behaved like superiors when in Africa. The Islamization of Africa was not the peaceful affair many Muslim authors are fond of depicting. Even Samuel Kodjo concedes that "certainly Islam and its representatives have demonstratively displayed their feelings of superiority and possibly also arrogance to the rest of Africa. This led to the merciless subjugation and conversion of some areas of Africa, among other things."[41] Nevertheless, we cannot speak of an Arab Islamic colonization of Africa. Colonization occurred only at the hands of those nations which had science and technology at their disposal and made use of them to establish their world domination. As I mentioned before, the Arab Islamic and African cultures were both preindustrial and without a technological-scientific foundation.

Although Arab Islamic culture was far more developed than African culture, the two shared in common their preindustrial character and thus were not mutually exclusive. Kodjo evaluates the intercultural processes of communication between Africa and Islam in the following way:

Relatively equal cultures and civilizations, precisely because they cannot shut each other out given this equality, tolerate and promote each other and might therefore be able to induce a contact situation, in spite of the possibility that one might superimpose its dominance over the other. . . . The superimposition of Islam over wide areas of Africa can be viewed as particularly characteristic of this condition of cultural encounter.[42]

In this sense African Islam can be interpreted as a form of preindustrial culture assimilated into indigenous African cultures. Recent attempts by Arab oil-producing countries to gain political influence in Africa both materially, with the help of petro-dollars, and ideologically, with the help of orthodox Arab Islam, have to be distinguished, as day-to-day political events, from the intercultural process of communication between Islam and Africa and the attendant Islamization of broad African regions. The study of African Islam clearly shows that Islam has been fully integrated into the animistic cultures of Africa. It has become, in effect, an African religion, and does not represent a political weapon in the hands of oil monarchs or dictators.

The intercultural process of communication between Europe and Africa on the one hand and the Muslim Middle East on the other displays in each case different traits from those observable in the process of communication between two preindustrial cultures. Contemporary acculturation is completely different from the latter process. The superimposition of Western European industrial culture on the non-European regions of the world occurs in the course of the encounter between "diametrically polarized cultures," as Kodjo would put it. The question here involves the encounter between one industrial culture and many nonindustrial cultures which are all integrated into the same World Society, structured now by power relations (see the discussion in chapter 1).

I have modified the reference to the preindustrial communality of African and Arab Islamic cultures by stressing the fact that the latter is a relatively developed culture, whereas the animistic cultures of Africa have no written traditions. This differentiation is of great relevance for the evaluation of the cultural encounter with Europe, or, of acculturation. In their collision with the modern Occident the animistic cultures of West Africa found themselves confronted with cultural configurations in state, economy, law, and so on, "for which there was no correspondence in their own tradition,"[43] as Uwe Simson, who has investigated this process of acculturation, notes. According to Simson the intercultural communication between Europe and the Arab Middle East is determined by the fact that the Middle East "can, in principle, counter all cultural elements of the partner with its own corresponding elements."[44] Kodjo can be understood in this way if he is seen as equating acculturation with cultural annihilation rather than with communication, even if he generalizes the African case, as I have shown in chapter 1. Western European culture could be completely superimposed on African traditions because, to use as an example the case of legal systems, there was no written African law. In the Middle East the process had a somewhat different complexion because equivalent elements existed for the configurations of the new culture. European law, for example, could not be firmly established because the *Shari'a* was available. Nevertheless, Islamic law cannot really be understood unless European influences are taken into consideration, as Noel Coulsen, the British expert on Islamic law, points out.[45]

In spite of this qualification the indisputable thesis remains that both cultures, the Arab Islamic and the animistic African (including the Afro-Islamic), are preindustrial and face similar problems in trying to master the developmental demands of our technological-scientific age.

PART THREE

ISLAM AND THE PROCESSES OF TRANSFORMATION
IN THE MODERN MIDDLE EAST

In part one I dealt with the meaning of modern Islam in World Society and attempted to analyze the asymmetrical structure of the acculturation processes which take place within this international society. Seen in the context of the superimposed framework of World Society, modern Islam appears as a preindustrial culture subordinate to the dominant technological-scientific culture. I have interpreted the repoliticization of Islam in this context as a counteracculturation.

In order to show that the backwardness of modern Islam is only an historical phenomenon, and thus not the essence of Islam, I returned in part two to the founding of the Islamic religion which, when considered from the perspective of the history of civilization, can be seen as the beginning of an extraordinarily important, world high culture. I stressed that *the* Islam does not exist, given that the original Arab Islam underwent considerable internal religious and especially cultural differentiation in the process of universalization. Today there are widely divergent variants of Islam—a fact which I illustrated with the example of West African Islam in chapter 5.

However, all variants of modern Islam share a commonality in that they are preindustrial cultures under challenge in a scientific-technological age. My central thesis in this study is that the predominant reaction to this threat is the adoption of a culturally defensive posture. However, to use a culturally analytical position to attempt an understanding of modern Islam is inappropriate and inadequate—a point central in my own criticism of traditional Islamic scholarship, which treats Islam as merely an object for exegetic and interpretative source studies, with interdisciplinary methodologies being foreign territories. Modern Islam is a social reality, not a literary source. My task in the third and last part of this study is the elucidation of this thesis.

In chapter 6 I shall try to define modern Islam from a theory-of-religion standpoint and to explain its place in the processes of social change from the viewpoint of a theory of society.

The Islamic Middle East has undergone transformational processes since the nineteenth century which have significantly changed its social structures. The promoters of social change were the new social forces which emerged from these processes. I shall examine the two most important forces for change here: students, whom I shall discuss in chapter 7, and the oil workers, whose importance I shall illustrate in chapter 8, using the examples of the petroleum economies in Iran and Saudi Arabia.

The transformational processes discussed here as problematic also condition the manifestations of Westernization in the modern Middle East, which are predominantly normative and not structural, as I shall elaborate further in chapter 7. This does not mean that the structures themselves are immutable; but it does mean that change is limited to a modification of the structures of underdevelopment which are so baldly apparent in the modern Islamic Middle East, as I shall demonstrate in chapter 8 apropos the changes conditioned by the production of oil.

CHAPTER 6

ISLAM AND SOCIAL CHANGE IN THE MODERN MIDDLE EAST

Two antithetical positions (which nevertheless share a tendency toward reductionism) are encountered when one studies the relationship between religion and the processes of social change. Proponents of an earlier position embraced by the humanities, as well as contemporary advocates of modernization theory, locate religious phenomena in the world of ideas; whereas Marxist authors dispute the autonomy of the normative realm and simply reduce religion to economics.

For Gustav E. von Grunebaum, the preeminent Orientalist of his time, religion embodies a special ideal force. He writes of the exceptional ability of "a religious movement to bring about cultural change" and ascribes this to the fact that "an alteration in religious position frequently aims at a revision of fundamental values, or even attempts to replace and thus to change the ordering principles of a cultural system more profoundly than any other complex of ideas would be capable of doing."[1] The opposite position can be found in Engels who, contrary to Marx, always displayed an inclination toward reductionism. For all that, the Eurocentric von Grunebaum does award Islam high marks for producing a high culture, whereas Engels regards Islamic history as circular and static. According to Engels it manifests itself in a "periodically recurring collision" between nomads and the craftsmen living in the cities. If the bedouins conquer the city dwellers they are themselves transformed in the course of historical development into city dwellers: "After a hundred years, of course, they are exactly at the point where those apostates stood [and] a new purification of the faith is necessary."[2] This "periodically recurring collision," according to Engels, is robed in religion and does not lead to a higher stage of development because the victorious nomads

leave the old economic conditions untouched. Things go on as usual and the collisions continue to occur periodically. By contrast, in the popular uprisings of the Christian West the religious wrapping serves only as banner and camouflage for attacks on an aging economic order. This order is finally overthrown and a new one arises, the world moves forward.[3]

Engels classifies the rise of Islam within these circular processes of social change: "Islam is a religion tailored for Orientals, especially Arabs, thus on the one hand to city dwellers engaged in trade and the crafts and on the other to nomadic bedouins."[4] In his letter to Marx of 24 May 1853 Engels emphasizes that "Mohammed's religious revolution, like *any* religious movement, was *formally a reaction*, [a] futile return to the old, [the] simple."[5] As one reads these passages it is particularly striking how precarious Engels's knowledge of Islamic history was and how much he tended to draw on the few data on Islam at his disposal and use them as the foundation for a universal interpretation of Islamic history. It should be noted here in passing that the thesis in which the nomadic-urban conflict serves as the model for a circular explanation of history was already developed by the Arab social philosopher Ibn Khaldun during the fourteenth century in his *Prolegomena (Muqaddima)*. Ibn Khaldun's *Muqaddima* was discussed widely in nineteenth-century Europe, thanks to the French translation by Baron McGuckin de Slane (three volumes, Paris, 1863–68).[6]

Interestingly enough, Engels's interpretation of Islamic history as circular and of European history as dynamic is in harmony with the Eurocentric typology of dynamic and static peoples (Europe and America versus non-Westerners) propounded by the leading sociologist of development during the 1960s, Richard F. Behrendt,[7] famous for his anti-Marxism.[8]

We know from the research of Maxime Rodinson (whose interpretation of Islam is "consciously and openly Marxist-oriented") that Islamic history did not proceed in a circular fashion. Although Rodinson describes his study as "Marxist" he is careful to add: "This does not mean that I subjugate my research to dogmas of doubtful value and suspect origin, as many may believe."[9] Rodinson's theses were discussed in detail in chapter 4 where I described early Islam as a "mobilizing ideology" and showed that a world empire possessing a highly developed culture emerged in the course of the rise of Islam.[10] But I am concerned at the moment only with the interpretation of the religious phenomenon: that is, with the relationship of ideology (Islam) to the social process. In my opinion no automatic reductionism exists between the normative and the historical, either as a reduction of history to the world of ideas or, in a crudely materialistic way, as a reduction of ideology to economy. Islam as an ideology could not have appeared without a supportive sociostructural framework. The changes in the social structure during the sixth and seventh centuries "caused a certain dissatisfaction to arise. With this the soil was prepared for the preachings of a prophet whose thinking was conditioned by his personal history, by his knowledge of older ideologies and by the same social circumstances."[11] But the existence of this sociostructural frame in itself would not have sufficed for things to develop the way they subsequently did. Rodinson questions the scholarly value of a "low level Marxism," which would impute this kind of determinism to the rise of Islam: "If Mohammed had not come into the world, another Mohammed would have been thrust into his place by the situation itself. No, events would have proceeded quite differently."[12] This position is reminiscent of Theodor Adorno's maxim, in which theory belongs "in the context of society and is simultaneously autonomous."[13]

I question the value of schematic interpretations of history. There is no peculiarly European, predictable road of development, just as there is no peculiarly Islamic evolution. Middle East history is not circular; Islam assisted the Arabs in developing from primitive bedouins into bearers of a high culture. However, this very important historical achievement[14] cannot be traced back to Islam alone, as both von Grunebaum and Islamic apologists seem to think. It is rather the result of a complex social evolution, a cooperation between ideology and sociostructural constructs. I shall deal with modern Islam and its historical position in an historically inspired, conceptual discussion of the relationship between religion and social change.

The Importance of Religion as a Political Ideology in Social Change

Religious movements are directly or indirectly political movements. They can be described as Ernst Bloch has, "as the ecstasy of walking upright, as the chafing, rebellious, most ardent will to Paradise."[15] Religious uprisings also have economic origins, but insofar as human dreams and inclinations enter into the religious, religion cannot be explained as being merely the "superstructure" of an extant economic base:

For [although] the economic desire is certainly the most sober and steady, it is not the only one, not the permanently strongest, [and] not the exclusive motivation of the human soul, especially not during religiously agitated times.[16]

Bloch emphasizes the importance of the social power of religious convictions, making reference to Max Weber. These convictions are historically powerful "in such a fashion that economic action is itself soon enough charged with a superstructure and, as it functions autonomously, conditions the entry of cultural religious substance, but by no means produces this substance all by itself."[17]

Religion is simultaneously both "mobilizing" and transforming, legitimizing and preserving. Consequently, the religious phenomenon is also political. Political movements with a religious character are more effective politically than are those without it. Furthermore, political systems which are religiously legitimized exhibit a more stable base.[18] Georges Balandier has reflected on both political functions of religion: "Religion can be an instrument of power, a guarantee of its legitimacy, something to be used in the political struggle,"[19] particularly since religions are always also political ideologies. "It is part of the essence of power that . . . it cultivates a thoroughgoing political religion."[20] The concepts of the political and the sacred coincide with each other in this situation and are by a third concept, that of order, the *ordo rerum*.[21] Religion can also serve as an instrument to challenge the powers-that-be "whenever the prophetic and messianic movements question the existing order during times of crisis and rise up as rival powers,"[22] as the current situation in Iran demonstrates. The Shah's regime was not religiously legitimized and his power therefore not sanctified; whereas the prophetic-messianic character of the mullahs movement was, dooming the Shah. In contrast, power in Saudi Arabia, based as it is on the correlation between the sacred and the political, remains stable.

Religious movements are encountered most frequently today in the underdeveloped Third World. Many social scientists explain this by citing the misery produced by underdevelopment which provides a fertile soil for salvation ideologies. However, if we recognize, as Bloch does, that the economic "is not the most characteristic motive of the human soul" and that "inclinations, dreams, grave and pure impulses, purposeful raptures," which always recur in the religious, "are nourished by something other than the most tangible need, yet are also never merely shadowy ideology,"[23] then we must realize that a purely socioeconomic engagement with the Third World is inadequate. The study of the religious-cultural sphere acquires a central significance.

The need to alleviate structurally conditioned misery becomes no less pressing even when we recognize that misery in itself does not necessarily engender religiosity. This remark has a methodological importance— the social function of religion as a political ideology must be analyzed. The French sociologist of religion Henri Desroche has discussed the relationship between religion and social development and has constructed the following schemata:

1. Defined positively: Religion is a factor in social development. This includes the rise and renewal of religion.
2. Defined negatively: Religion is an obstacle to social development
3. Defined complexly: Their relations depend on the kinds, phases or the stage of religion; or on the kinds, phases or the stage of social development. Or positive and negative definitions get entangled with each other.[24]

Desroche has also investigated the social effects of religion and emphasizes in the same vein

that the development of religion is to be inferred less from the state or even the structure of economic development. . . . *Homo religiosus* was and remains a man, . . . even though he belongs to a socioprofessional status probably assigned before birth. Likewise, he is and remains a man of an historical, national and cultural tradition.[25]

In a more recent study Desroche warns against religiosocial monisms with regard to the relationship between religion and development and mentions the apologetic and polemical monisms as noteworthy offenders. The first stresses rather unilaterally the positive social significance of religion and insists that religiosity is beneficial for development; whereas the second asserts the exact opposite.[26] This hint from Desroche requires further elaboration of the third possible model cited above, particularly considering that no religion functions in an exclusively positive or negative way relative to social development. Assertions about religion can be made only in conjunction with others concerning the role played by religion in the process of social evolution. This is especially true for Islam, which has at its disposal, as I have mentioned, a completely developed doctrine of law (*Sharia*) and a complex literary tradition. Many Islamic scholars prove themselves incapable of interpreting modern Islam, in spite of their extensive learning, because they attempt to understand social evolution through the study of the sources of Islamic dogmatics. Desroche argues that "a sociological scrutiny of any given religion cannot exhaust itself in an investigation of its essence," especially since this kind of examination cannot explain the social effect of a religion: "The same religion which appears here as a means of national identification, thereby contributing to cultural liberation, appears elsewhere as an instrument of political alienation and cultural suppression."[27] Clearly such different, historically conditioned forms of religious effectiveness cannot be comprehended through studying sources.

No uniform Islam has ever existed even in the Islamic, normatively oriented doctrine of law (*Sharia*) and certainly not in social reality. Islam was assimilated into the respective cultures which adopted it. In its dominant form orthodox Sunni Islam has remained Arab even though it is also embraced by many non-Arab peoples. Within Islam itself there was an internal division which took the form of rival legal schools within Sunni Islam.[28] An important distinction within the religious history of Islam is that between *Shari'a* and *Tariqa*.

> In essence, both have similar meanings, both deal with the path taken by the believer. But *Shari'a* is the path of the legal scholars and consequently the term stands today for the totality of the norms derived from the history of religion; in short, the Islam of the ulama. . . . *Tariqa* is the path of the mystical knowledge of God, today synonymous with the "religious brotherhoods," that is, with the lay orders[29]

writes Detlev Khalid, who tellingly translates "*Shari'a* Islam" as "legal Islam" and "*Tariqa* Islam" as "popular Islam." Alongside the main currents of Islam in its Sunni, Arab and Shi'i, Persian forms, numerous variants exist, emerging out of the adaptation of Islam to other cultures. African Islam is an ideal example[30] of this process of adaptation which produces something unique and incomprehensible if approached only through the *Shari'a* or via knowledge of the nativistic forms of African culture.[31]

These references to the multiple forms of Islam, as well as to Desroche's sociology of religion, indicate why a religioanalytical mode of procedure which exhausts itself in the study of the dogmatic sources of Islam (the Qur'an and the *Sunna*) remains inadequate for the understanding of modern Islam, even though knowledge of these sources is always a condition for any analysis. The following exposition on Islam and the place it occupies in the processes of social change in the modern Middle East derives from this position.

Attempts to Revitalize Islam: Modern Islam

The modern age is what it is because of the Industrial Revolution. Those regions of the world where this revolution took root grew into highly developed, complex societies. Europe penetrated the world or, as Hegel put it in his *Philosophy of Law*, bourgeois society was impelled by its own dialectic to expand, "in order to search around outside itself among other peoples . . . for consumers and thereby for the necessary means of subsistence" (paragraph 246). "This expanded context also provides the soil for colonization, toward which the fully developed bourgeois society is pushed" (paragraph 248). World Society proceeds from bourgeois society, which Johan Galtung has divided into a developed center and an underdeveloped periphery. The structure linking center and periphery is one of power and dominance.[32] This is the historical framework of modern Islam. The Muslims, whose Arab Empire once spread its borders "from the banks of the Loire to beyond the Indus, from Poitiers to Samarkand,"[33] belong in contemporary World Society among those who inhabit the periphery, to the underdogs.

Napoleon went to Egypt in 1798 in order to sever his rival England's route to India and announced to the Ottoman-ruled Egyptians that the blessing of *Liberté* from the French Republic was at hand:

In the name of God, . . . in the name of the French Republic, based upon the foundations of Liberty and Equality, Bonaparte, the Commander-in-Chief of the French Forces, informs all the population of Egypt: For a long time, those in power in Egypt have insulted the French Nation. . . . I came only to rescue your rights from the oppressors.[34]

With this the history of the modern Middle East began.

One of the first Egyptian students in Paris, Rifaʿa Tahtawi, who after his return to Egypt also became the first important modern Arab intellectual, appears not to have perceived this initial acculturation[35] between the East and the West as a relationship based on power and domination. For one thing, the Islamic Middle East at that time had not yet been colonized. In the Paris diary he began in 1826, Tahtawi justifies the adoption of European progress as an act of repossession. The Muslim peoples

need foreign countries in order to acquire what they do not know. . . . However, they [the Europeans] admit that we were their teacher in all manner of sciences and recognize our prominence vis-à-vis them. Now it is certain and patent that merit is due to whoever is first to effect an accomplishment.[36]

But this situation soon changed. In 1830 France conquered Algiers and in 1882 Egypt became a British colony. Europe now exerted direct control over the Islamic world.

Arab Islamic high culture manifested a strong Hellenistic influence.[37] Von Grunebaum emphasizes that the acceptance of Greek philosophy, Indian medicine, and Iranian administrative principles and their integration into Arab Islamic culture did not provoke any "disquiet." However, "The imprint of the Westernization of the last 150 years is completely different. . . . The purpose behind the admission of Western influences was not the completion of an indigenous heritage . . . but the elimination of a situation felt as backwardness."[38] He remarks, furthermore, that "the greatest difficulty which the Muslim world has encountered in its struggle with Westernization is found in the contradiction between a successful adoption of the foreign objectives and an inability to leave the traditional nidus."[39] This contradiction is reflected in the writings of contemporary Islamic intellectuals, who no longer perceive acculturation as an act of repossession but as an admission of inferiority. For them Westernization signifies self-surrender.

Modern Islam was at first supported by two movements which Hani Srour, basing himself on Arnold Toynbee, calls "zealots" and "Herodians."[40] Zealots were fanatics who tried to defend the autochthonous culture with archaic weapons; whereas the Herodians coopted the enemy's weapons in order to fight him. The Islamic zealots included in their ranks the movements of the Wahhabis[41] on the Arabian peninsula (today Saudi Arabia) and the Sanusis[42] in Libya, supported by the bedouins.[43] For Srour, the Herodians were the first unconditionally Westernized Islamic intellectuals. Srour sees in the Islamic modernism of the second half of the nineteenth century a victory of "creative Islam" over Herodian Islam.

In my scholarly work I have divided modern Islam into two types, both of which aim equally at a revitalization of Islam: the archaic chiliastic variant (a return to the Ur-Islam of the Prophet) and the modernistic variant (pan-Islamism). Both the Wahhabis and the Sanusis belong to the first type and the two great nineteenth-century Muslim intellectuals, Afghani and his disciple ʿAbduh, belong to the second. The Wahhabis created the present kingdom of Saudi Arabia, which was honored in a Nazi publication as the "Third Reich of Islam."[44] The Sanusis founded the kingdom of Libya, which was toppled by young officers in a 1969 coup d'etat.[45]

Afghani's attempt to reactivate Islam as a "mobilizing ideology" in order to overcome the backwardness of the Islamic Middle East failed. Yet the same effort is being repeated within the framework of current repoliticization, so that Afghani's *oeuvre* can now lay claim to a renewed relevance. Without being familiar with either the original writings, or even with more recent secondary literature, Michael Wolffsohn asserts that "for Afghani, Islam was a means to a political end,"[46] a thesis which cannot be maintained in a serious study of Afghani. For Afghani, Islamic high culture was identical with Islam itself; the Muslim peoples were backward only because they did not have an adequate understanding of Islam. "The oppression of Muslims by the European hegemonic powers was for the reformers a result of a religious value orientation."[47] Afghani believed that a correct value orientation, that is, Islam, was sufficient to bring about change. In my opinion the reasons for the failure of Islamic modernism lie in this normative attitude. Afghani's thinking never transcended the confines of Islamic dogmatics. Niklas Luhmann describes the social function of religious dogmatics:

Dogmatics interprets in order to give answers. On the one hand it works with functionally unanalyzed abstractions and in this respect is unreflective. It does not thematize its social function but understands itself, its concept of dogma, in turn in a dogmatic fashion. . . . It rests, on the other hand, on the context-free availability of its materials: that is, on a distance from the connections which it interprets.[48]

Islam as a system of norms is here used as the context-free material. The underdevelopment of World Society's framework is conditioned and encouraged by the dominance exercised by the center over the periphery and the "interaction" between top dogs and underdogs. These are structural adhesives of modern Islam from which Islamic dogmatists distance themselves in order to interpret their "material" free of context.

I think that it might be useful to discuss this thesis in greater depth by using the original Afghani text. In the Qur'an it is said: "God does not change a people's lot unless they change what is in their hearts" (13:11). This Qur'anic verse, which Islamic modernists cite indefatigably, is said to mean that contemporary Muslims are themselves responsible for their misery. Not structural conditions but the deviation from the correct system of norms, from the true Islam, is the cause behind the pauperization of the Islamic peoples. "We Muslims," Afghani writes,

can build our renaissance and our civilization only on the foundation of our religion and our Qur'an. Only this path can help us overcome our backwardness. Even the good things which we posses [that is, the adaptation to modern civilization] are proofs of our inferiority and decadence. We civilize ourselves by imitating the Europeans. . . . Through this, Islam loses its essential characteristics of dominance and superiority.[49]

The difference between the archaic Wahhabis, who want to return to Ur-Islam, and Afghani lies in the fact that the former disparage any civilizational achievements as "innovation" (bid'a) and cultivate nomadic values; whereas for Afghani reform is the road to the true Islam. It is striking that Afghani takes pains in his writings to use Martin Luther's

Reformation as the model for religious renewal.[50] The Oxford scholar Albert Hourani clearly alludes to this when he writes that Afghani meant "Islam needed a Luther: this indeed was a favorite theme of al-Afghani's, and perhaps he saw himself in the role."[51]

In the evolutionist tradition employed in research on acculturation during the nineteenth century, European culture was viewed as being superior vis-à-vis the "natives," because it could be confirmed scientifically. Although in classical colonization (Phoenician or Greek) the heroic and esthetic aspects of conquest were emphasized, modern colonialism regards itself as superior by virtue of its scientifically grounded character.[52] Classical anthropology championed this argumentation. It is interesting and at the same time remarkable that this particular argument[53] is also central for Afghani. "Colonialism is *in nuce* the dominance of those states and peoples having science at their disposal over weak and ignorant people [who do not]. Superiority rests on power and science which are always triumphant over weakness and ignorance. This is a cosmic law."[54]

This discussion of Afghani's original texts makes clear that while on the one hand Afghani aimed for a revitalization of Islam on the normative level, on the other hand he could not envisage this goal being realized through either an archaic movement or an imitative Westernization. Afghani's Islam can be interpreted as a product of an active, syncretistic (in contrast to a passive, imitative) acculturation.[55] Afghani wanted both to acquire European scientific culture and at the same time to cling to Islam. This is the contradiction von Grunebaum mentions in the passage cited above. Afghani rejected an unconditional Westernization as being merely passive and imitative.

Srour grasps an essential dimension of Afghani's thought when he emphasizes (using Toynbee's terms "zealots" and "Herodians") that "Afghani attempts to counter this challenge [of Europe, B.T.] with 'zealous' fervor and 'Herodian' reason. His synthesis consists of a reconciliation between 'dogma' and 'ratio.'"[56] However, this is correct only with reference to Afghani's intention. I characterized Afghani's thought above, in conjunction with Luhmann's definition of religious dogmatics, as a body of thought that does not reflect on its social function and rests on the context-free availability of its material, thereby keeping a distance from actual conditions. In short, I characterize it as thought arrested in religious dogmatics. The postulated synthesis between dogma and reason remains a postulate; it is unattainable. Islamic modernism failed and had to make room (at the latest after World War I) for other acculturative, more strongly

Westernized ideologies, especially for nationalism[57] and non-Marxist socialism.[58] This ideological formation, however, evolved out of a process of normative Westernization and not from a sociostructural transformation. The adopted ideas had no resonance or counterparts in the already extant societies of the Muslim Middle East. Repoliticization of Islam as a counter-acculturation is an understandable reaction, as I have discussed at length in chapter 3.

It seems to me critically important at this point to investigate closely the instrument for such a solely normative Westernization; that is, the structure of education. I shall attempt this in the next chapter.

CHAPTER 7

Modern Education and the Emergence of a Westernized Islamic Intelligentsia: Students as a Potential for Change in the Islamic Middle East

The central problem confronting modern Islam is the overcoming of the asymmetry in a World Society where the Islamic Middle East constitutes the dominated pole. Following the lead of von Grunebaum, I tried in chapter 6 to differentiate between two quite different historical situations in which Islam was confronted by a superior culture. In the case of high Islam, when the Islamic Middle East was itself dominant, the ancient Greek cultural heritage, particularly rational Greek philosophy, was easily integrated into Islam. Through this integration Islam was enriched and the Hellenization of Islam was a constituent part of high Islam.[1] In modern Islam, however, the integration of Western European techno-logical-scientific culture is not an easy undertaking. The Islamic Middle East of the modern period is, contrary to the classical Islamic Middle East, an underdeveloped region.

An educational system always mirrors the society which produces it. After the downfall of the Arab Islamic Empire in 1258, the Islamic Orient fell into profound stagnation and backwardness. The literary, philosophi-cal, and theological debates, available in such abundance to scholars dealing with high Islam, disappear altogether after the successful destruction of the Arab Islamic Empire by the Mongol barbarians. This literary poverty was not changed by the reunification of most areas of the Islamic world in the sixteenth century under the Turkish Ottomans, particularly given that the new empire, since its foundation in the fourteenth century along military, feudal, and bureaucratic lines,[2] had never harbored a high culture inside its borders. The educational system during this period was monopolized by the Islamic clergy, the *ulama*.[3] This monopoly in instruction and all other intellectual activities led to a situation in which the four pillars of religious education—Qur'an, *Hadith*, *Shari'a* and Arabic grammar—became the

95

only sources of pedagogy. The central feature of this Islamic education was the memorization of the sources of Islamic thought.[4] But problem-oriented thinking cannot be learned through raw memorization. This form of education corresponded to the absence of participation in a traditional society[5] whose hierarchy consisted of the *ulama*, the military, and the political authorities.

The Industrial Revolution,[6] which made Europe the figurative and actual center of the world, contributed to the military superiority of the European armies over the Islamically legitimated Turco-Ottoman Empire by providing new technology. Repeated military defeats made it expedient for the authorities "to adopt European weapons, training and techniques,"[7] as Bernard Lewis writes, adding that

with European weapons and technology came another importation, European ideas, which were to prove at least equally disruptive of the old social and political order. Until the eighteenth century, the world of Islam had been cut off from almost all intellectual and cultural contact with the West.[8]

But by the beginning of the nineteenth century, envoys of the Ottoman sultan were traveling through Europe and in time, thanks to the information they had gleaned in Europe, became even more influential than the *ulama* at the court of the sultan:

After the diplomats, the second—and in the long run more important—group of Middle Easterners to appear in Europe were the students. . . . By 1818 there were 23 Egyptian students in Europe. . . . In the course of the years hundreds of others followed them—the forerunners of the countless thousands that were still to come. . . . In the universities of Europe in the eighteen twenties, thirties, and forties there was much to learn.[9]

The appropriation of modern Western education became possible in the Muslim Middle East itself during the nineteenth century following the establishment of modern educational institutions in which European education was dispensed. The acquisition of such an education was no longer the privilege of students living abroad. In Egypt under the rule of Muhammad ʿAli (1805–48), and also in the Ottoman heartland during the *Tanzimat* (reform) period (1839–76), prominent Muslims tried to bridge the gap between Europe and the backward Islamic Middle East by opening channels in their region to Western educational influences. In the colonial age, officially introduced in the Islamic Middle East by the French colonial occupation of Algeria in 1830, Western education acquired a different complexion. It was exercised everywhere outside Europe "as a sociopolitical instrument of foreign rule,"[10] as Samuel Kodjo expressed it in his inaugural lecture at the University of Cologne.

Kodjo also notes that Western education continues today to constitute in the traditional societies of the Third World an "invasion into the psychic and social life of people, and creates through school attendance a complicated vacuum, in that schools in developing countries dispense a culture and an attendant life-style shorn of their substratum."[11] A new elite is brought up with a modern education only normatively Westernized, and must move within a traditional and in some areas a still archaic social structure. European and American writers usually deal with this question instrumentally. It is quite clear that within the perspective of educational economy, as it were, modern education was established to serve at the pleasure of the colonial rulers and that it continues to perform this function today. Horst Beyer has dealt with this question in the case of India, and is certainly correct in confirming that through modern education

an Anglicized class of Indian colonial assistants was [supposed to be] created to perform administrative and social functions. . . . The English constitutional system, in the context of the political and economic ruling system of imperialism, led to a dimension of colonial dependence, to the ideological indoctrination of an assistant class, and to the establishment of cultural foreign rule."[12]

This description, however, deals with just one dimension of the problem posed here and is, moreover, only in a limited sense correct in that it reflects the intention of the colonial system which employs education as a "sociopolitical instrument of foreign rule" (Kodjo). But it is false if it presumes to explain the extremely complex process of the diffusion of Western education in non-Western societies.

In the following sections of chapter 7 I shall use the example of the Islamic Middle East to show how the diffusion of modern education contributed to the disintegration of a traditional society and to identify the elite that has emerged from this process. Then I shall attempt, in a refutation of Horst Beyer's partially correct evaluation of colonial educational policies (which is simply wrong in many of its unreflected generalizations), to illustrate through the example of Iranian students abroad a case in which Westernized elites have not accepted the subordinate social function of "colonial assistants."

Modern Education and the New Forms of Socialization

When I define intellectuals in what follows as a modern social stratum and a new political elite in the modern Middle East, the term "intellectual" is not being used synonymously with "educated." In their own society the Islamic *ulama* are an educated stratum, but they have never been and still are not today intellectuals in the sense meant by Antonio Gramsci, who uses the term in the context of the industrial "higher culture":

The characteristic feature of the new intellectual may no longer be eloquence as the exterior and immediate driving force of the emotions and passions. Instead, he must immerse himself actively in practical life, not as a mere orator but as a *designer, organizer,* "permanent persuader."[13]

Some might detect the odor of Eurocentrism in this definition of the intellectual, especially coming as it does from a European scholar. However, without knowledge of Gramsci the Malayan social scientist Syed H. Alatas declares that the absence of a "functioning intellectual group" is a factor in underdevelopment and pleads urgently for the organization of such a group in that this has to be considered "a developmental necessity."[14] For Alatas the ability to pose problems, to define them, to analyze them and finally to solve them is the essential and characteristic quality of the intellectual. He adds: "the most important distinguishing trait of the non-intellectual is the absence of the will to think and the inability to see the consequence."[15] Alatas even refers to the *spiritus rector* of Islamic modernism, Afghani, who regarded the lack of the "intellectual spirit" to be one of the most important reasons for the backwardness of the Muslim Middle East, and amplifies: "The spirit of inquiry, the sense of the enchantment of intellectual pursuit, and the reverence for scientific and rational knowledge are not widespread in the developing societies."[16] Alatas, while remarking on the absence of intellectuals in the technological-scientific cultural sense in the Third World and while pleading how important it is that this lack be remedied, anticipates the possible reproach that he is promoting an imitative Westernization. But he rejects this reproach, pointing out that "the need for a functioning intellectual group is not a modern Western import. We are not reading Western history into Asian societies."[17] It should be clear by now that the type of intellectual described here cannot be produced by a traditional education which expends its energies not in creative thinking but in memorization and reproduction. The immediate question suggested by this is whether modern education, as originally introduced in the colonial context, was capable of producing this new intellectual and whether the diffusion of modern education could produce new forms of socialization.

As James Coleman has shown, the establishment of the new educational system in the colonies was primarily tailored to the requirements of the colonial system.[18] Western education under colonial conditions constituted a form of imitative Westernization. Alatas describes it as follows:

The significance of colonial education lies in its blocking the emergence of an intellectual tradition even in a society with such a tradition at an earlier period. . . . The colonial regime created the habits of horse racing, beer drinking, club life, a taste for Western music, interest in Western sports, and a host of other things. It could have stimulated intellectual interest on a big scale, *but it did not.*[19]

Traditional educational systems were dismantled and partially dissolved, new forms were introduced, but those that were Westernized stood there "without the infrastructure necessary for intellectual activity."[20] And this intellectual activity cannot exist in an underdeveloped society.

For political scientists the study of the diffusion of modern education in underdeveloped societies is particularly important in terms of the question of political socialization. We know from the available empirical studies, to which Coleman[21] refers, that the family remains the most crucial agent of socialization in preindustrial societies. Therefore the sociocultural framework needs to be discussed in order to see whether the forms of modern education also encourage new forms of social exchange.

Especially in the Middle East the family plays the primary role as a socializing institution in the political socialization of individuals. In his transregional empirical study, Donald Emmerson points out that new influences would have a greater effect if the students lived in dormitories during their education and not in their parents' homes.[22] As a rule, however, only students from rural areas live in dormitories. Universities in developing countries exist only in large cities and students of urban origin continue to live in the parents' home during their studies. In order to answer the question of how a successful transfer of new values "ensues," the scholar has to investigate the degree to which the students are integrated within the family system. In this context the concepts which Stephen Douglas developed, using the example of Indonesia (that is, continuity and discontinuity in the process of political socialization) are quite helpful.[23] They can explain, for example, the paradox illustrated in chapter 1 by the case of a science student who prays fervently and perhaps even exercises magic formulae in order to pass his exams. The introduction of modern sciences in this case was a "diffusion"; it had no infrastructure.

The existing scientific and technological institutions in the periphery, the so-called Third World,

provide ready-made knowledge, isolated from any cultural background. Although the methods of science are increasingly adopted, they exist side by side with archaic forms of thought. In developing societies the vast majority, including scientists and educated men, still believe in magic. . . . Hence science and archaic forms of thought are not felt to be in conflict; they are two different things, each valid in its respective sphere.[24]

This dualism is not perceived by the people concerned and governs the attitudes of those with only a surface Westernization. However, even students who study abroad and develop new attitudes because of the spatial distance between them and the institutions of their primary socialization reintegrate themselves very quickly into the old family structure. They thus unconsciously bridge the gap between their modern education and archaic forms of thought and life. The dualism described above remains in force. This may explain the social fact described by Alatas as an absence of intellectual spirit and capacity for inquiry among the educated of the Third World.

Students, Political Development, and Social Change

In spite of the qualifications made above concerning the effectiveness of the new forms of political socialization, it can be said that a new stratum of intellectuals has emerged in peripheral societies from the modern sector of education. This stratum finds itself in a struggle for authority with the supporters of the traditional structures. The discontinuities in the processes of political socialization are correlated with the structural heterogeneity of the social structures and the sociocultural fragmentation of society. When discussing Alatas I pointed out that the call for a new type of intellectual and for a modern technological culture is not intended to promote Eurocentrism. Edward Shils also speaks of the worldwide "modern intellectual culture" and says that to possess it is "vital because it carries with it a partial transformation of the self and a changed relationship to the authority of the dead and the living."[25]

If the discontinuities of political socialization are disregarded (for example, the acquisition of an egalitarian, rational education together with the continued existence of an authoritarian, traditional family structure), then the new education can be seen as a source for authority conflicts which provoke rebellion against the existing structures. Shils writes that

this has been especially pronounced in those who were brought up in a traditionally oppressive environment and were indulged with a spell of freedom from that environment—above all from the control of their elders and kinsmen. Once, however, the new tradition of rebellion was established among students, it became self-reproducing.[26]

Shils also points out that the solution to these conflicts often depends on the ability of the respective political system to integrate the rebellious students into existing institutional and cultural structures. In view of the meager resources of the political systems in peripheral societies, the possibilities of the governments to make the students conform after they have been awakened into rebellion by the new forms of political socialization are minimal. Donald Emmerson calls this problem "the professional frustration of the students" and defines it in the following way:

One of the sources of this insecurity is the contrast between what the student wants out of life and what he expects to get, for it is here that he feels most deeply the dislocative effects of socio-economic change. . . . He may be able to identify more fully with calls for sweeping, radical change because he feels he has nothing to lose and everything to gain by shaking up the status quo.[27]

The Iran specialist Norman Jacobs, as early as 1967, pointed to the political significance of the Iranian students as a potential for political unrest:

The ideological control of the Iranian students overseas is considered a special problem by the political authority. For such students may leave Iran to study abroad at too early an age; that is, at an age when they *morally* are vulnerable to a way of life that is radically different from that to be found in Iran, and at an age before they have interiorized the Iranian religious, social, and cultural traditions to the extent that they forever will be bound to Iran and the Iranian way of doing things. Also, as returnees they may not adjust to the realities of Iranian society. For they (too often) expect as a right, prestigeful occupational opportunities . . . comparable to what they have become accustomed abroad, which do not exist in Iran. And when they do not receive these opportunities, they grumble and create dissatisfaction and political unrest in the society.[28]

However, the Iranian example shows that student frustrations cannot be reduced only to concerns about their professional future. Under the Shah, Iran possessed a resourceful political system which, viewed from an economic perspective, was capable of integration. Modern education provides students, especially those who study abroad (to be discussed further below), the possibility of learning that modern, structurally and functionally differentiated societies grant personal liberties which are unknown in underdeveloped societies. The Shah's regime could integrate the students occupationally but not politically, as I shall show below. Professional frustration as a determinant of the behavior of students in underdeveloped societies should therefore not be overestimated.

Emmerson proposes three levels of analysis for the investigation of behavior and attitudes of students in underdeveloped societies: (1) biographical variables on the individual level; (2) institutional and discipline-specific variables on the university level; and (3) the more comprehensive social level providing the context for political and social change.[29]

On the individual biographical level, data would have to be collected on the age, sex, social background, and family environment, as well as religious preference, which allow generalizations through aggregation. On the second level, distinctions must be made not only between disciplines but also between the degrees of Westernization of the respective university institutions. Within the same country these distinctions are important; for example, in Egypt the political behavior of the students of the ʿAyn Shams University deviates strongly from that of the students of the Islamic Al-Azhar University. The distinction between students at indigenous universities and those at European or American universities is particularly important. On the third level of analysis appropriate monographic research on each country is necessary. Emmerson correctly emphasizes that the study of the political role of students in the political development of Third World countries is decidedly complicated because each student operates on two separate levels of interaction: he is a member of a traditional family and at the same time a member of a modern institution, the university:

His age, religion, and personality, the proximity, social origins, and political attitudes of his family, the location, auspices, and quality of his university, his career preparations and perceived life chances, the politicians who proselytize him, the balance of stability and change in his nation—all these factors define the terms of the student's entrance into, or avoidance of, the political realm.[30]

The student is active in a sociocultural as well as a socioeconomic, structurally heterogenous society. His political behavior is determined by the cultural fragmentation of his society.

Study Abroad and Students as a Polarizing Force in Social Conflict

It was pointed out above that the first Islamic student delegations to Europe at the beginning of the nineteenth century contributed substantially to the establishment of Western European cultural influences. The Arab American historian Hisham Sharabi has investigated this phase of Middle East history and writes that "the rise of the intellectuals and the elaboration of ideological functions must be seen as a manifestation of the process of education and enlightenment brought about by increasing contact with Europe."[31] Rifaʿa Tahtawi, the Islamic scholar who accompanied the first large group of Egyptian students to Paris in 1826 as prayer leader (*imam*), after returning to Egypt became a pioneer in the cultural Westernization of the entire Middle East. His biography documents problems experienced by students abroad which are still pertinent in today's situation. The problem at issue is that of a person with his feet in two cultures of radically different degrees of development: he is enlightened by the foreign culture and wants to appropriate from it without abandoning his attachment to his own culture. Tahtawi wrote in his Paris diary: "Naturally I consent to only what does not contradict the text of our Islamic law."[32] Tahtawi became an intellectual through his studies in Paris, which he completed while continuing to fulfill his duties as *imam*. He became an intellectual because, as he says himself, he dared to contemplate and carry out the adoption of the new in contrast to other Islamic scholars who wrote only "commentaries and supercommentaries" on inherited religious sources. In his diary he describes the difference between traditional scholars and modern intellectuals:

If one says of somebody in France that he is a scholar, one does not mean with this that he knows about religion but that he has knowledge of one of the other scholarly disciplines. It is not difficult to recognize the superiority of these Christians in the sciences and therefore to realize that many of these sciences do not even exist in our countries.[33]

Albert Hourani, the Oxford scholar who has written the most comprehensive and knowledgeable study so far on modern Arab-Islamic history of ideas, comes to this conclusion in his chapter on Tahtawi:

Tahtawi's ideas about society and the state are neither a mere restatement of a traditional view nor a simple reflection of the ideas he had learnt in Paris. The way in which his ideas are formulated is on the whole traditional: at every point he makes appeal to the example of the Prophet and his Companions, and his conception of political authority is within the tradition of Islamic thought. But at points he gives them a new and significant development.[34]

Tahtawi is an ideal example of an intellectual who begins as a student abroad, becomes a cultural modernizer, and lives in two irreconcilable worlds as a consequence of his Westernization. He is a product, in short, of the contemporary process of acculturation.

The time spent by Islamically socialized students in Western countries took on a political significance in the course of the nineteenth and twentieth centuries (in addition to the cultural aspects described above). The students abroad did not remain confined to their role as cultural mediators in the acculturation process; they also became a political factor. In the West they learned the values and forms of political opposition, and as a result were no longer willing to submit uncritically to the existing order. Samuel Huntington regards university students, particularly those who studied abroad, as one of the most progressive groups in underdeveloped, traditional, or transitory societies.[35]

In the next section, which concludes this chapter, I want to test Huntington's thesis using the example of an Islamic society, Iran. The background to this discussion is the assumption I criticized earlier which holds that Westernized intellectuals are "assistants of colonialism"—the absurdity of which can easily be demonstrated through the example of Iranian students abroad.[36]

Iranian Students Abroad as a Reservoir for Social Change and Their Place in the Political System

Muslim students in the West, like all other students from underdeveloped societies studying at European and American universities, make up an intellectual elite (and are also provided with material privileges). Proportionally these students are an infinitesimal minority, but they are most definitely not a *quantité négligeable*. For developmental specialists the importance of these students as a potential for change is a well-known phenomenon, for which numerous examples can be trotted out.

The origins of the Young Turks, who seriously threatened the Ottoman Empire as a political system well before Kemal Ataturk appeared, go back to secret associations of Turkish students abroad. It was out of these that the "Committee of Union and Progress," the secret association behind the revolution of 1908, emerged.[37] The Arab students in Europe before World War I also had their share of secret associations which infiltrated the Ottoman Empire and helped organize the Arab revolt of 1916. This event led to the secession of the Arab Middle East from the Ottoman Empire and contributed to its disintegration.[38] African students in Europe were in the same manner supporters and agents of the decolonization process.[39]

That the Iranian students in Europe and America played an important role in the fall of the Shah's regime can be assumed with considerable certainty; although no concrete assertions can be made about this, given that scholars usually gain access to the materials necessary for their research only when the historical process has come to its end and rests in the distant past.

At the moment one can only analyze and draw one's conclusions from those publications of the Iranian students abroad which are accessible, although specialists know how difficult it is to collect and interpret these materials adequately. Small sects have always played a decisive role in history, but tend to grossly overrate themselves during their formative phase. The autism of the sectarians who live outside the actual political process is recognizable in their publications, which usually appear in pamphlet form. This autism exhibits itself in a verbal radicalism not infrequently repellent.

If the Iranian students are no exception, and if their publication *Iran Report* (no longer published) can be judged as typical for this autism, a legitimate question arises: why should such a verbal radicalism be taken so seriously? And this calls into doubt the hypothesis mentioned above according to which the students from underdeveloped societies at European and American universities form a social and political potential for change.

Nevertheless, it should have become clear from the above discussion that the students who were "awakened" in the course of their Westernization do present a force of unrest in a traditional society in which participation is unknown or discredited or even actively combated by the dominant elites. Islamic societies of the modern Middle East are not participatory, even though classical Islam originally celebrated the democratic principle of consultation (*shura*). But even in high Islam this tradition was already being bracketed out after the caliphate had become dynastic and authoritarian following the assassination of the fourth caliph, who was elected according to the *shura* principle.[40] The traditional Islamic education dominant prior to the process of acculturation mirrored these authoritarian political norms.

A change in political socialization first occurs as a result of studying abroad, although the new forms of socialization are not without problems, as I demonstrated in the first section of this chapter. Nevertheless, it is indisputable that modern university students break through the barriers of traditional political socialization because of their academic studies. As a rule, the intelligentsia is a product of the processes of acculturation and Westernization, although there is also a traditionally oriented educated class.

A Western education can also be acquired in the Middle East at local universities. Thus the consequences of Westernization are not limited to students studying abroad. Usually the political organizations of the intellectuals forge the vehicle for the processes of communication to take place between the two groups of intellectuals, those in the Middle East and those abroad. According to my information the pan-Arab Ba°th party, for example, has an apparatus abroad which is supported by Arab students. Iranian political groups also once had their factions in the political organization of Iranian students abroad, the CISNU, and through this channel they exerted political influence in their homeland.

The new forms of political socialization of the students abroad are conditioned by the new model of education produced by Westernization. These students familiarize themselves with new norms and internalize them in the course of their education. These norms, however, collide with the traditional education they acquired in childhood and to a certain extent through school socialization. They become the potential for change.

The westernized students are

by their very nature . . . against the existing order, and they are generally incapable of constituting authority or establishing principles of legitimacy. There are numerous cases of student and religious demonstrations, riots and revolts, but none of student governments.[41]

Even though Huntington stresses here that students cannot seize political power, as can the military, for instance, he continues to consider them a weighty factor in political change. Although they clearly cannot win political power using their weapons of riots and demonstrations, nevertheless these weapons can force governments to make concessions because they must be taken seriously. Through unrest and demonstrations, and through remote control of the politically more alert students abroad, local student organizations develop the ability "to polarize a situation and to compel other social groups to support or to oppose the government."[42] This pattern was indeed successfully followed in the case of Iran. Without the student unrest the situation could not have come to the crisis point it actually did.

The toppled Pahlavi dynasty had been founded by a charismatic leader and carried on by the Shah. To be sure, the ruling system erected by this dynasty was not Islamically legitimized but it had maintained the tradition of Oriental despotism in which participation is impermissible and the ruler rules unencumbered. In democratic systems the ruler is an elected official and a professional politician[43] who is bound by "established rules" (Max Weber). By contrast, the Oriental despot acknowledges no restraints. He rules by virtue of force and "controls absolutely the army, the police and the secret service, prison wardens, torturers, executioners, and all instruments necessary to arrest, torture, and kill a suspected person."[44]

Iran is an Islamic society. Thus a question arises about the relationship existing between Islam (which is not only a religion but also a political ideology; see chapter 2) and the state; and a further question arises as to whether Islam recognizes the right of resistance against despotic authorities, a right based on the theory of natural law in the emerging bourgeois societies of Europe.[45]

In Islam the state is the political incarnation of religion. Muhammad was not only the founder of a religion but also a politician and strategist. Islam as a political strategy is also a political legitimation of the theocratic state (see chapter 4). Islam does not recognize the right to resistance. The successors of Muhammad were caliphs, the executors of God's will. Muhammad explicitly excluded the right to resistance against Islamic rulers: "Whether he wants to or not, the Muslim must hear and obey, except if he is ordered to disobey God."[46] In the Qur'an it says: "Believers, obey the Prophet and those in authority among you" (4:59). Islamic law recognizes a number of legal sources, the most important of which apart from the Qur'an and the *Sunna* is *ijtihad*, or the effort to expand the concepts for developing new legal norms adjusted to the Qur'an and the *Sunna*. The ruler needs the Islamic scholars, the body of *mujtahid*s, the interpreters of Islamic law, as his advisors. These are "the people who bind and loose" (*ahl al-ʿaqd wal-hall*).

Islamic apologists cite this as proof that Islam is democratic and legitimizes the constitutional state. But Islam does not admit of a division of powers. "The people who bind and loose" were deputized as judges during the period of high Islam and were devoted to the Oriental despot who ruled them. Fritz Steppat alludes to the transformation of the Islamic scholars (the *ulama*) into judges and *qadi*s:

But this legal court system was, on the contrary, not an institution independent from the caliphate. The judges were subject to the orders of the authorities. . . . This procedure at first won a majority of the *ulama* over to the state, it is true, but as officials, as pliant, dependent tools.[47]

Nevertheless, during early Islam a Muslim could refuse obedience to an impious ruler. In high Islam, when the *ulama* were put into positions as state jurists and ideologues, Islamic law excluded even this possibility. Authority came from God, and only God could punish rulers for their sinful behavior. In a legal commentary by the classical Islamic constitutional lawyer Abu Yusuf, one reads:

Do not revile the rulers when they behave well for they deserve divine rewards and you are obliged to be thankful. If they act badly, sin weighs on them and you are obliged to be patient. They are the scourge with which God afflicts whom he wants to afflict. Do not oppose this affliction with wrath and indignation but accept it with meekness.[48]

Steppat, who has investigated Islamic legal tradition, shows how "in orthodox Islam a clear tendency toward an almost unconditional submission to the authorities, a theologically justified quietism,"[49] arose.

However, the transition referred to here is applicable only to orthodox Sunni Islam. Shiʿi sectarian Islam grew out of an opposition movement, and the objection could be raised that these explanations are not valid for Iran. When the Persian Safavids established their dynasty in 1502 they drew on the principle of the imamate of Shiʿi Islam to legitimate their rule. They encouraged the promulgation of the doctrine which permits political power to be delegated to secular rulers prior to the return of the Mahdi (the Twelfth Imam) on the Day of Judgment, by calling on the eighth-century Imam Jaʿfari and the teachings of the Twelver Shiʿa. Through this maneuver Shiʿi Islam was employed as the religious legitimization of a political authority, as Norman Jacobs remarks.[50] The ruler is supposed to be controlled by the Shiʿi Islamic scholars of Qum, although the latter are also part of the ruling authorities. Thus, the oppositional character of Shiʿi Islam was lost.

The Pahlavi dynasty, which emerged from the ruins of the Qajar dynasty, was originally established with the support of the Shiʿi clergy. Although it is true that the founder of this new dynasty, Reza Khan, did not formally suspend the constitutional mooring of authority in the principle of the Twelver Shiʿa, which allowed for the delegation of power to a secular person until the return of the Twelfth Imam (see the Constitution of 1907),[51] he did introduce a political secularization, continued by his unfortunate son, the toppled Shah, with little success. The Westernization accompanying these measures failed to go deeper than the surface. Bahman Nirumand, a prominent Persian living abroad, has described this secularization: "Similar to Ataturk in Turkey, Reza Shah, too, carried out a number of reforms which, admittedly, produced a momentary melioration in the country, but which were too superficially applied to bring about any permanent improvement."[52]

The Pahlavi dynasty did not bother with a sacralization of politics in order to legitimize its rule. But Iran is an underdeveloped society which must still function somehow while bridging this transitional period and deal with the transformation and absorption of disappointments resulting from unfulfilled expectations. According to Niklas Luhmann, to function in this way is the most important task of religion in simple religious systems.[53] Whereas an Oriental despotism in Saudi Arabia, whose political authority is sacralized, remained stable, a secularizing Oriental despot in Iran was overthrown. The Shah depended on his executioners, his torturers and his prison wardens—to repeat the words of Wittfogel—but neglected the necessary correspondence of the sacred and the political. When Westernized intellectuals, especially the students studying abroad, challenged the principles of Oriental despotism he could only appeal to his machine of repression, the SAVAK, and not to the officialdom of the Islamic clergy. If religion is not used to legitimize power it is apt to become subversive and serve as the basis for rebellion. Shiᶜi Islam, with its doctrine of the returning Mahdi, is a messianic religion; and it is precisely such prophetic-messianic religions which are able, according to Balandier, to "question the existing order in times of crisis and rise up as competing powers."[54]

The British Islamic scholar Erwin Rosenthal observed the following during a visit to Iran in the 1960s:

Yet my impression was that Islam as a force in public life was not much in evidence, and that the separation of state and religion was a fact. The people at large are observant and fervent believers. The intellectuals are, like elsewhere, divided.[55]

This is evidence that secularization remained superficial. It contributed not to modernization but rather to the convulsion and eventual destruction of the Pahlavi dynasty's power. If the Shah had had the Shiᶜi clergy as allies, the Westernized intellectuals could not have succeeded in polarizing the country and ousting him.

In the third section of this chapter I discussed the thesis espoused by American social scientists which holds that "occupational frustrations" are frequently the cause for unrest among students. This thesis has only a limited applicability for Iran, especially considering that the Pahlavi regime was rich in resources and thus potentially possessed the material means for integrating students who had studied abroad. Iran under the Shah was an authoritarian society in which academicians who had completed their education abroad belonged to an exclusive political elite as long as they assented to the political system. As a result it was not difficult to integrate this new social group by providing it with material privileges. Difficulties arise, however, if returning students demand the same rights in their homeland which they enjoyed in the Western democracies, such as freedom of expression, of the press, and of assembly. This was the case in Iran under the Shah, where such dangerous liberties could not be granted. Of course it should be noted that these liberties are also not allowed in today's Islam-dominated Iran.

The Confederation of Iranian Students (CISNU) was the covering organization of Iranian students abroad. Its annual meetings took place in Frankfurt. The independently and irregularly published issues of *Iran Report* provided some information on these meetings. The issues could usually be obtained only in leftist bookstores; they were generally inaccessible through public interlibrary loan. I have at hand a rather incomplete selection of issues, and those I have are excessively repetitive.[56] However, it is interesting to follow the shifting positions taken in these publications. In the early issues it sufficed to denounce the torture methods practiced by the despotic Shah's regime with a moral vehemence, thus carrying out the publicity work regarded as the gravest duty of Iranian students abroad. In later issues contacts with underground organizations are reported, particularly contacts with the Mujahidin, which probably spawned the Fedayin Khalq, or People's Fedayin. During the climax of the Iranian crisis the idea of armed struggle was embraced.

An analysis of the *Iran Report* issues confirms the hypothesis formulated at the beginning of this chapter that students abroad represent a political potential for change; their level of consciousness has been changed with the help of progressive European culture. An example for this is an article in the *Iran Report* of September 1978 which espouses the party of the Islamic movement in Iran without a religious position being taken in the article itself. The Iranian students rejected criticism of Islam in these publications: "Whoever argues against Islam would have to judge similarly or even condemn those social movements in Europe which had appeared in a religious garment and under the religious guidance of, for example, a Thomas Munzer."[57] We have seen that orthodox Islam does not recognize the right of resistance and that Shiʿi Islam has developed in the same direction ever since the Safawid dynasty in the sixteenth century. When an Iranian student comes to Europe and reads Ernst Bloch's book, *Thomas Münzer als Theologe der Revolution* (Thomas Münzer as a Theologian of Revolution), he is forced to reflect whether such ideas could not also be incorporated into Islam. The new ideas are transferred via the communication routes connecting Iranians abroad with their homeland and affect a political system constructed on the Middle Eastern pattern much more dangerously than any bombs could. Democratic as well as revolutionary ideas find no welcome in either an Islamic or a secular Oriental despotism, but cannot be fought with "the torturers, the executioners and the prison wardens" of the despot, to invoke Wittfogel's enumeration once again.

If we recall that the students did not always play a modernizing role in the recent events in Iran even after the downfall of the Shah, it seems questionable whether the thesis promoting the students as one of the decisive forces in the process of modernization can still be advocated. Norman Jacobs, the Iranian specialist cited above, insisted in the 1960s that the students, although admittedly a threat to the existing order, should not be regarded as elements in the process of modernization without qualification:

Regardless of the negative trouble certain students have created, and it has been considerable, yet, it must not be thought that these students are necessarily agents of positive change that many overenthusiastic economists, political scientists, and sociologists have made them out to be. This premise does *not* preclude the fact that these students are, or may be, agents of "modernization" and other innovations . . . which do not challenge the essentials of the basic Iranian institutional structure.[58]

We might recall here the earlier exposition of the political socialization of students in underdeveloped societies and remember that for these students, including those who had studied abroad, the family continues to count as the primary socializing institution. Because of this, Westernization remains a superficial overlay, for the society in which these students live and operate is itself not modern. Allow me to repeat here once again that the process of Westernization in the modern Middle East has been an essentially normative affair. Although Western norms were introduced, Middle Eastern society neither modernized nor industrialized itself.

Clearly, Western education leads to cultural anomie, as I explained in chapter 3.

If Westernized students in the Middle East are discussed here as a modernizing elite, this must be understood in the context of my earlier explanations regarding the nature of political socialization. It should also be remembered that Westernization takes place normatively and not structurally. If the student and his social and political activities are located within this more comprehensive context it can be said in conclusion that

the student is not an isolate. His ties to family and community are not somehow magically severed by matriculation. Nor is he automatically an enthusiast in the vanguard of change. In part a product of modernization, he is psychologically exposed to its dislocations; often its prime beneficiary, he can number among its casualties as well.[59]

CHAPTER 8

OIL PRODUCTION AND THE EMERGENCE OF A
NEW SOCIAL STRATUM: THE OIL WORKERS.
THE ISLAMIC SOCIAL SYSTEM AND
TRADE UNION ORGANIZATION

A central conclusion to be drawn from the above discussion regarding modern Islamic intellectuals who have come from a Western or Westernized educational system is that the process of the diffusion of modern educational institutions in the Middle East produces a normative but not a structural Westernization. Westernized intellectuals interiorize European norms in the course of their Western-oriented education, but they have to live in a traditional, backward society.

These arguments might create the impression that I am defining the transformation processes which the modern Middle East is passing through idealistically and am overlooking very real structural changes. Indeed, the Middle East of today can hardly be compared with the Middle East which Napoleon entered in 1798. Change has taken place, although only within the existing structures of a preindustrial culture. In disputing the claim that there was a structural Westernization, I intend to emphasize that no structural mooring of technological-scientific culture has taken place in the modern Middle East. To be sure, existing structures have changed and partially new structures have emerged; had they not, the new social strata—modern intellectuals and laborers—would be inconceivable, especially since they are the components of these new structures. Nevertheless, the new structures are fully integrated into the social formations of underdevelopment. I have attempted to illustrate this fact earlier, using the dualism which typifies modern education in the Middle East as an example.

Iran can serve as a prototype for the importance of students and oil workers as social forces. Without the strikes of the oil workers and the demonstrations of the students the Shiʿi Iranian clergy would have had great difficulty in reactivating Islam as the substance of a "mobilizing ideology" and in employing it to topple the despotic Shah, destroy his regime, and proclaim the new Islamic social order ("Islamic Republic").

Like the majority of OPEC countries Iran is an Islamic country.[1] The oil workers and the university students, whose actions polarized the situation and led to the present state of affairs, are nevertheless new social forces in a traditional Islamic society. Through their predominantly Western education, modern university students import foreign influences which are profoundly disturbing to the traditional, internally integrated social order.[2] For their part, the oil workers confront a nonindustrial society with new norms and forms of action (strikes), derived from the history of industrial societies with their attendant labor movements. In Iran and in the other OPEC countries the labor movement arose out of oil production. It lays claim to a modern form of organization for itself, the trade union, but under the conditions imposed by a traditional Islamic system of order. And here the question of the compatibility of these contradictory principles arises. The regime of the Shah was overthrown through strikes, among other events, but as we saw earlier, Islam does not recognize the right to resistance. According to Islamic interpretation, a strike is a form of disobedience which Islam strictly forbids.[3]

The periphery of World Society—today's developing countries—although displaying widely divergent social structures, nevertheless shares in common the structure of underdevelopment. Thus, we are dealing with societies which cannot be considered as industrial. This means that all these societies represent noncomplex social systems, although the lack of complexity varies in degree from one region to another. In the process of the dissolution of traditional structures and the conquest of underdevelopment, trade unions are a social and political force propelling this process along. Jürgen Büse, who has investigated this *problème* from a systems-theory position, has shown that the traditional system of an underdeveloped society exhibits models of association and action which either circumscribe the autonomy of social subunits or deny it altogether. Such social systems do not recognize organizations like trade unions. Wherever these social institutions exist in the Middle East, one is dealing with a transference, with an adoption of the offspring from some other, foreign society. Büse has studied West African trade unions and reports that their rise can be explained as a "process of activating collectivities or subcollectivities."[4] Trade unions can make an important contribution to social change by accelerating the disintegration of traditional structures. But the diffusion of trade unions alone cannot accomplish this task:

The continual reduction of an awareness of traditional limits can be effected only at a place and in a measure where the specialization through education, training and experience reaches a degree and volume which condition not only a tie to the profession, that is, the internalization of corresponding values and norms . . . but also the readiness to be incorporated into the emerging modern, that is, change-oriented, urban system.[5]

In this chapter I want to examine what effect the discovery and production of oil has had on traditional Islamic societies, together with the emergence of a new factor, industrial labor, in order to interpret the relationship between Islam and trade unions. In the conclusion I shall discuss the significance of the oil workers in the most important oil-producing countries, Iran and Saudi Arabia.

Labor and Oil Production

Prior to their contact with industrialized Europe (within a colonial context) Islamic societies were traditional and predominantly agrarian. The economic penetration of the Middle East by the European colonial powers led to a weakening of inherited social structures and to the genesis of new structures. Social change usually entails a loosening, if not to say dissolution, of traditional society.[6] This process was marked by economic, sociocultural and political influences from the more developed (because industrialized) West.[7]

The discovery of oil in the Middle East at the beginning of this century and its exploitation soon thereafter accelerated the process of societal restructuring. What occurred was not industrialization in the sense of the development of society toward a higher level, but rather industrialization in the sense of an industrial exploitation of raw materials (oil) and its distribution in the metropolis.

The American political scientist George Lenczowski, who has analyzed the effects of oil production on the existing structures, has come to the conclusion that

The employment of thousands of workers by the oil industry has had multifarious effects on the socioeconomic processes of the Middle East. It has meant a massive drift of the population from the villages to the oil camps or cities. The uprooting of old loyalties and the shaking of traditional values have been an inevitable consequence of this movement.[8]

Oil production destroyed traditional society and, through the new mobilization processes, changed population structures. Oil workers were a product of this process, and employment in the new economic sector became the most important source of occupation in the entire economy of the various countries. Moneir Nasr writes:

The oil industry makes additional employment possible, which leads to a relative augmentation of incomes and consumption, which in turn leads—according to the principle of acceleration—to higher employment. The amount of total incomes in the oil countries is a function, among others, of the number of employees which in turn is dependent on the level of the entire demand triggered by the employees of the oil economy. Above all it is the influence of the oil industry in the Middle East which determines the level of income in these countries.[9]

The oil workers are recruited from the village populations and from bedouins and are employed in an industrial production which conflicts with their previous agrarian or nomadic understanding of the labor process. It is patent that these deracinated peasants and bedouins make up an army of unskilled workers. The technical personnel are brought in from the metropolis. In addition, foreign skilled workers—Indians, Pakistanis and more recently Koreans—are also employed. The imported work force in the Arab emirates and Saudi Arabia is today a source of continually worsening social and economic problems.[10] The hierarchy of the work process in oil production, structured according to national origin and differing qualifications, is correlated with a corresponding wage hierarchy. The strikingly wide divergences in living standards of the employees involved in oil production create a further source of social unrest. "Both these wage differences and the generally low wage levels help explain why today in almost the entire petroleum industry of the Near East small and larger strikes are constantly breaking out."[11] Strikes are a weapon used by organized labor in labor struggles; and since the concept of strikes was developed by labor movements in the industrialized societies, the significance of the new social and political influence from the West needs consideration.

Before I deal with this question, however, I want to conclude my discussion of the emergence of this new social factor, *labor*, as another product of oil production in traditional Islamic societies. I will try, with the help of Lenczowski, to discover the common characteristics of the new social factor and to summarize the social changes triggered by the new production.

To begin with, it can be stated that the oil workers lack an effective trade union organization. Lenczowski points out that this deficiency mirrors the more general condition of labor in these countries and contends that we are dealing here with "the result of the conscious policies of the governments concerned, regardless of what the laws say."[12] In spite of the absence of an effective labor organization, the oil workers, although mostly unskilled and characterized by a low level of awareness, do indeed organize themselves and take action. Political motives for action are often interwoven with economic and social ones.

It is true that the Islamic societies of the nineteenth century were thoroughly shaken by colonial penetration, but *no new structures for society as a whole could emerge*. For example, the effects of oil production are sectorially circumscribed: not only does the oil industry create jobs almost exclusively for unskilled workers but the number of these jobs are also relatively modest in terms of the economy as a whole. "The oil sector gets its technology and its capital goods from abroad and therefore does not create jobs in other domestic areas of the economy."[13] The significance of the acceleration principle, cited by Moneir Nasr for a policy of employment, is sectorially limited. Algeria, which pursues the construction of its own industrial sector coordinated with oil production, is, unfortunately, a special case in this respect. The new social structure in the oil-producing countries is by no means homogenous and is subdivided into various ununiformly developed sectors. These societies are structurally heterogenous and are, collectively, underdeveloped both socioeconomically and socioculturally. Integrated into an inequitable international division of labor, they play the role of raw-materials producers.

Islam and the Unionized Organization of Labor

The Industrial Revolution helped those societies in which it took place evolve into socially differentiated systems whose subunits enjoy autonomy.[14] The trade union in pluralistic industrial societies is an autonomous subunit of a complex (because industrial) social system. But Islamic societies are not yet industrial and still have relatively simple social systems which, not having undergone differentiation, cannot grant their subunits autonomy. Wherever trade unions were formed, they were either a mouthpiece of the government or were persecuted for insubordination. Those labor unions daring enough to demand autonomy in developing countries understandably run into increasing conflict with the government's strategy of control which attempts . . . to bring the labor movement under its control by replacing the militant autonomous union leaders with leaders dependent on the party leadership and develops the head organization into an implementing mechanism.[15]

Under these conditions it is clear that labor unions cannot fulfill their function in the social system; they can exert a modernizing influence only if permitted to operate as autonomous units of action.

The classification of societies into complex and simple systems, those which are industrialized and those which are still preindustrial, can be refined further if they are more precisely described. Simple systems in which the degree of dominion over nature is very low are characterized, according to Balandier, by a congruence of the sacred and the political,[16] whereas complex systems are generally secularized. The secularization of Christianity in Europe is a consequence of industrialization and the evolution of a corresponding open society. Islam remains innocent of this phenomenon so far because it has remained a preindustrial culture.

In developing his theory of social change, Shmuel Eisenstadt points to the position of religious leaders in preindustrial cultures. These leaders were confronted with the need

to formalize and formulate their faith and tradition in such a way that they could be fully articulated and organized on a relatively differentiated cultural plan. They were also confronted by the necessity to regulate and channel the different dynamic orientations and elements which had developed in the very bosom of their religion itself and to maintain internal organization and discipline. In conjunction with internal problems such as these, specific patterns of action of the religious elites and organizations evolved within these societies.[17]

Such patterns of action are based on loyalty vis-à-vis the prevailing authorities and cannot allow any opposition. In this respect they stand in contradiction to the models of association and action cited above which a modern system offers its subunits; it is here that the autonomy of social organizations belongs. Without such autonomy a trade union cannot fulfill its social duties. In a traditional system, where the political and the sacred coincide, religious leaders always want

to preserve traditional orientations and to control the development of an independent, critical public opinion. They often see a threat to political loyalty in uncontrolled religious and intellectual activity and therefore attempt to control this activity and to maintain loyalty vis-à-vis the regime and the resources it provides.[18]

Eisenstadt makes these general assertions more specific in the case of Islam and recognizes that the Islamic "religious leadership [was] not organized as a separate church: it did not form an organized corporate body and was heavily dependent on the rulers."[19]

In view of the fact that the religious leadership in a traditional system is decisive in determining cultural and political value orientation, I think the thesis can be safely advanced that the dependency of the Islamic religious leadership on those in power became the norm in Islamic history. The members of such a society cannot be citizens in the sense of *citoyens*, but can only be subjects with all that implies of their relationship to those in authority. Fritz Steppat has established this thesis as being true for Islam. After an investigation of appropriate sources he has concluded

that the theologians prohibit rebellion against the authorities to the believer and dictate for him that he obey the orders of the authorities without enquiring about the legitimacy of the authorities. . . . Thus, in orthodox Islam a clear tendency toward an almost unconditional subjugation to the authorities, a theologically justified quietism, has arisen.[20]

Steppat also points out that Islam does not have a tradition of resistance.[21] Admittedly, the relationship between a Muslim and the authorities analyzed by Steppat refers to the classical Islamic Empire,

but is nevertheless of significance for the contemporary Islamic world. It explains why the masses, clinging to tradition in the Islamic countries, regard the state in part as a paternalistic authority, in part as a hostile power, but in any event have scant hopes of being able to influence it—this is why they submit, even though it obviously does not serve their interests.[22]

Labor union mentality cannot be integrated into such an asymmetrical structure of relations between subjects and rulers. In this sense the emergence of such a mentality in the Middle East means a "continuous destruction of the consciousness of traditional boundaries" (Büse) and a break with the traditional models of association and action.

At the apex of its development (750–1258) the researcher can detect in the ᶜAbbasid Empire commercial capitalist structures.[23] It was also during that period that new forms of professional association, which might be described as protolabor unions, came into being. ᶜAbd al-ᶜAziz al-Duri writes of this new tendency:

In that period socioeconomic development brought out a new social force: the common people. The cities had expanded appreciably and both population and varieties of labor had increased correspondingly. The cities were centers of labor and the crafts and thus became a stage for a distinct labor movement which manifested itself in the organization of labor and the crafts.[24]

It must be said that the use of the term "labor movement" for this period, however accurate one may consider Duri's description to be, is very problematic.

In a teaching manual from the law faculty at the University of Aleppo in Syria, the author, Muhsin Shishakli, emphasizes that Arab Islamic culture does not acknowledge the phenomenon of the *labor union*:

The labor union is the product of modern industry. The Arab countries find themselves still in a transitional state—that is, on the way from a traditional to a modern economic system. The inherited system is rapidly dissolving and losing its very essence.[25]

After a short overview of preindustrial forms of labor organization and the present state of development of labor unions in individual Arab countries, Shishakli acknowledges—in what was at the time an official university manual—that even though trade unions already exist in the Arab world no freedom exists for organized labor:

Indeed, we cannot assert that labor union freedom exists anywhere in the Arab world. For the labor unions are usually subordinated to the state administration and are always exposed to the arbitrariness of governmental policies. The wording of the labor laws, which guarantees the freedom of the workers, allows the right to form unions and submits conflicts between unions and the government to an independent judiciary, is usually of no consequence. But these laws are nevertheless one step forward. The general political situation in the Arab world and the predominant forms of government cannot cope with the traditional freedom of the unions granted by some of the more progressive societies.[26]

Even though Shishakli's work is a university manual, it contains social challenges which seem to me worth citing:

In the present phase of development the foundation of rural unions and the granting of union freedom should be pursued as goals. The unions belong to the primary social supports of modern society. The labor union can acquire great positive significance if it is freed of any governmental caprice. The union could be part of the natural, correct configuration of a developed Arab society.[27]

During the still unfolding phase of the repoliticization of Islam in the Middle East today, the warning cry against imitation of the West is ubiquitous. Even the demand for labor union autonomy is incriminated as an imitation of the West. Modern industrial society is a complex social system which has a technological-scientific cultural base. Islam remains a preindustrial culture based on the correlation existing between the sacred and the political.[28] Islamic societies are fundamentalistic and refuse autonomy to their subunits which are, in any case, very simple. The demand for autonomous trade unions in the Middle East is not an imitative gesture, but rather a plea in the defense of a modern industrial society. At the same time it is also a call for secularization, because no union autonomy can be achieved on the basis of a correlation between the sacred and the political. Islam carries on, as we have seen above, the tradition of obedience of subjects to their rulers and does not admit of an open society which guarantees autonomy to its subsystems.

If one calls for the establishment of liberties, such as those so self-evident in Western European societies, in non-Western societies, one runs up against more than warning cries from religious fanatics. It has become fashionable today among social scientists to warn of Eurocentrism when the question revolves around the appropriation of Western European achievements by non-Western societies. The reproach of Eurocentrism is certainly justified when it is a question of dealing with paternalistic or neocolonial attitudes, but it becomes farcical if handled in a fashionable or slovenly manner.[29]

Oil Production and the Condition of Labor in Iran and Saudi Arabia

Saudi Arabia and Iran, in that order, are the largest oil-exporting countries of the world. Their modern political and economic histories are almost identical with the history of the discovery and exploitation of petroleum.[30] Before the inauguration of oil production in 1908, Iran was close to being a segmentary society with a very weak central government. The new economic transformation contributed, in part, to the downfall of the Qajar dynasty and to the foundation of the strongly centralized Pahlavi state, whose central institutions could not have been financed without the oil revenues.[31] In Saudi Arabia the discovery and exploitation of oil in the 1930s coincided with the foundation of the Saudi Kingdom which likewise neutralized the segmentary tribal structures of the Arabian peninsula in favor of a strong central government.[32]

I mentioned above that the disintegration of traditional social structures was one consequence of the production of petroleum. A corresponding transition from rural to nonagrarian occupations can be observed in the region's structure of employment.[33] At the beginning of this century the portion of the population occupied in agriculture was 90 percent, whereas toward the end of the 1970s this figure was reduced to 33 percent. But the effects of employment in the oil sector, as pointed out above, are "always an important factor. . . . When oil creates jobs, and when it has significant consequences for the formation of a working class, it happens indirectly, through the creation of jobs by the state, from the revenues received [from oil]."[34] The structure of employment in construction, which expands disproportionally, and also in the embryonic industrial sector cannot be understood without taking into consideration the oil revenues.

The emergence of a new stratum, that of wage earners, in a preponderantly agrarian society creates new problems for the political system. The first labor law was issued in Iran in 1936 and was followed by the first labor legislation in 1946.[35] This legislation was amended several times and a new labor law was passed in 1959. Iran has the longest history of industrial relations among the Islamic oil-producing countries. Iranian labor law formally allows for the foundation of labor unions but thwarts industrial action (strikes) and refers labor conflicts to commissions. The attempts of the Pahlavi regime to keep the labor unions under government control only furthered conspirational activities and a parallel communist penetration of the Iranian labor unions by the Tudeh party,[36] which relentlessly tried to transform labor demands for wage increases into political conflicts. The return of the Shah to Iran in 1953 after the American-contrived overthrow of the nationalist Mossadeq regime was accompanied by an attempt to control the labor unions through more effective governmental policies. But even before the events of 1953, a three-day general strike had erupted in 1946, centering around demands for higher wages and the improvement of working conditions:

In view of the importance of the oil industry, this action, in which the workers succeeded with most of their demands, was of enormous significance and demonstrated the important role a small but strategically well-positioned working class can play in an economy such as that of Iran.[37]

The foundation of a state-controlled and loyal labor union followed from this action. Control and loyalty, however, failed to prevent the labor struggles of 1978 and the consequent ruin of the Pahlavi dynasty.

Now the question arises whether the Iranian labor movement which contributed to the overcoming of one despotic regime can continue to exist in an equally despotic Islamic regime hostile to conflicts and abhorring the organization of labor through unions as an imitation of the West. We have seen in the second part of this study that the Islamic system of social order preaches social homogeneity and submission to authority and does not allow any concept of the labor union as a lobby within a pluralistic society. We can only anticipate, therefore, that a grave conflict will erupt between the Iranian labor movement and the currently dominant clergy after this seemingly endless transitional period comes to an end.

The Shah attempted to secularize Iran through reform from the top and in the process ignited a rage in the Islamic clergy—the guardians of religious legitimacy—against his regime. The story is somewhat different in Saudi Arabia, where the authority of the Saudi dynasty is Islamically legitimized. Even a transient alliance between the oil workers and the clergy (*ulama*) is precluded in this case because the *ulama* figure importantly among the pillars supporting the political order of the Saudi monarchy. Both the Saudi labor movement and the oil sector are younger than those of Iran. In Saudi Arabia the political system controls society more effectively than did that of the Shah in Iran, because Saudi society remains tenaciously archaic and functionally undifferentiated. If a Saudi subject wants to take a wage labor job, for example, he needs permission from the government. The oil consortium ARAMCO introduced the first mass employment of this kind in the region. The first labor decree in which the restriction cited above can be found comes from the year 1947. In it there is no mention of the word "labor union." Only after the spontaneous wage-demand strikes of the oil workers in 1953 and again in 1956 was this decree amended by the royal decree of 1956, which expressly forbids strikes and threatens severer punishment for strike organizers than for strikers.[38] In 1969 the Saudi government issued a new labor law which, similarly, strictly prohibits strikes but provides for local labor offices commissioned to resolve labor conflicts. However, these conflicts are considered *only on an individual basis*: collective grievances are punishable.[39] There are, admittedly, conspirational secret labor organizations in Saudi Arabia, but no precise information on them exists.[40]

Labor migration (the importation of foreign labor) is supported by the state in Saudi Arabia, not only because the Saudi population is primarily nomadic and provides no pool of qualified workers for recruitment but also because of political reasons. According to official statistics the number of Saudi workers in 1975 amounted to 1,286 million, whereas the number of foreign workers was indicated as having been only 314,000. Since about two million migrant workers from Yemen live in Saudi Arabia and are not included in the statistics, Helen Lackner contends that the figures cited above for foreign workers are unrealistic.[41] The Yemenis constitute the core of the foreign workers. If one assumes a 3 percent increase in Saudi employment, the proportion of foreign workers should have amounted to 35 percent of the labor force by 1980. For years the Saudi government has attempted strenuously to reduce the proportion of Arabs (especially Palestinians and Yemenis) among the labor migrants in favor of Indians, South Koreans, and Taiwanese Chinese, especially since the latter do not carry any political baggage and thus do not represent any political danger. Moreover, the presence of these foreign workers is tied to specific projects, whereas Yemenis and Palestinians tend to integrate themselves into the country.

The spectacular events surrounding the occupation of the Mecca Mosque in November 1979 set off a chilling alarm signal for the Saudi dynasty, particularly since deracinated bedouins and foreign workers supported the assault, which was a religious performance by a political sect. The Middle East specialist of the *Neue Zürcher Zeitung*, Arnold Hottinger, wrote of the Mosque occupation that

obviously the bedouins and the participating foreigners, who were probably "guest workers," expressed their dissatisfaction with existing conditions through a "religious" war action, as has happened time and time again in the Islamic world. . . . The event of the Mosque occupation was most probably a mixture of deracinated bedouins and foreign workers.[42]

In the long term the fate of the Saudi dynasty might be similar to that of the Pahlavis; although it must be repeated that the religious legitimacy of the Saudi regime will most probably prolong its continued existence. However, the structural effects of the oil industry cannot be captured and controlled within the framework of an Islamic system of social order. Islam recognizes the community of believers in the form of the Islamic *Umma*. This *Umma* is a homogeneous, internally integrated, and thus functionally undifferentiated structure which classifies the indulgence in conflict as disobedience. This communal ideal corresponds to preindustrial agrarian values which cannot be realized in an open, industrial society. Petroleum production has existed in Iran since 1908; and in spite of state repression a labor movement developed which contributed significantly to Iran's political evolution, although no labor union tradition was allowed to take root.[43] In Saudi Arabia

the labour force, even when the migrants are included, is small and divided. The division is between the privileged workers in oil and the others. Non-oil workers have better conditions if they are Saudi Arabian than if they are migrant. . . . Migrant workers have the worst conditions, . . . the South Korean in particular.[44]

Although the Saudi Arabs are cosseted compared to the foreign workers, privilege does not secure loyalty: work in the production of oil deracinates the bedouins and transplants them into new living conditions. They cannot be integrated through wage privileges alone, especially when they see that a puritanical morality is preached and strictly sanctioned but not observed by the kingdom's rulers. To continue with Hottinger's *NZZ* report:

The people of Saudi Arabia have long known that the ruling strata indulge in drinking, gambling and carnal pleasures behind the high walls of their palaces; whereas the local and foreign subjects who are guilty of these "infractions" are requited with the harsh punishments of the religious law.[45]

No archaic social order can survive the industrial effects of oil production and the attendant structural changes. The "Islamic Republic" of Iran, too, will be unable to resolve the social problems which the production of oil raises.[46]

CONCLUSIONS

Future Prospects for Islam as a
Preindustrial Culture in the
Scientific-Technological Age:
The Secularization of Islam

A leading German Orientalist of the Weimar Republic asserted in his 1924 two-volume collection of papers, in a manner both Eurocentric and full of faith in progress: "The future of Islam can only consist in an adaptation to European intellectual life [!? B.T.], otherwise its days are numbered."[1] However, we are witnessing today a current of Islamic reinvigoration on an international scale. This current is being called "the repoliticization of Islam" because the Islam which was once forced into retreat by the normatively (but not structurally) oriented Westernization process is now enjoying a revitalization. I have described these processes above as acculturation and counter-acculturation.

For me, as a scholar whose cultural identity is located in the Middle East, it is neither sufficient nor satisfactory to diagnose modern Islam as a defensive culture. I also feel compelled to reflect on which course the modern Middle East should take in order to overcome its inferiority vis-à-vis that industrialized portion of our World Society representing scientific-technological culture. In spite of all the efforts by Islamic apologists, this inferiority is an obdurate fact which cannot be ignored or glossed over. Industrialization is no doubt the only solution. Cultural retrospection, a dominant feature in the phenomenon of Islamic repoliticization, can produce certain sociopsychological effects, but it certainly cannot contribute to the conquest of underdeveloped structures and the concomitant inequalities in World Society.

The industrialization of a society means the functional differentiation of its social structures, and for its system of religion this means secularization. But many Muslim scholars point to the correlation between the sacred and the political in Islam since the time of Muhammad's *pax islamica* and contend that this connection is an immutable and essential feature of

127

Islam. I want to let some of these authors speak for themselves before discussing the question of Islam and secularization.

The generic group of apologetic publications in modern Islamic literature is so voluminous and prominent that it would be unpardonable to pass over it and focus only on the few open-minded and innovative Muslim authors who are, unfortunately, without influence. The fallacious vision the apologetic authors present to their readers is particularly striking in this species of literature. Even serious scholars seem transfixed by the assumption that secularization portends the extinction of religion. I shall demonstrate below how wrong this conviction is when I develop my definition of secularization as a diminution of the religious system to a subsystem of society. What is distressing is that in many Islamic publications secularization is equated with promiscuity, homosexuality, or simply sexual freedom as such; this degeneracy leads to the emasculation of religion and behind it all lurks a worldwide "Jewish conspiracy" whose primary goal is the combating of Islam. These voices, being so numerous, cannot be ignored. I would like to quote a few examples:

The Egyptian scholar Faruq ᶜAbd al-Salam believes he can already observe the "fruits" of the depoliticization of religion in Europe:

Entire countries, which allegedly acknowledge Christ the Prophet, admit of homosexuality and actually regulate it by law. They even make prostitution, atheism, nudism, and also abortion and the taking of interest legal. Distinctions are no longer made between monotheists and atheists, between the church builder and the builder of brothels.[2]

After many long-winded passages of this sort the author comes to the point and asserts his ability to establish the fact that "Jewish-Zionist planning stands behind the spread of this [pernicious] idea of the separation of religion and politics and its institutional anchoring in the political system, especially through the introduction of the multiparty system."[3] In harmony with this Egyptian scholar, two Saudi professors at the University of Mecca, ᶜAli Garisha and M. S. Zaybaq, see "the Jews as propagators of secularization . . . in order to annihilate religion by keeping it imprisoned behind the walls of the churches."[4] Lest the above flowering of sexual fantasy appear singular, I shall quote the two Saudi professors at greater length:

If religion [in the West] is kept imprisoned behind church walls then we are not surprised to learn that religion changes there accordingly. People pray as music is being played. Then dancing events follow in which both sexes participate. Dancing is done under dimmed lights while warm and heated melodies are played. The clergy watch all this and even offer instructions.[5]

All these things could not take place in Islam "because the Islamic religion does not admit of any separation between state and religion. According to the Islamic doctrine of moral duties (*fiqh*), the state is an inseparable part of religion; state and religion are one.[6]

If a Muslim scholar publishes in a European language and lives beyond the reach of Islamic sanctions (and thus does not have to fear for his life), he can easily dismiss these ideas as not being serious and turn to more important things. In his critical study of religion, "Die Zukunft einer Illusion" (The Future of an Illusion), Sigmund Freud called for a "rational foundation for cultural prescriptions" and considered it no longer dangerous to express such thoughts:

In earlier times it was different, of course. One earned with such utterances a certain abbreviation of one's earthly existence and an excellent acceleration of the opportunity to have a personal experience of the life beyond. But, I repeat, those times are past and today this kind of writing is safe for the author.[7]

But this improvement in the intellectual climate is only valid for Europe, which has the Enlightenment behind it. Herbert Marcuse's criticism of Freud, that none of his writings shows "him more clearly in the grips of the dialectics of Enlightenment"[8] than the one cited above, makes the limitations of the critique of European Enlightenment clear. Because Islam has not experienced an Enlightenment, both the principle of tolerance, in the sense of the freedom allowed to those who think differently,[9] as well as the priority of reason are foreign to it. We can see evidence of this in the persecution of the Hellenized Muslim philosophers.[10]

The association of secularization with forbidden sexual fantasies may have its origin in the fact that religion and sexuality in the Islamic Middle East are the two central taboos. As a critical Arab writer said in an essay published in 1970, when the single remaining literary island in the Middle East (Beirut) still existed without censorship:

In our society there are two taboos about which one cannot be critical . . . and which one cannot investigate intellectually. If one dares, nevertheless, the literary product is either not published at all or the publishing organ which risked publication is confiscated and prosecuted. The dazed author is excluded from society and has to count on [encountering] every conceivable kind of unpleasantnesses. *The two taboos* of which I am speaking *are religion and sexuality.*[11]

Because I entitled my paper for the First Conference of Islamic Philosophy on Islam and Civilization (Cairo, November 1979) "Islam and secularism" and was consequently suspected of wanting to establish a positive connection between the two, Muslim fundamentalists argued for the cancellation of my paper. They failed in their efforts, thanks to the resolute intervention of the secularly oriented chairman of the conference, Mourad Wahba.[12] In the following I would like to present my Cairo theses in a more condensed and heightened form and discuss the problem of the secularization of Islam within a broad framework.

The concept of secularization comes from the Latin. *Saeculum* means "age"; "to be secular" means "to be oriented toward this age, that is, toward this present world." In Europe the process of secularization took place parallel to the development of modern industrial society and was originally advanced and sustained by the forces pushing for change in the Christian church itself. The peasant revolts led by the theologian Thomas Münzer[13] against the feudal lords and allied clergy, together with the Reformation initiated by Martin Luther,[14] ushered in the subsequent secularization. Although this historical development in Europe is approbatively viewed as progress, the concept of secularization in the Islamic world usually carries negative connotations. The enlightened Muslim author Detlev Khalid points to the prejudice disseminated among Muslims which holds that secularization concerns only Christianity:

In the apologetic literature we find the indefatigably repeated assertion that Islam does not recognize a clergy and that, therefore, a conflict between state and religion would be foreign in an Islamic milieu. This argument is wishful thinking and nothing other than the supplanting of reality by ideals. If we set aside the pronouncements of the Prophet concerning this problem, we can confidently assert that the clergy is a reality in Islamic societies today.[15]

Nikki Keddie has provided evidence from her research on Islamic history for the existence of religious institutions in Islam through which an Islamic clergy reproduced itself.[16]

Let me first explain the concept "secularization" in terms of the sociology of religion and raise the question of why secularization is a by-product of the birth of modern industrial society in Europe. This will be followed by a discussion dealing with whether the concept of secularization has any relevance for Islamic history. If the thesis which holds that secularization is a prerequisite for modern societies is indeed convincing, then it appears to me legitimate to pose the question whether attempts have been made on the

Islamic side to secularize modern Islam and whether Islam, as a sociocultural system and as a religion, is compatible with secularization. In short, what form might a secularized Islamic Middle East take on in the future? Niklas Luhmann points out that modern societies are to be explained as fully differentiated social systems. Secularization is associated with the full differentiation of a function; that is, secularization is "correlated with sociostructural evolution in the direction of a functional differentiation."[17] According to the religiosociological interpretation of Luhmann, secularization appears only

when the religious system is no longer primarily oriented as a society toward the personal environment of the social system, but as a subsystem of society oriented toward the internal social environment. . . . Then secularization appears as a consequence of the high degree of differentiation which modern society has attained.[18]

Secularization as used here describes the repercussions that social transformation, moving in the direction of modern industrial society, has on both the religious system and the social environment of this system; repercussions most precisely described by this concept.[19]

Opponents of secularization in the Islamic world often misunderstand the meaning of this concept and quite incorrectly interpret it as presaging the extinction of religion. Secularization is not a voluntary act but the product of a complicated social evolution, represented at its zenith by modern industrial society. Furthermore, secularization does not mean the abrogation of religion, because in a functionally differentiated system religion merely takes on social significance of a different nature and thus maintains meaning. To sum up, I want to emphasize, in tandem with Luhmann, that

secularization is one of the consequences of the transformation of society in the direction of a primarily functionally differentiated system in which each functional sphere gains greater self-reliance and autonomy but also becomes more dependent on how the other functions are fulfilled.[20]

In a system that is not functionally fully differentiated, there is an observable congruence between the sacred and the political. There is a correlation between this congruence and the absence of a full differentiation of the social system. George Balandier divides societies into those exhibiting an advanced degree of domination over nature and those in which control over nature is underdeveloped. "The kinship existing between the sacred and the political is quite unequivocal in societies which are not oriented toward dominating nature but are linked to it and see themselves continued and reflected in it."[21] I am in agreement with Balandier in explaining the process of industrialization and the development of science and technology, the necessary precursors of industrialization, as a process of acquiring power over nature. Out of this process functionally, fully differentiated social systems emerge which are, as a rule, secularized industrial societies.

Islam produced one of the most highly developed civilizations of the preindustrial age. Such preindustrial civilizations can be classified as empires. Shmuel Eisenstadt, a modernization theorist and sociologist, has studied these empires in the process of social change and insists that they were not functionally, fully differentiated social systems.[22] To refer to Balandier again, one encounters in these empires the congruence of the sacred and the political. Political power in these empires was borne by an alliance of the religious and political leaders in which the former provided religious legitimation for the political respectability of the latter. Actually, religious leaders always supplied political legitimacy to these imperial systems.

The distinction between organic and ecclesiastical religious systems is central, in religiosociological terms, to the discussion of secularization,[23] and I agree with Detlev Khalid when he identifies Islamic religious scholars (the *ulama*) as a clergy. In contrast to Christianity, however, Islam is organic not ecclesiastical:

Organic systems tend to equate religion and society; sacral law and social structure are at the heart of religion. Church systems, on the other hand, posit a structure that is within society but clearly separate from it; primary attention is given to the internal ordering of the church.[24]

Khalid overlooks this extremely important religiotheoretical differentiation. To be sure, dogmatic Islam admits of no clergy and it is to this fact that apologists and opponents of secularization generally make their appeal. Nevertheless a clergy *has* developed, complete with appropriate religious institutions, in the course of Islamic history. However, the Islamic clergy never possessed a separate church and never established an autonomous political power over the secular rulers, as was the case in ecclesiastical religious systems. In his study on secularization attempts in modern Egypt, Daniel Crecelius examines the traditional religiopolitical system and shows that in reality, the ruler dominated the learned men of religion . . . for the ulama did not attempt to *wield* political power so much as to *manipulate* it, hoping to influence state and society through their teachings and pious conduct. . . . This traditional self-view the ulama held of themselves as advisers and not rulers.[25]

The *ulama* were called upon by the political authorities to religiously indoctrinate all spheres of society. To be sure, they had no political power, but they did have the monopoly over the religiopolitical legitimation of rule. Bruce M. Borthwick, who has done research on the political function of the *ulama*, also comes to the conclusion that in the traditional organic system of Islamic religion

religious and political functions were fused and were performed by a unitary structure. . . . Religious institutions and officials have been as fully a part of the state as the army and generals. . . . The Sunni ulama . . . were expected to preach obedience to the ruler. . . . This they did.[26]

Even today a secularized social system is not to be found in the Middle East, if one disregards the politically secularized judicial systems in Tunisia and Turkey, whose social systems nevertheless exhibit strong religious traits. This absence is understandable if one bears in mind that although only a few Islamic countries have even relatively developed branches of industry at their disposal, even these, taken collectively, cannot as yet be classified as industrialized societies in which the process of complete social differentiation has reached an advanced stage. This lack of secularization should be interpreted here as the correlate of a low degree of differentiation.

Social scientists and historians who study social change, or who work specifically on Islamic social change, concur that secularization is an inevitable consequence of the high degree of differentiation in modern industrial society. But the question here is what industrialization and secularization have to do with the crisis of Islam and the North-South conflict. The term "North-South gradient" describes the conditioning factors of the social conflict between the privileged and underprivileged in our World Society: that is, the North-South conflict. For Galtung this important historical gradient is found "in the gap between levels of industrial manufacturing."[27] In the case of the Middle East this means that the Islamic countries will attain their long-fought-for equality of rights relative to the developed countries of Europe only when they industrialize and thereby secularize their social systems. This problem has been of acute concern to Islamic reformers, especially Afghani, since the nineteenth

century. But before I go into Islamic reform I think it important to deal
first with the problem of the correlation of the sacred and the political in
medieval Islam when Arab Islamic culture had reached its zenith and could
have supported an industrial revolution. Even though preindustrial, the
Islamic Empire displayed a relatively high degree of social differentiation
which favored the development of science and technology.[28] Tayeb Tisini,
a contemporary Arab philosopher, after a long study of the history of
Islamic philosophy, has attempted to develop a model for a new historiography. It becomes clear from his model that high Islamic philosophy
prepared the ground for a secular interpretation of the cosmos constructed
on a scientific foundation:

> The political and social content of those ideas of the Arab Islamic thinkers . . . was
> expressed in an attitude hostile toward the dominant feudal, intellectual orienta-
> tion. This attitude had its social base in the then comprehensive vertical and
> horizontal development of commodity production and in the economic activities
> that went hand in hand with the development of sciences, such as chemistry,
> astronomy, medicine, and mathematics.[29]

This was one strand in the early, interrupted evolution of Islamic society in
the direction of secularization, and it manifested itself in the philosophical
works of Avicenna, Averroës, Farabi, Ibn Tufayl, and others as well as in the
philosophy of history and social philosophy of Ibn Khaldun. The other
strand, revealing a tendency towards secularization, was the tradition of
Sufi Islam which embodied rebellion against the ascendancy of the Islamic
clergy and their alliance with the feudal aristocracy of the time. Sufi
Islam[30] evidenced a secularizing tendency insofar as it emphasized inwardness (batiniyya) in religiosity and aggressively questioned the role of the
ulama as mediators between God and the believer. Tisini has put forward
the interesting thesis that had heretical Islamic philosophy and Sufi Islam
been able to gain the upper hand in Islamic history, and had they not been
so successfully combated by the ulama, they could have made an important
contribution to the industrial development of what was at that time a
socioeconomically developed Islamic society.[31] But the transition from
a developed merchant capitalism to an industrial society was not effected
and the Arab Islamic Empire was submerged by history.

Secularization is not an intellectual phenomenon and cannot mean that
the Muslim Middle East must accommodate itself to "European intellectual life" (C. H. Becker) or must master the "intellectual problem of
Westernization" (von Grunebaum). In any case, this is the intention

of Orientalists in the humanities who "are still unwilling to make use of the benefits of modern theories on power, authority and political structures, confining themselves to interpretation of documents and the usual methods of cultural history," as the American social scientist and Middle East specialist Amos Perlmutter asserts in censuring Orientalists as the "factologists of dusty old world academies whose roots go back to the turn of the century."[32] In Europe, secularization was intimately bound up with the Industrial Revolution and thus had a sociostructural context which cannot be adequately understood or explained through intellectual history.

Shmuel Eisenstadt, in discussing Max Weber's thesis of the secularizing Protestant ethic and its explanatory value for the origins of modern capitalism, rejects the hypothesis that the Protestant ethic, as an *economic* ethic, singlehandedly brought about social change, particularly since this ethic coincided with other social factors. I think the results of Eisenstadt's research deserve to be quoted at length here because they may contribute to a better understanding of Islamic reformism than can methods employed by humanists, especially given that Luther's Reformation is the model Islamic modernists want to emulate:

> The Reformation was, of course, not originally a modernization movement. It had no modernizing impulses but wanted to set up a new and purely medieval, sociopolitical, religious order. Originally, Protestantism was indeed a religious movement, and as such wanted to restructure the world. But since it also possessed strong worldly impulses, these two were mingled together from the very beginning with the most important sociopolitical, economic and cultural tendencies for change in the European . . . societies at the end of the seventeenth century, that is, with the development of capitalism, the Renaissance states, absolutism, secularism and science.[33]

It is regrettable that Islamic modernists have chosen to ignore both these sociohistorical conditions as well as the results of the Reformation. They do not see secularization as a social process that lies beyond conviction.

The Lutheran Reformation was not only a struggle against religious offices and the clergy as such. It also implied the depoliticization of religion ("God cannot and will not allow anyone to govern the soul except for the soul alone." Martin Luther, *Of Worldly Authorities,* 1523) and the laying of the foundation for a new religious ethic. One of the climaxes of this development was the European Enlightenment and a concomitant secularization of all areas of life. With the help of their scientific-technological achievements, the Europeans liberated themselves from the tyranny of nature. Mastery over nature was one of the most distinctive features of the new European culture. In contrast, one of the central features of Islamic culture was the conflation of the sacred and the political.

Freud makes it clear in his theory of culture that the renunciation of blind drives is a prerequisite for every culture. In his critical writings on religion he reminds us of the following: "Religion has obviously rendered human culture great services, [has] contributed much to the subduing of the societal drives.[34] In another place he points out that the religious foundation of Islam "led to great worldly successes."[35] However, in a scientific age in which all areas of life have been secularized, religion as a custodian of culture becomes superfluous. Freud calls for "a rational foundation for cultural prescriptions."[36] I see no reason why this should exclude a religious ethic.

In the evolution of European history sketched here, stretching from Luther's struggle against the clergy and the Reformation to Freud's plea for a rational foundation for cultural prescriptions, a continuity which Islamic scholars tend to overlook holds sway. Afghani, the spiritual father of modern Islam, discussed at length above, ascribed the highest value to the Lutheran Reformation and attributed all European achievements to it.

In the course of its development Islam produced a fundamental schism (the split into an orthodox Sunni and a sectarian Shi'i Islam in the seventh century) and a number of religious variants (the most important being mystical Sufi Islam, out of which *Tariqa* Islam evolved). *But Islam has never known either a Reformation or an Enlightenment.*

Afghani writes in one of his most important texts on Luther:

If we reflect on the causes of the revolutionary transition of Europe from barbarism to civilization, we recognize that this change became possible only through the religious movement which Luther initiated and executed. This great man saw that Europeans were crippled by their ambitions and dominated by the clergy. He also saw that irrational traditions were dominant and as a consequence became the leader of this religious movement. He indefatigably called the Europeans into adopting a reformed value orientation. He explained to them that they were born free and yet remained in bondage.[37]

Luther was the model for Islamic modernism and Afghani presumably saw himself as the Islamic Luther. According to Afghani, only a new, reformed Islamic movement actively engaged in the struggle against both the colonizing European powers and the Islamic clergy could bring about a development in the Middle East similar to that of Europe. The Protestant ethic initiated a substantial change which exploded religious dogma and thus introduced a new tradition into Christianity. Afghani did not question the dogmatic fundaments of Islam, but rather believed that the Middle East could overcome its backwardness only on the basis of orthodox religion.

Afghani's friend, confederate, and cofounder of reformist Islamic modernism, Muhammad ᶜAbduh, whose work is far more voluminous than that of Afghani, attempted to think through the problem of the Middle East's civilizational backwardness within the confines of Islamic dogmatics. According to the foremost ᶜAbduh scholar, Charles Adams, two questions stand at the center of ᶜAbduh's work: the relationship between reason and religion on the one hand and science and Islam on the other.[38] My study of ᶜAbduh has led me to the same conclusion. ᶜAbduh criticizes the *ulama*'s rigidified understanding of Islam and reminds us that Islam recognizes *taqlid* as well as *ijtihad* as maxims of orientation for action. Literally, *taqlid* means "imitation" and *ijtihad*, "effort." Mohammed Arkoun translates *taqlid* as "submission to authority" and *ijtihad* as "independent legal findings."[39] ᶜAbduh contends that it is not structural conditions which have caused the backwardness of the Middle East; normative orientation alone is the decisive element. If Muslims exerted themselves, followed the path of *ijtihad*, and desisted from *taqlid*, then all their problems would be solved. These are the central arguments of ᶜAbduh's modernism.

Traces of this attitude can still be found today in the writings of the Islamic modernists. Rashid Rida, the editor of the Islamic journal *Al-Manar* (published in Cairo), stood firmly in this tradition.[40] A contemporary of Rida's, Shekib Arslan (1869–1946), was a Europeanized Islamic modernist and scholar who was also active in Europe. In 1929 Rida referred a question from an Islamic cleric from Indonesia to Shekib Arslan. In this question, which the Indonesian cleric had directed to the editorial office of *Al-Manar*, it was asked why the Muslims were backward, in spite of following the commands of God, whereas other people were developed. Arslan composed an answer which appeared in book form in 1930 with the title *A Treatise on Why the Muslims Are Backward While Others Have Developed*. This essay continues to be published and read even today. Here, too, as for all Islamic modernists, this verse from the Qur'an holds good: "God does not change a people's lot unless they change what is in their hearts" (13:11). In other words, the Muslims are underdeveloped because they undervalue the characteristic feature of Islam which, according to Afghani, "consists of dominance and superiority."[41] Arslan summarizes this idea of Afghani's at the end of his treatise by writing that the reader would be in error if expecting him to say that the salvation of the Muslims can be found through the appropriation of Einstein's relativity theory, the study of X rays, the inventions of Thomas Edison, or the chemical procedures of Louis Pasteur. For Arslan these achievements are

in reality only offshoots and nothing original; they are products and not initia-tions. Sacrifice [*tadhiyya*] or exertion [*jihad*] are the highest kinds of knowledge and tower over all other forms of knowledge. If a community [*umma*] has complete command of this knowledge and acts accordingly, then it can master all the other sciences, including their branches, and can appropriate all conceivable fruits and achievements from them. . . . The Muslims would have to, if they chose to, strive and behave as the Holy Scripture commands them to. Then they would reach the ranks of the Europeans, Americans and Japanese in both science and prosperity, while still preserving their Islam.[42]

The passage cited here is important not only because it is taken from a very influential Islamic work but also because it expresses the typical attitude of a modernized Islamic scholar who is as biased against the conservative Islamic clergy as was his spiritual predecessor, Afghani. However, ortho-doxy remains the common denominator connecting the Islamic modernists with the traditional *ulama*, whom I have called here "clergy." Both argue with the Qur'anic verse cited above and explain the backwardness of the Islamic Middle East as a consequence of Muslims not acting according to the commands of the Qur'an and not carrying out a holy war (*jihad*). It is important to mention that *jihad* in Islam means "holy struggle" in the sense of "exertion" and not "holy war" in a military sense, as ignorant journalists often incorrectly translate the term. Modern Islamic intellec-tuals have failed to recognize that Islam is a preindustrial culture which is incapable of meeting the requirements of our technological-scientific age. Their thinking remains imprisoned in apologetics and dogmatics.[43]

Islamic modernism, as a form of dogmatism, is eager to provide an answer to the question of why Muslims are today so backward and Euro-peans, who are obviously not Muslims, are so advanced. The social function of Islamic dogmatics reveals a defensive-culture and is a reaction to the penetration of the world by a superior technological-scientific culture. But this social function is not reflected in contemporary Islamic thought. Dogma, that is, the testimony of the Qur'an and the *Sunna*, is at the center of their reflections and perhaps this explains why Muslims remain back-ward. The declarations of the Qur'an and the *Sunna* from which the dog-matic material is constituted are used out of context. They are applied in a technological-scientific age even though they originated in a nomadic society in the process of transformation. But these linkages of the modern era which contemporary Islamic thought wants to explain are ignored—a distance is maintained. The thinking of Islamic modernism remains enclosed within the confines of dogmatics and thus remains reactive. It is merely the expression of a *defensive-culture*.

The development of technological-scientific culture and the transformation of Europe in the modern age led to a victory over the powerful conjunction of the sacred and the political which, as we have seen earlier, is a characteristic feature of preindustrial cultures. Today, cultural precepts are founded on reason rather than religion, which should make Freud rest easier. Viewed from this perspective, it must be conceded that Islamic culture is preindustrial and still based on a congruence of the sacred and the political. Islam is also a political ideology, containing the definitive groundwork for a system of social order. It is here one finds Islamic law, the *Shari'a*, which governs all areas of life. As early as the classical period of Islam under the ʿAbbasids (750–1258) pious Muslims felt the deficiency in their religion of a religious "inwardness." This inwardness formed the background from which a new course was set in Islam—Sufism—usually interpreted as Islamic mysticism. Islam contains not only a form of government but also a basis for a social identity. Orthodox Sunni Islam originated as an Arab identity and remains one today. The Shiʿi variant of Islam fashions the substance of an Iranian identity today in the form of an Iranized Islam. These aspects of Islam cannot be ignored when the accusation is made that Islam is inadequate to meet the demands of the modern age. Islam is not only a sociocultural system of order but, since the emergence of Sufism, it also contains a basis for religious interiority.

In Europe the Industrial Revolution and the technological-scientific culture it produced have not led to the extinction of Christianity in spite of this culture's rational underpinnings. But religion *is* secularized and, as an ethic, is primarily relegated to the internal sphere. Afghani makes a vigorous appeal to Luther and uses his Reformation as a model for the Islamic peoples; he ignores, however, the crucial fact that the Protestant ethic has been primarily domiciled within the sphere of interiority and that, for Luther, the religious man, as a personally accountable Christian individual, is dependent upon himself. The future of Islam seems to lie in a parallel direction.

The question of whether Islam can be reconciled to technological-scientific culture is one that also engages Muslim intellectuals. Unfortunately, however, it is very difficult to find fertile starting points for analysis in their writings because they cannot seem to escape the confines of religious dogmatics which I described above.

As an example, it seems worthwhile to quote here a characteristic assertion of an Islamic scholar found in a book entitled *The Imputed Chasm between Science and Religion*. The author, Muhammad ᶜAli Yusuf, concedes that Christianity is incompatible with a scientific culture, adding that

in the Islamic Middle East the state of affairs has a completely different aspect. Between Islam and science neither a conflict nor a chasm exists. Therefore, we can observe that the efforts in the Islamic Middle East concentrate on overcoming the illusion that there is a gap between science and religion. . . . Religion is from God. But Allah has called himself "the truth" [*al-ḥaqq*]. Truth cannot contain contradictions within itself. There is thus no contradiction between religion and truth. For science is based naturally on the truth.[44]

This assertion fulfills all the criteria of religious dogmatics. The Qur'an states that God is *al-ḥaqq*, the Truth. Since science is said to search for truth it cannot stand in opposition to Islamic religious writings.

The secularly oriented Arab philosopher Sadiq Jalal al-ᶜAzm, who received his Ph.D. degree from Yale University, emphasizes in his book, *Critique of Religious Thought* (published 1969 in Beirut in Arabic), that the debate over whether specific, isolated portions of Islamic doctrine are in conformity with or in contradiction to this or that scientific insight is fundamentally unfruitful. Unfortunately, debate within Islamic writings takes precisely this form. According to al-ᶜAzm the chasm is much deeper:

It concerns the method which we employ in order to arrive at our insights and convictions. . . . In this respect there is a fundamental contradiction between Islam and science. For Islam, as for any other religion, the correct method consists in using certain "revealed" religious texts, or the writings of scholars who have studied and commented upon these texts, as the source of truth. . . . It is superfluous to mention that the scientific method stands in complete contradiction to this religious, exegetically dogmatic method.[45]

The author recognizes that the efforts of Muslim intellectuals to reconcile Islam with scientific culture remain confined in the methodological cage of religious dogmatics described by al-ᶜAzm.

Al-ᶜAzm is himself a Muslim and a descendant of a famous family of Damascene notables. His criticism of Islam is limited to the assertion that modern scientific culture is rationally based and incompatible with Islam. But for al-ᶜAzm it is important to differentiate between religion as the content of a particular culture and religious consciousness as a form of inwardness. In the Islamic Middle East

this religious consciousness is crushed by the petrified traditional forms of belief and by stagnant religious customs. This religious consciousness must free itself from its fetters in order to express itself in forms adapted to the conditions and requirements of civilization in the twentieth century.[46]

Al-ᶜAzm was taken to court following the publication of his book,[47] but was later exonerated and now is allowed to teach again as a university professor; although in order not to endanger himself or his position as a professor, he is no longer active as a critic.

A similar fate befell ᶜAli ᶜAbd al-Raziq, an al-Azhar scholar and judge, still detested today, who published his book *Islam and the Forms of Government* in Cairo in 1925.[48] In this book he attempts to prove, with the help of Islamic texts, that Islam is not a form of government but a religion which concerns people in their interiority. Because of his publication ᶜAbd al-Raziq lost his positions as professor and judge but was later vindicated, albeit only formally. His book seems to me to be very timely, given the current repoliticization of Islam in the Middle East, because it appears to have an answer to the question whether Islam can indeed provide a system of government for the present age. From a purely scholarly position one could dismiss as problematical ᶜAbd al-Raziq's attempt to interpret Islam as an unpolitical religion, as a species of religious consciousness, because it is an historical certainty that the founder of Islam, Muhammad, was also a statesman and the creator of the *pax islamica* (see chapter 4). However, the critical point here does not concern religioanalytical insights but the appropriation of the rationally based technological-scientific culture in the Islamic Middle East together with the rescue of Islam as a religious form of awareness. In this situation, in which secularization is ineluctable, ᶜAbd al-Raziq's interpretation of Islam as the source of internal religious awareness rather than as a pattern for government appears to provide an adequate solution.

Islamic history is not only religious history but also political history. ᶜAbd al-Raziq, who, as I mentioned above, once held a professorship at Al-Azhar University, is distinguished from other Islamic modernists by his strict separation of the two historical definitions of Islam. ᶜAbd al-Raziq acknowledges that the Arab Muslims built up a powerful empire in the course of the spread of Islam, but emphasizes that this was an *Arab* accomplishment. The Arabs acted as "rulers and colonizers" during this imperial foundation, not as Muslims. "The new state which was founded by the Arabs and governed in the Arab way was an Arab state. By contrast, Islam, as I know it, is a religion for all mankind. It is neither Arab nor foreign."[49]

One rarely finds among contemporary authors in our era of Islamic repoliticization a scholar of the intellectual quality of either Afghani or ʿAbduh or even of the latter's disciples. Apologetic literature is ascendant. Marshall G. S. Hodgson writes in the epilogue to his three volume history of Islam that Islam was once a vision and needs another vision for its renewal. "We cannot say that the religious heritages are in fact able to offer such vision."[50] The wishful thinking which Hodgson criticizes in the revitalization of this inheritance is the striking feature of the literary attempts at repoliticization. If we look, for example, at the widely distributed publication of Yusuf Qurdawi, *Al-hal al-islami (The Islamic Solution)*, we find only an apologetic self-congratulation but no *solution* for the problems at hand.[51]

In the course of my studies of Islam I have been particularly impressed by only two Islamic scholars among the numerous writers in the field (and these two—characteristically and unfortunately—have published only in English or French): the Pakistani Fazlur Rahman, who teaches in Chicago, and the Algerian Muhammad Arkoun, who teaches in Paris. I assume that both would have just as little opportunity as I do to address an Islamic public because the censors in the respective despotically governed societies would stand in the way.[52]

A German reviewer wrote apropos a remarkable publication by Arkoun: "For the time being it appears that radical analyses such as the one by Arkoun are more apt to be published and discussed by both Muslims and non-Muslims in Europe rather than in the Islamic world."[53] Arkoun calls for an adaptation of Islam to the scientific age and criticizes the fact that "the general Islamic consciousness . . . remains content with dogma."[54] Arkoun sees no contradiction between Islam and science. Fazlur Rahman also calls for a radically new vision of Islam:

Muslims must decide what exactly is to be conserved, what is essential and relevant for the erection of an Islamic future, what is fundamentally Islamic and what is purely "historical." In other words they must develop an enlightened conservatism. . . . The task of rethinking and reformulating Islam at the present juncture is much more acute and radical than has faced the Muslims since the 3rd/9th century. . . . And this is exactly what the conservatives, who still largely control the mainsprings of power in the community, not only refuse to do but completely fail even to recognize the need to do. . . . Indeed, the need to cultivate a sound historical thinking about Islam is the first desideratum and prerequisite of any successful process of the reformulation of Islam."[55]

Rotraud Wielandt, a German Orientalist, discusses in her Ph.D. dissertation the problems, not to mention the repressions, with which Muslims are confronted when they dare to interpret elements of Islam as historically conditioned and not as ontological truths.[56]

The main currents of Islam since the nineteenth century can be divided into two alignments: the modernists, who want to integrate technological-scientific achievements into Islam without accepting their consequences; and the fundamentalists, who refuse the new as such and cling to Ur-Islam as their standard. Today, the second orientation is completely dominant. The central problem of the first current, modernism, is not specifically Islamic: the illusion that the diffusion of innovations is compatible with the preservation of the old can also be observed at work in other traditional societies. Gerd Zimmermann writes in conjunction with his discussion of the problem of diffusion that

the leaders of the developing countries of course want to take over the machines and the accompanying technical "know-how," but for understandable reasons consider any "sociocultural Westernization" going beyond a technical takeover a threat to their national identity. In extreme cases they want economic and technological development without social change.[57]

During the First Conference of Islamic Philosophy on Islam and Civilization that I mentioned above, the distinguished Islamic scholar Richard Mitchell presented a paper on "Islam and Technology," in which he strongly emphasized that technology is not value-neutral and implies a value system.[58] One cannot make an appeal for a diffusion of modern technology and at the same time refuse its social implications. Unfortunately, Mitchell found no concurrence among the Islamic members of his audience.

I would like to conclude my plea for the secularization of Islam with a few remarks on the social character of secularization and modernization. In chapter 1 I emphasized that industrialization is not a value in itself. I argue both against Marxists who reduce history to the development of modes of production and against growth ideologies, and contend that industrialization is to be striven for only as a human quality, as a means for liberating human beings from the tyranny of nature. In Europe, where the evolution of emancipatory ideas in bourgeois society occurred parallel to the Industrial Revolution, social development is no longer analyzed with the help of social theory and bound up with the elaboration of emancipatory social blueprints, but is regarded merely as a problem to be conquered by social technology. Social development is reduced to economic growth. Daniel Bell is correct in noting that economic growth has become "the secular religion of all highly developed industrial societies."[59] The consequences are incalculable: "the withering of *civitas*"; in other words, "terrorism, struggles among groups and political anomie appear, or . . . all public intercourse disintegrates into cynical transactions."[60] Bell's solution is the return of Western society to a religious conception: "Religion can restore generational continuity. It refers us back to the existential categories which are the basis for modesty and respect for others."[61] Bell must certainly mean with this a religious ethic and not the religious system as a political order.

Islamic societies can learn much by reflecting on Western European development, but this acquired wisdom should not be equated with imitation. In chapter 1 I argued from the perspective of a theory of civilization, with reference to Norbert Elias, and presented the evolution of European society as the most progressive and advanced development in the history of humankind so far. It has become fashionable in Europe today to formulate and discuss self-accusations. Anti-institutional posturing and ecological romanticism have supplanted rigorous social criticism which could help in making certain discriminations. The romantically regressive protest against a ludicrous ideology of growth and its inhumane application overlooks the fact that existing institutions in the developed Western industrial societies guarantee for the first time in the history of the world an institutionalization of human dignity through a corresponding safeguarding of the individual against possible attacks from either state or church.

Islam has no tradition either of autonomous institutions designed to protect human dignity or of tolerance toward dissenters. The Islamic notion of "tolerance," *al-tasamuh*, refers exclusively to *ahl al-kitab* (adherents of monotheistic religions—Christians and Jews) and this is not as comprehensive as is the European concept of tolerance in terms of the Age of Enlightenment. The modern concept lacking in Islamic tradition is based on the right to be different (*le droit à la différence*) that applies to all religions as well as to nonreligious views and convictions. My appeal for a cultural authenticity in Islam in an age of world-societal communication should not be seen as standing in contradiction to the integration of European Enlightenment values into Islam in the form of a religious ethic. The Hellenized Islamic philosophers are for me examples of the possibility of wise appropriation. Averroës and Avicenna were Islamic philosophers for whom there was no contradiction between membership within the sphere of Islam and the adoption of Greek philosophy with its attendant rationalization of the cosmos. Only Islamic fundamentalists, for whom Islam is an inviolable, organic religious system, could reject such a cultural enrichment and the reduction of the Islamic system to a religious ethic more appropriate for our time. Such a secularization does not imply the extinction of religion, as I have repeatedly emphasized. An industrial society with a "rational foundation for its cultural precepts" (Freud) is not in contradiction to the preservation of religion as an ethic. In modern Western societies, where instrumental reason holds sway, the consequences of attempts to repress such an ethic are clearly visible. Both the communist and the "alternative romantic" sects, whose rites smack of pseudoreligions, document above all a deep need for religion in the West. Bell's plea for a resuscitation of religion in the industrial societies corresponds to an objective need and also to the spirit of the times in these societies.

Muhammad Arkoun notes that "there is talk in the West of a crisis of faith and even of a threat from the new proliferation of magic rites and deviant sects."[62] Arkoun, who advocates an Islamic ethic, does not neglect to warn his Muslim contemporaries against abusing this religious need in the West as an argument for reinforcing apologetic Islamic positions.

This first concluding remark, which holds that industrialization should not be seen as simply a technical process involving the development of productive forces and therefore not as an imitative retrieval of European history, is connected to a second concluding observation on secularization. The industrialization of a society implies a functional differentiation and thus a diminution of religion to a subsystem of that society. However, this conceptual definition needs to be refined through historical analysis. In terms of the distinction I made earlier between ecclesiastical and organic systems of religion, the process of secularization has to assume historically diverse forms. I am in agreement with British sociologist Brian Turner's criticism of modernization theories which try to universalize the model of Western development, and I emphasize with him that the secularization of Islam cannot come about along the lines of the Western pattern.[63] That Turner does not provide concrete suggestions but remains content with this rather general observation probably has to do with the fact that Islam is an organic system of religion whose central element is its sacred law, the *Shari'a*.

Modern law in an industrial society has to be capable of both regulating and formalizing industrial relations. The *Shariʿa* contains no departure points for such formalizations; nor does it offer as it now stands any reference points for the "institutionalization of social change,"[64] to use Frank Rotter's phrase. In the apologetic literature, for example in Sabir Tuʿayma's *Al-Shariʿa al-islamiyya fi ʿasr al-ʿilm* (*Islamic Law in a Scientific Age*), Islamic law is interpreted as timelessly applicable to all social problems, including the regulation of international relations.[65] The work of the Western-educated lawyer Subhi al-Salih, who wrote in Arabic, is noteworthy in this regard. (Al-Salih, who had a French Ph.D. degree and was the former vice Mufti of Lebanon, was killed by Shiʿi gunmen in 1986.) Al-Salih also offers apologetic arguments, but recognizes certain lacunae in Islamic law which he thinks can be overcome by following the path of *ijtihad*, or, in other words, through independent legal findings. His solution enjoins the "opening of all gates of *ijtihad*" and the proscription of *taqlid*, or, subjection to the authority of tradition.[66] Al-Salih points out that we live in a scientific-technological age but is of the opinion that the Islamic *Shariʿa* is completely adequate to meet the demands of this age.[67] I am inclined to dispute this but want to leave open the discussion of the future of Islamic law in a secularized Islam because an answer would require exhaustive research in the sociology of law and religion, and would have to be connected with an analysis of legal forms in the Islamic countries.[68]

For the time being I simply want to note that the answer cannot come out of traditional, exegetically inclined Orientalism. Although I always try to keep my distance from the apologetic literature, I have to agree here with one apologetic author, Muhammad Muslehuddin, who has studied Orientalist works on Islamic law. Muslehuddin correctly argues that Orientalists are not legal scholars and thus do not even understand their own law, but nevertheless presume to disseminate crucial opinions on this law.[69] To this it might be added that law cannot be understood merely through literary exegesis; understanding it presupposes a knowledge of legal theory and sociology. In order to be fair I should mention that the two standard works on Islamic law cited above (note 71 in chapter 1) come from the pens of British Orientalists Noel Coulsen and Joseph Schacht. In spite of their limits these works still appear useful for the study of Islamic law. We cannot escape the observation that most of the Western Orientalists and their Middle Eastern fundamentalist contenders alike share scripturalism; that is, they view Islam in the medium of religious scripture and not as a

THE CRISIS OF MODERN ISLAM   147

reality. In this study, real Islam and not scriptural Islam has been subjected to scrutiny.

The preoccupation with modern Islam in its current phase arises from the fact that the contemporary Islamic Middle East finds itself in a crisis—actually, in a double crisis produced by both the pauperization of the Muslim peoples and the identity crisis brought on by Westernization. In their despair Muslims are turning to Islam as the promise for a better future and as the basis for a cultural identity. The product of this development is a repoliticization of Islam, which can be observed today throughout the entire Islamic Middle East.

The conclusion to be drawn from the above discussion is that the modern era rests on a rationally based technological-scientific culture. Europeans are developed because they possess this culture, whereas Muslims are backward because they have not yet appropriated the technological-scientific culture and *not* because they have been inattentive toward the Qur'anic verse quoted earlier: "God does not change a people's lot unless they change what is in their hearts" (13:11). The Christian West went through a Reformation of Christianity whose end product was the severance of the sacred from the political. Islam however remains based on an equation of the sacred and the political. Al-Afghani, the first and still today the intellectually most formidable Islamic thinker of modern times, found fault with the fact that Islam had not yet produced a Luther and believed he could assume the role of a Muslim Luther himself. This audacious assertion of Afghani's is often overlooked by his Muslim readers. Islam still requires a transforming reformulation out of which secularization could materialize.

We have learned from both the not strikingly successful secularization attempts in Kemalist Turkey and the frustrated, not to say boomeranged efforts of the toppled Shah, who tried to neutralize religion by fiat, that a "rational foundation for cultural prescriptions" can occur only on the basis of the structural evolution of society toward an industrial, functionally differentiated social organization. The Westernized and secularly oriented Muslim intellectuals want to introduce modern structures for which no social basis exists in Islam. A scientific- and technological-oriented culture cannot flourish in an agrarian or peripherally capitalist society. To project the industrialization of the Islamic Middle East and the attendant secularization of its organic religious system as the perspective of the future—I repeat—is not inimical to the preservation of one's own cultural authenticity. Just as the Europeans developed an Occidental Christian variant of technological-scientific culture, so Muslims can create their own Oriental Islamic variant of this stage of civilization in which Islam would be reduced to a subsystem of the greater, whole social system: that is, to a religious ethic. Muslims have historical parallels for such a development. As I mentioned above, during the ᶜAbbasid period (750–1258) Hellenized Muslim philosophers explained the world rationally, and adherents of Sufi Islam protested fiercely against this misuse of religion to legitimate governmental authority. The cultural authenticity of Islam was not questioned at that time. Nor does the secularization of Islam in our modern age necessarily portend its extinction.

NOTES

Introduction. Islam as a Defensive Culture in a Scientific-Technological Age

1. Ernst Bloch, *Subjekt, Objekt: Erläuterungen zu Hegel*, 2d ed. (Frankfurt 1972), 32.

2. See Klaus-Jürgen Gantzel, ed., *Herrschaft und Befreiung in der Weltgesellschaft* (Frankfurt 1975), esp. chap. 2.

3. An extreme example is Klaus Busch, *Die multinationalen Konzerne: Zur Analyse der Weltmarktbewegung des Kapitals* (Frankfurt 1974).

4. Ernst Bloch, *Thomas Münzer als Theologe der Revolution*, reprint (Frankfurt 1972), 55.

5. A discussion of this interpretation can be found in Bassam Tibi, "Die feudalistische Weltordnung und die Neue Internationale Wirtschaftsordnung," *Die Neue Gesellschaft* 25, no. 9 (1978): 718–27.

6. It is therefore problematical when Senghor speaks of the *culture universelle* and at the same time develops an anti-industrial, romantic attitude glorifying agrarian cultures. See chapter 1 on "Romantische Entwicklungsideologien" *in* Bassam Tibi, *Internationale Politik und Entwicklungsländer-Forschung* (Frankfurt 1979), 29–66.

7. For examples, see Armando Cordova, *Strukturelle Heterogenität und wirtschaftliches Wachstum* (Frankfurt 1973), and Dieter Senghaas, "Strukturelle Abhängigkeit und Unterentwicklung" *in* Bassam Tibi and V. Brandes, eds., *Unterentwicklung. Handbuch II, Politische Ökonomie* (Frankfurt and Cologne 1975), 120ff.

8. See Syed M. Alatas, *Intellectuals in Developing Countries* (London 1977), 56.

9. See Frantz Fanon, *Black Skin, White Masks: The Experience of a Black Man in a White World* (New York 1967), 83ff. Ethnopsychoanalysis is still a wide-open field. See, for example, Georges Devereux, *Ethnopsychoanalyse* (Frankfurt 1978), and the collection of articles by the Swiss author Paul Parin, *Der Widerspruch im Subjekt: Ethnopsychoanalytische Studien* (Frankfurt 1978).

10. See James S. Coleman, ed., *Education and Political Development* (Princeton 1965).

11. Eric Hoffer, *The True Believer: Thoughts on the Nature of Mass Movements* (New York and Evanston 1951), 37.

12. Ibid., 39.

13. See Nikki Keddie, "Oil, Economic Policy and Social Conflict in Iran," *Race and Class* 21, no. 1 (1979): 13–29. Robert Graham, *Iran: Die Illusion der Macht* (Frankfurt 1979), 12ff., describes the squatter urbanization which he was able to follow during a two-year stay in Iran.

14. A good example is Seyyed H. Nasr, *Islam and the Plight of Modern Man* (London 1975), 83ff.

15. Besandniah of the Iranian Ministry of National Guidance writes in a letter to the editor of *Der Spiegel* (32 [1979]), that "all Muhammadans are brothers and do not intend to violate borders. But if there are any clashes they are the result of an imperialist conspiracy."

16. Anthony F. C. Wallace, *Religion: An Anthropological View* (New York 1966), 126ff., 157ff.

17. Bryce Ryan, "Die Bedeutung der Revitalisierungsbewegungen für den sozialen Wandel in den Entwicklungsländern," *in* René König, ed., *Aspekte der Entwicklungssoziologie* (Cologne and Opladen 1969), 37–65, esp. 62.

18. ʿAbd al-ʿAziz al-Duri, *Muqaddima fi al-taʾrikh al-iqtisadi al-ʿarabi* (Beirut 1969).

19. Nasr, *Islam and the Plight of Modern Man*, 148.

20. Muhammad El-Bahey, *Al-fikr al-islami al-hadith wa silatuhu bi al-istiʿmar al-gharbi*, 4th ed. (Cairo 1964), 483. The correct transliteration of the author's name is al-Bahi. Al-Bahi, a former head sheikh of al-Azhar, submitted his Ph.D. dissertation at the University of Hamburg in 1936 with his name transliterated as el-Bahey, the form used and known ever since.

21. René König, "Über einige offene Fragen und ungelöste Probleme der Entwicklungsforschung," *in* König, *Aspekte der Entwicklungssoziologie*, 9–36, esp. 30.

22. For the caliphate see Sir Thomas W. Arnold, *The Caliphate*, 2d ed. (London 1965); for the imamate see S. Husain M. Jafri, *The Origins and Early Development of Shiʿa Islam* (London 1979), 289ff.

23. Johan Galtung describes this structure of world society in "Eine strukturelle Theorie des Imperialismus," *in* Dieter Senghaas, ed., *Imperialismus und strukturelle Gewalt*, 4th ed. (Frankfurt 1978), 190; see also note 2.

24. See chapter 4.

25. Maxime Rodinson, *Mohammed*, trans. Anne Carter (New York 1971), 295.

26. Gustav E. von Grunebaum, *Studien zum Kulturbild und Selbstverständnis des Islam* (Zürich and Stuttgart 1969), 118.

27. Arnold Hottinger, "Islamische Revolution? Die Muslime im Konflikt mit der westlichen Moderne," *Merkur* 16, no. 3 (1979): 204–16, esp. 216.

28. Galtung, "Strukturelle Theorie des Imperialismus," 43.

29. Von Grunebaum, *Kulturbild und Selbstverständnis des Islam*, 118.

30. Ibid., 119.

Chapter 1. ACCULTURATION, WESTERNIZATION,
AND INTERCULTURAL COMMUNICATION IN
WORLD SOCIETY AND IN ISLAM

1. See my inaugural lecture at the University of Göttingen in 1974 on the problem of acculturation, published in *Internationale Politik und Entwicklungsländer-Forschung: Materialien zu einer ideologiekritischen Entwicklungssoziologie*, Edition Suhr-

kamp, no. 983 (Frankfurt 1979), 176ff. This chapter contains revised portions of my article, "Akkulturation und interkulturelle Kommunikation," *Gegenwartskunde* 2 (1980): 173–90.

2. See Gérard Leclerc, *Anthropologie und Kolonialismus* (Munich 1973), 57ff., 60ff.

3. See James M. Coleman, ed., *Education and Political Development* (Princeton 1965), chap. 3, 353ff.

4. This rather undifferentiated thesis can be found, for example, in Bjorn Pätzold, *Ausländerstudium in der BRD: Ein Beitrag zur Imperialismuskritik* (Cologne 1972), 175ff, a published version of his Hamburg dissertation.

5. Darcy Ribeiro, *Der zivilisatorische Prozess* (Frankfurt 1971), 198ff.

6. Johan Galtung, *Strukturelle Gewalt: Beiträge zur Friedens- und Konfliktforschung* (Reinbek, Hamburg 1975), 119.

7. Ibid., 120.

8. Ibid., 121.

9. Samuel Kodjo, *Probleme der Akkulturation in Afrika* (Meisenheim/Glan 1973), 71.

10. Ibid., 47.

11. Ibid., 262.

12. Ibid., 266f.; emphasis mine.

13. See Bassam Tibi, *Nationalismus in der Dritten Welt am arabischen Beispiel* (Frankfurt 1971). English translation: *Arab Nationalism: A Critical Enquiry*, Marion Farouk-Sluglett and Peter Sluglett, eds. and trans. (London 1981), 33ff., 40ff., 62ff.

14. See Maria Mies, "Kulturanomie als Folge westlicher Bildung," *Die Dritte Welt* 1, no. 1 (1972): 23–38. The concept of anomie was originally coined by Emile Durkheim in his innovative study, *Le suicide: Etude de Sociologie* (Paris 1897).

15. See chapter 3.

16. Kodjo, *Akkulturation in Afrika*, 241.

17. Ibid., 266.

18. Ibid., 267.

19. Ibid., 266.

20. Ibid., 276.

21. Uwe Simson, *Auswärtige Kulturpolitik als Entwicklungspolitik* (Meisenheim/Glan 1975), 33.

22. Ibid., 34.

23. Tibi, *Arab Nationalism*, 64ff.

24. Richard F. Behrendt, *Soziale Strategie für Entwicklungsländer: Entwurf einer Entwicklungssoziologie* (Frankfurt 1965), 250ff.

25. See the chapter on romantic ideologies of development in West Africa, in Tibi, *Internationale Politik und Entwicklungsländer-Forschung*, 32–66.

26. Gerd Zimmermann, *Sozialer Wandel und ökonomische Entwicklung* (Stuttgart 1969), 73, characterizes the relations between non-Occidental intellectuals and European culture with the term "love-hate."

27. See Gustavo L. Matus, "Der Status der Nation und das internationale Schichtungssystem," *in* Peter Heintz, ed., *Soziologie der Entwicklungsländer* (Cologne and Berlin 1962), 45–69.

28. Johan Galtung, "Eine strukturelle Theorie des Imperialismus," *in* Dieter Senghaas, ed., *Imperialismus und strukturelle Gewalt*, 4th ed. (Frankfurt 1978), 29ff., 55ff.

29. See the chapter on "Kolonisation als Akkulturation" in Leclerc, *Anthropologie und Kolonialismus*, 52ff.

30. Cited from Johanna Eggert, *Missionsschule und sozialer Wandel in Ostafrika* (Bielefeld 1970), 46.

31. Ibid., 49.

32. Ibid., 275.

33. Ibid., 277.

34. Galtung, "Strukturelle Theorie des Imperialismus," 75.

35. Leclerc, *Anthropologie und Kolonialismus*, 60.

36. Galtung, "Strukturelle Theorie des Imperialismus," 36f.

37. Dieter Oberndörfer, "Methoden der Aussenpolitik," *in* Karl Dietrich Bracher and Ernst Fraenkel, eds., *Internationale Beziehungen*, Fischer-Lexikon, vol. 7 (Frankfurt 1969), 176.

38. Norbert Lechner, "Sozialwissenschaftliches Krisenmanagement in Lateinamerika," *in* Dankwart Danckwerts et al., *Die Sozialwissenschaften in der Strategie der Entwicklungspolitik* (Frankfurt 1970), 131.

39. Maria Mies, "Warum Deutsch? Eine Untersuchung des sozioökonomischen Hintergrunds der Studienmotivation von Deutsch-Studenten in Poona/ Indien," *in* Wolfgang S. Freund and Uwe Simson, eds., *Aspekte der auswärtigen Kulturpolitik in Entwicklungsländern* (Meisenheim/Glan 1973): 262ff., esp. 262.

40. Ibid.

41. Ibid., 279.

42. Ibid., 280.

43. Ibid., 281.

44. Norbert Elias, *Über den Prozess der Zivilisation: Soziogenetische und psychogenetische Untersuchungen*, vol. 2, *Wandlungen der Gesellschaft: Entwurf zu einer Theorie der Zivilisation*, 2d ed. (Bern and Munich 1969), 312.

45. Ibid., 318.

46. See my discussion of this in Bassam Tibi, "Widerstandsrecht in rechtlosen Gesellschaften: Friedensforschung und Dritte Welt," *Gegenwartskunde* 28, no. 3 (1979): 283–97.

47. Elias, *Prozess der Zivilisation*, 317.

48. Ibid., 321.

49. Ibid., 343.

50. Ibid., 342ff.

51. Ibid., 336, my emphasis.

52. Ibid., 348, my emphasis.

53. Ibid., 344f.

54. Ibid., 347.

55. Ibid., 348, my emphasis.

56. Ribeiro, *Zivilisatorische Prozess*, 199.

57. Ibid.

58. Ibid., 200.

59. Elias, *Prozess der Zivilisation*, 351.
60. Edward W. Said, *Orientalism* (London 1978), 5.
61. Ibid., 3.
62. Ibid., 328.
63. ʿAli M. Garisha and Muhammad S. Zaybaq, *Asalib al-ghazu al-fikri li al-ʿalam al-islami*, 2d ed. (Medina 1978), 211.
64. Ibid., 6.
65. Yusuf al-Qurdawi, *Al-hal al-islami, farida wa darura* (Beirut 1974), 47.
66. Ibid., 88f.
67. Max Horkheimer, *Kritische Theorie*, vol. 1, 2d ed. (Frankfurt 1972), xiii, my emphasis.
68. Ibid.
69. Barrington Moore, Jr., *Social Origins of Dictatorship and Democracy: Lord and Peasant in the Making of the Modern World* (Boston 1966), 415.
70. See Fritz Steppat, "Der Muslim und die Obrigkeit," *Zeitschrift für Politik*, 12 (1965): 319–33, and the discussion in my "Widerstandsrecht in rechtlosen Gesellschaften," 291ff.
71. See the introductory studies on Islamic law by Noel J. Coulsen, *A History of Islamic Law* (Edinburgh 1971), and Joseph Schacht, *An Introduction to Islamic Law*, 5th ed. (London 1979).
72. Ansgar Skriver, "Kommt der Süd-Süd-Dialog? Lehren der UNCTAD-Konferenz von Manila," *Merkur* 33, no. 8 (1979): 754–62, esp. 762.
73. See Helen Lackner, *A House Built on Sand: A Political Economy of Saudi Arabia* (London 1978), 32ff., 120ff.

Chapter 2. ACCULTURATION AND NON-WESTERN IDEOLOGIES.
MODERN ISLAM AS A POLITICAL IDEOLOGY

1. Anthony F. C. Wallace, *Religion: An Anthropological View* (New York 1966), 126f.
2. The historical transformations of Islam are documented in the comprehensive, three-volume work of Marshall G. S. Hodgson, *The Venture of Islam* (Chicago 1974), which appeared posthumously. Volume 1 is entitled *The Classical Age of Islam*; volume 2, *The Expansion of Islam in the Classical Age*; and volume 3, *The Gunpowder Empires and Modern Times*.
3. This is discussed at length by Rotraud Wielandt in *Offenbarung und Geschichte im Denken moderner Muslime* (Wiesbaden 1971). On this subject see my review in *Internationale Politik und Entwicklungsländer-Forschung*, Edition Suhrkamp, no. 983 (Frankfurt 1979), 163ff.
4. Herbert Schnädelbach, "Was ist Ideologie?" *Das Argument* 10, no. 50, special issue (1969): 71–92, esp. 72.
5. On this see Tibi, *Internationale Politik*, chapter 1.
6. Peter Christian Ludz, "Ideologieforschung: Eine Rückbesinnung und ein Neu-Beginn," *Kölner Zeitschrift für Soziologie und Sozialpsychologie* 29 (1977): 1–31, esp. 2.

7. Max Horkheimer, "Ideologie und Handeln," reprinted in Max Hork-heimer and Theodor W. Adorno, *Sociologica II*, 3d ed. (Frankfurt 1973), 38ff., esp. 38.

8. Ibid., 39.

9. Ibid., 41.

10. Helmuth Plessner, "Abwandlungen des Ideologiegedankens," reprinted in Kurt Lenk, ed., *Ideologie, Ideologiekritik und Wissenssoziologie*, 5th ed. (Neuwied 1971), 265ff., esp. 281.

11. Ibid.

12. Gerhard Brandt, "Industrialisierung, Modernisierung, gesellschaftliche Entwicklung: Anmerkungen zum Stand gesamtgesellschaftlicher Analysen," *Zeitschrift für Soziologie* 1, no. 1 (1972): 5ff., esp. 7.

13. An example for this is Klaus Busch, *Die multinationalen Konzerne: Zur Analyse der Weltmarktbewegung des Kapitals* (Frankfurt 1974).

14. Theodor W. Adorno, *Stichworte*, 3d ed. (Frankfurt 1970), 189.

15. See Thomas Mirbach, *Kritik der Herrschaft: Zum Verhältnis von Geschichts-philosophie, Ideologiekritik und Methodenreflexion in der Gesellschaftstheorie Adornos* (Frankfurt 1979), 114ff.

16. Schnädelbach, "Was ist Ideologie?" 87.

17. Ibid.

18. See Bassam Tibi, "Zur Kritik der sowjetmarxistischen Entwicklungs-theorie," *in* Bassam Tibi and Volkhard Brandes, eds., *Unterentwicklung, Handbuch II, Politische Ökonomie* (Frankfurt and Cologne 1975), 64–86.

19. Daniel Bell, *The End of Ideology* (Glendale Ill., 1960), 373.

20. David Apter, ed., *Ideology and Discontent* (London and New York 1964) 17, 22ff.

21. Paul S. Sigmund, *The Ideologies of Developing Nations*, 2d ed. (New York 1967), 39f.

22. Ibid., 32.

23. This form of reductionism is found even in revisionist modernization theorists, such as Shmuel N. Eisenstadt. See Bassam Tibi, "Unterentwicklung als kulturelle Traditionalität? Eisenstadts Beitrag zur makrosoziologischen For-schung," *Soziologische Revue* 3, no. 2 (1980): 121–31.

24. Ludz, "Ideologieforschung," 17ff., 26.

25. For more on this see, for example, Ibrahim Abu-Lughod, *The Arab Rediscovery of Europe: A Study in Cultural Encounters* (Princeton 1963).

26. Walther Braune, "Die Entwicklung des Nationalismus bei den Arabern," *in* Richard Hartmann and Helmuth Scheel, eds., *Beiträge zur Arabistik, Semitistik und Islamwissenschaft* (Leipzig 1944), 425ff., esp. 427.

27. On *négritude* see note 5.

28. Nikki Keddie, ed., *An Islamic Response to Imperialism* (Berkeley and Los Angeles 1968), and idem, *Sayyid Jamal ad-Din "al-Afghani"* (Berkeley and Los Angeles 1972).

29. On Ibn Khaldun and his concept of ʿasabiyya see Bassam Tibi, *Arab Nationalism: A Critical Enquiry*, Marion Farouk-Sluglett and Peter Sluglett, eds. and trans. (London 1981), 112ff.

30. For more detail on Husri: ibid., 90ff.

31. See, for example, Sami Hanna and George Gardner, eds., *Arab Socialism: A Documentary Survey* (Leiden 1969).

32. See, for example, Bassam Tibi, *Militär und Sozialismus in der Dritten Welt: Allgemeine Theorien und Regionalstudien über arabische Länder*, Edition Suhrkamp, no. 631 (Frankfurt 1973), esp. chap. 3.

33. Maxime Rodinson, *Islam und Kapitalismus* (Frankfurt 1971), 259. See also my review in *Archiv für Rechts- und Sozialphilosophie* 59, no. 1 (1973): 155–58.

34. Rodinson, *Islam und Kapitalismus*, 261.

35. For many years a critical occupation with Third World ideology, within the framework of international relations, has been at the center of my research. On this see my collection of articles cited in note 3.

Chapter 3. The Repoliticization of Islam as Cultural
Retrospection and Counter-Acculturation

1. See the contributions in Bassam Tibi and Volkhard Brandes, eds., *Unterentwicklung. Handbuch II, Politische Ökonomie* (Frankfurt and Cologne 1975).

2. Wilhelm E. Mühlmann, *Chiliasmus und Nativismus* (Berlin 1961), 386. In his article collection, *Rassen, Ethnien, Kulturen: Moderne Ethnologie* (Neuwied 1964), 324, Mühlmann speaks of "mere superficial phenomena: ideology without substance or without infrastructure."

3. Niklas Luhmann, *Funktion der Religion* (Frankfurt 1977), 115.

4. Georges Balandier, *Politische Anthropologie* (Munich 1972), 123.

5. See Samuel P. Huntington, *Political Order in Changing Societies*, 2d ed. (New Haven 1969); see also Bassam Tibi, "Schwache Institutionalisierung als politische Dimension der Unterentwicklung," *Verfassung und Recht in Übersee* 13, no. 1 (1980): 3–26.

6. See Nikki Keddie's forceful argument in "Oil, Economic Policy and Social Conflict in Iran," *Race and Class* 21, no. 1 (1979): 13–29.

7. See Bassam Tibi, "Zum Verhältnis von Religion, Politik und Staat in islamisch legitimierten Monarchien," *Orient* 21, no. 2 (1980): 158–74.

8. Fouad al-Farsy, *Saudi Arabia: A Case Study in Development* (London 1978), 63ff., 89ff.

9. René König, ed., *Aspekte der Entwicklungssoziologie* (Cologne and Opladen 1969), 19.

10. Cairo 1925, reprint Beirut 1966; French translation, "L'Islam et les bases du pouvoir," *Revue des Études islamiques* 7 (1933): 353–91, 8 (1934): 163–222.

11. Bassam Tibi, *Nationalismus in der Dritten Welt am arabischen Beispiel* (Frankfurt 1971). English translation: *Arab Nationalism: A Critical Inquiry*, Marion Farouk-Sluglett and Peter Sluglett, eds. and trans. (London 1981).

12. See Richard P. Mitchell's excellent study, *The Society of Muslim Brothers* (London 1969).

13. Gérard Leclerc, *Anthropologie und Kolonialismus* (Munich 1973), documents this in detail.

14. See my inaugural lecture at the University of Göttingen, in the appendix of my article collection, *Internationale Politik und Entwicklungsländer-Forschung*, Edition Suhrkamp, no. 983 (Frankfurt 1979), 176ff., where I discuss this problem.

15. This is how the phenomenon is usually understood in Islamic scholarship. See, for example, the article by Gustav E. von Grunebaum, "Das geistige Problem der Verwestlichung in der Selbstsicht der arabischen Welt," in his collection of articles, *Studien zum Kulturbild und Selbstverständnis des Islam* (Zurich 1969), 229ff. Von Grunebaum has been strongly criticized by the Moroccan intellectual Abdallah Laroui, *The Crisis of the Arab Intellectual: Traditionalism or Historism* (Berkeley and Los Angeles 1976), 44ff.

16. Urbanization in Iran with its rise of slums is vividly described in Robert Graham, *Iran: Die Illusion der Macht* (Frankfurt 1979), 12ff.

17. Bassam Tibi, "Die Wiederentdeckung der ägyptisch-nationalen, kulturellen Identität: Ägyptens Loslösung vom Panarabismus unter Sadat," *Dritte Welt* 6, no. 2 (1978): 253–65, esp. 261ff.

18. See the chapter on the Ottoman Empire in Tibi, *Arab Nationalism*, 50ff.

19. For the achievements of this "high culture" see the contributions in Joseph Schacht and Clifford E. Bosworth, eds., *The Legacy of Islam* (London 1974), esp. from chap. 6 on.

20. Nikki Keddie, ed., *An Islamic Response to Imperialism* (Berkeley and Los Angeles 1968).

21. See the old but still best study of Richard Hartmann, "Die Wahhabiten," *Zeitschrift der Deutschen Morgenländischen Gesellschaft* 78, no. 2 (1924): 176–213.

22. Gary Troeller, *The Birth of Saudi Arabia* (London 1976), and in greater detail John S. Habib, *Ibn Sa'ud's Warriors of Islam: The Ikhwan of Nagd and Their Role in the Creation of the Sa'udi Kingdom, 1910–1930* (Leiden 1978).

23. See Charles C. Adams, *Islam and Modernism in Egypt*, 2d ed. (New York 1968).

24. See E. E. Evans-Pritchard, *The Sanusi of Cyrenaica*, 3d ed. (London 1973).

25. Tibi, *Arab Nationalism*, 135ff.

26. See Michael C. Hudson, *Arab Politics: The Search for Legitimacy*, 2d ed. (New Haven 1979), esp. 1–30; also the review of Roger Owen, "Explaining Arab Politics," *Political Studies* 26, no. 4 (1978): 507–12.

27. Detlev Khalid, "Das Wiedererstarken des Islam als Faktor sozialer Umwälzung," *Aus Politik und Zeitgeschichte* (March, 1979): 3–17.

28. Muslims dispute the existence of an Islamic clergy, which is, however, an historical reality documented by, among others, Nikki Keddie, ed., *Scholars, Saints and Sufis: Muslim Religious Institutions in the Middle East since 1500* (Berkeley and Los Angeles 1972), esp. chap. 1 on the *ulama*, 17ff.

29. Thomas Hodgkin emphasizes the revolutionary tradition in Islam in his "The Revolutionary Tradition in Islam," *Race and Class* 21, no. 3 (1980): 221–37.

30. See note 1.

31. Maria Mies, "Kulturanomie als Folge westlicher Bildung," *Die Dritte Welt* 1, no. 1 (1972): 23–38.

32. Ibid., 25f.
33. Ibid., 26.
34. Henri Desroche, "Religion und gesellschaftliche Entwicklung," *in* Friedrich Fürstenberg, ed., *Religionssoziologie* (Neuwied 1964), 393ff.
35. Luhmann, *Funktion der Religion*, 26.
36. Ibid., 115.
37. Ibid.
38. Ibid., 120f.
39. The social function of religion is discussed in detail in chapter 6, in conjunction with Desroche's interpretation of religion.

Chapter 4. THE RELIGIOUS FOUNDATION OF ISLAM:
ISLAM AS AN ARAB IDEOLOGY AND CULTURE

1. See my conference report, "Islamische Weltkonferenz über islamische Philosophie," *Entwicklung und Zusammenarbeit* 21, no. 2 (1980): 10–11.
2. Fazlur Rahman, *Islam*, 2d ed. (Chicago 1979), 19, 24f.
3. Carl Heinrich Becker, *Islamstudien: Vom Werden und Wesen der islamischen Welt*, 2d ed. (Hildesheim 1967), vol. 1, 331. The first edition was published in Leipzig in 1924 and 1932.
4. Hamilton A. R. Gibb, *Islam*, 3d ed. (Oxford 1978), 74 (in the chapter "Orthodoxy and Schism"). The first edition was published in 1949 under the title *Mohammedanism*.
5. ʿAbd al-ʿAziz al-Duri, *Muqaddima fi al-taʾrikh al-iqtisadi al-ʿarabi* (Beirut 1969).
6. Elman R. Service, *Origins of the State and Civilization: The Process of Cultural Evolution* (New York 1975), 297. On the controversy between Service and Morton H. Fried on the history and theory of civilization see the summary by Klaus Eder in his review of Service, *Soziologische Revue* 2, no. 2 (1979): 135–43.
7. See the chapter by Irfan Shahid, "Pre-Islamic Arabia," *in* Peter M. Holt, Ann K. S. Lambton, and Bernard Lewis, eds., *The Cambridge History of Islam* (Cambridge, 1970), esp. vol. 1, 3–29.
8. Maxime Rodinson, *Mohammed*, Anne Carter, trans. (New York 1971), 27.
9. Ibid., 44.
10. Ibid., 70.
11. Ibid., 44.
12. Ibid., 69.
13. See the internationally recognized German translation of the Qurʾan by Rudi Paret (Stuttgart 1979). See also Rudi Paret, *Der Koran: Kommentar und Konkordanz*, 2d ed. (Stuttgart 1977), and the eminently readable introductory study by Paret, *Mohammed und der Koran: Geschichte und Verkündigung des arabischen Propheten*, 4th ed. (Stuttgart 1976). For more fastidious scholarly readers, Richard

Bell and W. Montgomery Watt, *Introduction to the Qur'an*, 2d ed. (Edinburgh 1977), with index, Qur'an index and bibliography, might be more suitable.

14. See Bassam Tibi, "Religionsstiftung, Islam und Psychoanalyse," *Psyche* 33, no. 8 (1979): 773–83.

15. Rodinson, *Mohammed*, 224.

16. Ibid., 283.

17. Ibid., 279; see also 207.

18. Ibid., 227.

19. Ibid., 112.

20. Ibid., 268.

21. W. Montgomery Watt, *Muhammad at Medina*, 6th ed. (London 1977), 78ff.

22. Sigmund Freud, "Das Unbehagen in der Kultur," *in* Sigmund Freud, *Studienausgabe*, vol. 9, *Fragen der Gesellschaft: Ursprünge der Religion*, 2d ed. (Frankfurt 1974), 191ff., esp. 232.

23. In the following citations from the Qur'an the first figure refers to the chapter (*sura*) and the second to the verse (*aya*). Translator's note: the English translation of the Qur'an used here is *The Koran*, N. J. Dawood, trans., 4th ed. (Harmondsworth, Sussex 1974).

24. Watt, *Muhammad at Medina*, 143.

25. See the article on Muhammad by W. Montgomery Watt *in* Holt et al., *Cambridge History of Islam*, vol. 1, 30–56, esp. 35.

26. Ibid., 55.

27. Elias Canetti, *Masse und Macht*, 3d ed. (Munich 1979) vol. 1, 162; see also 156ff.

28. Watt, *Muhammad at Medina*, 192ff. Jewish influences on the foundation of Islam are grossly exaggerated, to my mind, in the book by Patricia Crone and Michael Cook, *Hagarism: The Making of the Islamic World* (Cambridge 1977), esp. 10ff., in which the two authors translate the dialectical Arabic term *higra* (*hijra*, or the emigration of Muhammad from Mecca to Medina in 622) as "exodus" and, in a second wordplay, Islam as "hagarism" (from Hagar, concubine of Abraham and Qur'anic founder of Mecca). Watt's analysis seems to me to be truer to the materials.

29. Christian influences are discussed in Richard Bell, *The Origins of Islam in its Christian Environment*, 2d ed. (London 1968). First edition 1926.

30. W. Montgomery Watt, *Islamic Political Thought: The Basic Concepts* (Edinburgh 1968), 28f.

31. Marshall G. S. Hodgson, *The Venture of Islam* (Chicago 1974), esp. vol. 1, *The Classical Age of Islam*, 193.

32. Watt, *Muhammad at Medina*, 144.

33. Hodgson, *The Venture of Islam*, vol. 2, *The Expansion of Islam in the Middle Periods*, 12ff.

34. Helmut Böhme, *Europäische Wirtschafts- und Sozialgeschichte*, vol. 1, *Morgenland und Abendland: Staatsbürokratie, Völkerwanderung und römisch-christliches Reich (300–750)* (Frankfurt 1977), 177.

35. Ibid., 179.

36. See Hodgson, *Venture of Islam*, and Bernard Lewis, ed., *Islam*, 2 vols. (New York 1974), a collection of translated selections from Arabic sources. Volume 1 is *Religion and Society*; volume 2 is *Politics and War*.

37. On the question of enrichment through Hellenization see W. Montgomery Watt, *Islamic Philosophy and Theology*, 5th ed. (Edinburgh 1979), 37ff., 91ff.

38. Pierre Rondot, *Der Islam und die Mohammedaner von heute* (Stuttgart 1963), 211f.

39. Ibid., p. 218f.

40. Werner Ende, "The Flagellations of Muharram and the Shi῾ite Ulema," *Der Islam* 55, no. 1 (1978): 19–36.

41. See the Twelver Shi῾i description by the Iranian religious scholar Sayyid M. H. Tabataba'i, *Shi'ite Islam*, Seyyed H. Nasr, trans. (London 1975).

42. See Bassam Tibi, "Der Islam als politische Ideologie," *Die Neue Gesellschaft* 26, no. 3 (1979): 212–17, esp. 213f.

43. The early development of Shi῾i Islam is discussed by S. H. M. Jafri, *The Origins and Early Development of Shi'a Islam* (London 1979).

44. See Werner Ende, *Arabische Nation und islamische Geschichte* (Beirut 1977), 233ff.

45. ῾Abd al-Hadi Fakiki, *Al-Shu῾ubiyya wa al-qawmiyya al-῾arabiyya* (Beirut 1963?), 39.

46. ῾Abd al-῾Aziz al-Duri, *Al-ghudur al-ta'rikhiyya li al-qawmiyya al-῾arabiyya* (Beirut 1960), 35.

47. Ende, *Arabische Nation und islamische Geschichte*, 235f.

48. Ibid., 236.

Chapter 5. THE UNIVERSALIZATION OF ISLAM: THE CASE OF THE ISLAMIZATION OF THE NON-ARAB PEOPLES OF WEST AFRICA

1. Sigmund Freud, "Der Mann Moses und die monotheistische Religion," *in* Sigmund Freud, *Gesammelte Werke*, vol. 16 (London 1950), 101–246, esp. 242.

2. Ibid., 199. For further interpretation see Bassam Tibi, "Religionsstiftung, Islam und Psychoanalyse," *Psyche* 33, no. 8 (1979): 773–83.

3. See the Introduction of Joseph Schacht, *An Introduction to Islamic Law*, 5th ed. (London 1979).

4. Ernst Bloch, *Thomas Münzer als Theologe der Revolution* (Frankfurt 1972), 56.

5. See the Introduction of William Stoddart, *Sufism: The Mystical Doctrines and Methods of Islam* (Wellingborough, Nottinghamshire 1976), where the author, unfortunately, overlooks the central tension between *Shari῾a* and Sufi Islam.

6. Arthur J. Arberry, "Mysticism," *in* Peter M. Holt, Ann K. S. Lambton, and Bernard Lewis, eds. *The Cambridge History of Islam* (Cambridge 1970) vol. 2, 604ff., esp. 605.

7. An internationally recognized introduction to West African Islam is John S. Trimingham, *A History of Islam in West Africa*, 5th ed. (London 1978).

8. For this see Mervyn Hiskett, "The Development of Islam in Hausaland," *in* Michael Brett, ed., *Northern Africa: Islam and Modernization* (London 1973), 57–64.

9. Donal B. C. O'Brien, *The Mourides of Senegal: The Political and Economic Organization of an Islamic Brotherhood* (London 1971), 22.

10. Husayn Ibn Mansur al-Hallaj, *Märtyrer der Gottesliebe*, Annemarie Schimmel, trans. and ed. (Cologne 1968), 37.

11. O'Brien, *Mourides of Senegal*, 23.

12. Ibid.

13. Cited from Lucy C. Behrman, *Muslim Brotherhoods and Politics in Senegal* (Cambridge, Mass. 1970), 29.

14. Ibid., 27.

15. O'Brien, *Mourides of Senegal*, 35.

16. Concerning the concept of segmentary societies, see the authoritative study of Christian Sigrist, *Regulierte Anarchie: Untersuchungen zum Fehlen und zur Entstehung politischer Herrschaft in segmentären Gesellschaften Afrikas* (Freiburg/ Breisgau 1967), esp. 21ff.

17. On the African realms, in spite of its romantic bias, J. C. DeGraft-Johnson, *African Glory: The Story of Vanished Negro Civilizations*, 2d ed. (New York 1966), 77ff. The chapter (pages 58ff.) on "The Moslem Invasion of Africa" is still useful.

18. Gerd Spittler, *Herrschaft über Bauern: Die Ausbreitung staatlicher Herrschaft und einer islamisch-urbanen Kultur in Gobir (Niger)* (Frankfurt 1978), 103.

19. Ibid., 104ff.

20. Martin A. Klein, *Islam and Imperialism in Senegal* (Stanford 1968), 237.

21. Hiskett, "Islam in Hausaland," 64.

22. Humphrey Fischer, "The Western and Central Sudan," *in* Holt et al., *Cambridge History of Islam*, vol. 2, 345ff., esp. 396.

23. Ibid., 399.

24. O'Brien, *Mourides of Senegal*, 34.

25. Carl Heinrich Becker, *Islamstudien: Vom Werden und Wesen der islamischen Welt*, 2d ed. (Hildesheim 1967), vol. 2, 196.

26. Ibid., 201.

27. Ibid., 207. Christian missionaries also pursued this goal, of course, but Islam found better access to Africa. On African Christianity see Horst Bürkle, ed., *Theologie und Kirche in Afrika* (Stuttgart 1968).

28. The establishment of Islamic law (*Shari'a*) in the various African countries is the subject of the study by J. N. D. Anderson, *Islamic Law in Africa*, 3d ed. (London 1978).

29. Brun-Otto Bryde, *The Politics and Sociology of African Legal Development* (Frankfurt 1976), 86ff.; see also my review in *Archiv für Rechts- und Sozialphilosophie* 65, no. 2 (1979): 433f. and *Kölner Zeitschrift für Soziologie und Sozialpsychologie* 31, no. 4 (1979): 821.

30. Klein, *Islam and Imperialism in Senegal*, 238f.

31. Paul Parin, *Der Widerspruch im Subjekt: Ethnopsychoanalytische Studien* (Frankfurt 1978), 162.

32. Ibid., 163.

33. Maxime Rodinson, *Mohammed*, Anne Carter, trans. (New York 1971), 84.

34. Pierre Rondot, *Der Islam und die Mohammedaner von heute* (Stuttgart 1963), 406.

35. Ibid., 408.

36. Behrman, *Muslim Brotherhoods and Politics*, 14.

37. O'Brien, *Mourides of Senegal*, 33.

38. Ibid., 299.

39. Samuel Kodjo, *Probleme der Akkulturation in Afrika* (Meisenheim/Glan 1973), 259.

40. The Syrian philosopher Tayeb Tisini emphasizes this epistemological trait of Arab Islamic philosophy in *Die Materieauffassung in der islamisch-arabischen Philosophie des Mittelalters* (East Berlin 1972).

41. Kodjo, *Akkulturation in Afrika*, 256.

42. Ibid., 255.

43. Uwe Simson, *Auswärtige Kulturpolitik als Entwicklungspolitik: Probleme der kulturellen Kommunikation mit der Dritten Welt am Beispiel des arabischen Raums* (Meisenheim/Glan 1975), 33.

44. Ibid., 34.

45. See N. J. Coulson, *A History of Islamic Law*, 3d ed. (Edinburgh 1978), 149ff.; and Norman Anderson, *Law Reform in the Muslim World* (London 1976).

Chapter 6. Islam and Social Change in the
Modern Middle East

This chapter is based on my article, published under the same title, in *Archiv für Rechts- und Sozialphilosophie* 65, no. 4 (1979): 483–502. I have included a number of cuts and reformulations in order to integrate the article with some grace into the present volume.

1. Gustav E. von Grunebaum, *Studien zum Kulturbild und Selbstverständnis des Islam* (Zurich and Stuttgart 1969), 109.

2. Friedrich Engels, "Zur Geschichte des Urchristentums," *in* Friedrich Engels and Karl Marx, *Über Religion* (East Berlin 1958), 256.

3. Ibid.

4. Ibid.

5. Letter to Marx, dated 24 May 1853, *in* Engels and Marx, *Über Religion*, 96. (Emphasis in original.)

6. There are several complete (three volumes) translations in English and French of the *Muqaddima*. Among the numerous interpretations, the reader's attention is directed to Heinrich Simon, *Ibn Khalduns Wissenschaft von der menschlichen Kultur* (Leipzig 1959), and Muhsin Mahdi, *Ibn Khaldun's Philosophy of History* (London 1957) as well as Peter von Sivers, *Khalifat, Konigtum und Verfall: Die politische Theorie Ibn Khalduns* (Munich 1968).

7. Richard F. Behrendt, *Soziale Strategie für Entwicklungsländer: Entwurf einer Entwicklungssoziologie* (Frankfurt 1965), 11ff., 110ff., 250ff. See Bassam Tibi, *Arab*

Nationalism: A Critical Enquiry, Marion Farouk-Sluglett and Peter Sluglett, eds. and trans. (London 1981), 22–26, for a critical assessment.

8. See Richard F. Behrendt, "Die Zukunft der Entwicklungsländer als Problem des Spätmarxismus," *Futurum* 3 (1970): 574–616.

9. Maxime Rodinson, *Islam und Kapitalismus* (Frankfurt 1971). See also my review in *Archiv für Rechts- und Sozialphilosophie* 59, no. 1 (1973): 155–58.

10. Rodinson, *Mohammed*, Anne Carter, trans. (New York 1971).

11. Rodinson, *Islam und Kapitalismus*, 243. I am turning to Freud in my attempt to connect the biography of Muhammad with the psychoanalytical interpretation of monotheistic religions. See Bassam Tibi, "Religionsstiftung, Psychoanalyse und Islam," *Psyche* 33, no. 8 (1979): 773–83.

12. Rodinson, *Mohammed*, 283.

13. Theodor W. Adorno, *Stichworte: Kritische Modelle 2*, 3d ed. (Frankfurt 1970), 189.

14. The work by Peter M. Holt, Ann K. S. Lambton, and Bernard Lewis, eds., *The Cambridge History of Islam*, 2 vols. (Cambridge 1970), is fundamental for the study of Islamic history. On Islamic origins and early history see volume 1, *The Central Islamic Lands*, esp. part 1, "The Rise and Domination of the Arabs," 1–139.

15. Ernst Bloch, *Thomas Münzer als Theologe der Revolution*, reprint (Frankfurt 1976), 56.

16. Ibid., 55.

17. Ibid.

18. The thesis of the sacralization of power as a basis for the stability of the political system is, of course, valid only for pre- and nonindustrial societies and thus for modern developing countries. Balandier, too, emphasizes that the sacralization of politics is the case only in traditional societies. See Georges Balandier, *Politische Anthropologie* (Munich 1972), 122.

19. Ibid., 131.

20. Ibid., 115. Michael Wolffsohn, in his "Die politische Funktion der Religion. Ansätze zu einer vergleichenden Analyse," *Der Dritte Welt* 6, no. 1 (1978): 125–81, esp. 127, thinks that the expression "political religion" is a contradiction in terms; one should rather speak of "politicized religion." He cites Balandier as his authority, who, however, uses the expression "political religion" employed here.

21. Balandier, *Politische Anthropologie*, 123.

22. Ibid., 135.

23. Bloch, *Thomas Münzer*, 56.

24. Henri Desroche, "Religion und gesellschaftliche Entwicklung," *in* Friedrich Fürstenberg, ed., *Religionssoziologie* (Neuwied 1964), 393ff., esp. 397f. The French original of this chapter appeared in *Archives de Sociologie des religions*, no. 12 (1961): 3–34.

25. Desroche, "Religion und gesellschaftliche Entwicklung," 411f.

26. Henri Desroche, "Religionssoziologie und Entwicklungssoziologie," *Internationales Jahrbuch für Religionssoziologie* 5 (1969): 20–40, esp. 23.

27. Ibid., 27.

28. On the rise and significance of these law schools see Joseph Schacht, *An Introduction to Islamic Law*, 5th ed. (London 1979), 28ff., 57ff.

29. Detlev Khalid, "Das Wiedererstarken des Islam als Faktor sozialer Umwälzung," *Aus Politik und Zeitgeschichte* 10 (March 1979): 3–17, esp. 3.

30. See chapter 5.

31. See the contributions on Africa in Holt et al., *Cambridge History of Islam*, vol. 2, pt. 7, 209–405.

32. See Johan Galtung, "Eine strukturelle Theorie des Imperialismus," *in* Dieter Senghaas, ed., *Imperialismus und strukturelle Gewalt*, 4th ed. (Frankfurt 1978), 29–104.

33. Rodinson, *Mohammed*, 281.

34. The text of this leaflet is cited in Ibrahim Abu-Lugod, *The Arab Rediscovery of Europe* (Princeton 1963), 13f.

35. See Bassam Tibi, "Akkulturationsprozesse im modernen Orient," *Neue Politische Literatur* 15, no.1 (1970): 77–84.

36. Tahtawi's Paris diary was translated into German by Karl Stowasser in his 1968 University of Münster Ph.D. dissertation, *At-Tahtawi in Paris: Ein Dokument des arabischen Modernismus aus dem frühen 19. Jahrhundert*. See page 70.

37. The Hellenist influence was an occasion for racist authors to deny any originality to Islamic philosophy. Ernst Bloch defends Islamic philosophy against this racism in *Avicenna und die Aristotelische Linke* (Frankfurt 1963), esp. 9.

38. Von Grunebaum, *Kulturbild und Selbstverständnis des Islam*, 118.

39. Ibid., 119.

40. Hani Srour, *Die Staats- und Gesellschaftstheorie bei S. G. "Al-Afghani"* (Freiburg/Breisgau 1977), 18ff.

41. See Richard Hartmann, "Die Wahhabiten," *Zeitschrift der Deutschen Morgenländischen Gesellschaft* 78, no. 2 (1924): 176–213.

42. See E. E. Evans-Pritchard, *The Sanusi of Cyrenaica*, 5th ed. (London 1973).

43. For details see John S. Habib, *Ibn Saʿud's Warriors of Islam: The Ikhwan of Nagd and Their Role in the Creation of the Saʿudi Kingdom, 1910–1930* (Leiden 1978).

44. Arthur Rock, *Ibn Saud gründet das Gottesreich Arabien* (Berlin 1935), 9ff.

45. See Bassam Tibi, *Militär und Sozialismus in der Dritten Welt* (Frankfurt 1973), 303ff.

46. Wolffsohn, "Politische Funktion der Religion," 130.

47. Abdel Moneim Laban, *Einige Aspekte der Akkulturation und des sozialen Wandels in Ägypten von 1900 bis 1952* (Frankfurt 1977), 43. Laban was the first to demonstrate the influence of Auguste Comte on the Islamic reformers, especially Afghani.

48. Niklas Luhmann, *Funktion der Religion* (Frankfurt 1977), 87. A study of Islamic dogmatics strongly confirms this assertion of Luhmann's. See Rotraud Wielandt, *Offenbarung und Geschichte im Denken moderner Muslime* (Wiesbaden 1971), who arrives at the same conclusions. See my review of the book in *Internationale Politik und Entwicklungsländer-Forschung: Materialien zu einer ideologiekritischen Entwicklungssoziologie* (Frankfurt 1979), 16ff.

49. Afghani's writings are available in the one-volume work *Al-aʿmal al-*

kamila li Jamal al-Din al-Afghani, M. ʿAmmara, ed. (Cairo 1968); see esp. 327f.

50. Ibid., 328.

51. Albert Hourani, *Arabic Thought in the Liberal Age, 1798–1939* (London 1962), 122.

52. See Gérard Leclerc, *Anthropologie und Kolonialismus* (Munich 1973) and also my inaugural lecture at the University of Göttingen in Tibi, *Internationale Politik und Entwicklungsländer-Forschung*, 176ff.

53. Leclerc, *Anthropologie und Kolonialismus*, 25.

54. Al-Afghani, *Al-aʿmal al-kamila*, 448.

55. See Behrendt, *Soziale Strategie*, 250ff., where these concepts are developed.

56. Srour, *Staats- und Gesellschaftstheorie*, 48.

57. Tibi, *Arab Nationalism*, 133ff.

58. Bassam Tibi, "Skizze einer Geschichte des Sozialismus in den arabischen Ländern," *in* Bassam Tibi, ed., *Die arabische Linke* (Frankfurt 1969), 7–41.

Chapter 7. MODERN EDUCATION AND THE EMERGENCE OF A
WESTERNIZED ISLAMIC INTELLIGENTSIA: STUDENTS AS A POTENTIAL
FOR CHANGE IN THE ISLAMIC MIDDLE EAST

1. See Dominique Sourdel, "The Abbasid Caliphate," *in* Peter M. Holt, Ann K. S. Lambton and Bernard Lewis, eds., *The Cambridge History of Islam*, (Cambridge 1970), esp. vol. 1, 104–40; see also the chapters in vol. 2, pt. 8, "Islamic Society and Civilization," 441–889. On Hellenization specifically see W. Montgomery Watt, *Islamic Philosophy and Theology*, 5th ed. (Edinburgh 1979), 37ff., 91ff.

2. On the social structure of the Ottoman Empire see Kurt Steinhaus, *Soziologie der türkischen Revolution: Zum Problem der bürgerlichen Gesellschaft in sozio-ökonomisch schwach entwickelten Gesellschaften* (Frankfurt 1969), 11ff.; as well as Bassam Tibi, *Arab Nationalism: A Critical Enquiry*, Marion Farouk-Sluglett and Peter Sluglett, eds. and trans. (London 1981), 50ff.

3. On this see Nikki R. Keddie, ed., *Scholars, Saints and Sufis: Muslim Religious Institutions in the Middle East since 1500* (Berkeley and Los Angeles 1972), ch. 1.

4. This form of education, which occupies itself exclusively with the memorization of religious sources, can be documented through the pedagogical manual of Saʿid I. ʿAli, *Usul al-tarbiya al-islamiyya* (Cairo 1978). (Faculty of Education, ʿAyn Shams University, Cairo.)

5. See Samuel F. Huntington and J. M. Nelson, *No Easy Choice: Political Participation in Developing Countries* (Cambridge, Mass. 1976), 28.

6. See Peter Landes, *The Industrial Revolution: The Birth of the Modern Age* (London 1978).

7. Bernard Lewis, *The Middle East and the West*, 2d ed. (New York 1966).

8. Ibid., 37.

9. Ibid., 39.

10. Samuel Kodjo, "Bildungsqualität als Schwerpunkt künftiger entwicklungstheoretischer Diskussion und Forschung," *Kölner Zeitschrift für Soziologie und Sozialpsychologie* 26 (1974): 287–330, esp. 296.

11. Ibid., 297.

12. Horst Beyer, "Bildungssystem und Unterentwicklung in Indien," in G. Wurzbacher, ed., *Störfaktoren in der Entwicklungspolitik* (Stuttgart 1975), 183–212, esp. 184.

13. Antonio Gramsci, *Philosophie der Praxis: Eine Auswahl*, Christian Riechers, ed. (Frankfurt 1967), 410.

14. Syed H. Alatas, *Intellectuals in Developing Societies* (London 1977), 15.

15. Ibid., 16.

16. Ibid., 11.

17. Ibid., 53.

18. James S. Coleman, ed., *Education and Political Development* (Princeton 1965), Introduction and chap. 1, esp. 35ff.

19. Alatas, *Intellectuals*, 49.

20. Ibid.

21. See the Introduction of Coleman, *Education and Political Development*, 21.

22. See Donald K. Emmerson, ed., *Students and Politics in Developing Nations* (London 1968), Conclusion, 390–426, esp. 395.

23. Stephen A. Douglas, *Political Socialization and Student Activism in Indonesia* (Urbana 1970), 18.

24. Alatas, *Intellectuals*, 55f.

25. Edward Shils, "The Intellectuals in the Political Development of the New States," *in* John H. Kautsky, ed., *Political Change in Underdeveloped Countries*, 7th ed. (New York 1967), 195–234, esp. 199.

26. Ibid., 204.

27. Emmerson, *Students and Politics*, 409f.

28. Norman Jacobs, *The Sociology of Development: Iran as an Asian Case Study*, 2d ed. (New York 1967), 234.

29. Emmerson, *Students and Politics*, 392.

30. Ibid., 415.

31. Hisham Sharabi, *Arab Intellectuals and the West: The Formative Years, 1875–1914* (Baltimore and London 1970), 2.

32. Tahtawi's Paris diaries have been translated into German in an Orientalist dissertation. See Karl Stowasser, *At-Tahtawi in Paris. Ein Dokument des arabischen Modernismus aus dem frühen 19. Jahrhundert*, Ph.D. diss., University of Münster 1968, 65.

33. Ibid., 199f.

34. Albert Hourani, *Arabic Thought in the Liberal Age, 1798–1939* (London 1962), 73. See also the section on Tahtawi in Tibi, *Arab Nationalism*, 58ff.

35. Samuel P. Huntington, *Political Order in Changing Societies*, 2d ed. (New Haven 1969), 201.

36. The following section is based on a paper dealing with Iranian students abroad which I presented at the international Iran conference "Gesamtanalyse der

Ursachen und möglichen Perspektiven der Entwicklung in Iran," June 21–22, 1979, in Bonn and which was subsequently published in *Orient* 20, no. 3 (1979): 100–108. The text is presented here in an abridged and heavily revised form.

37. See Feroz Ahmad, *The Young Turks: The Committee of Union and Progress in Turkish Politics, 1908–1914* (Oxford 1969).

38. Richard Hartmann, "Arabische Politische Gesellschaften bis 1914," in Richard Hartmann and Helmuth Scheel, eds., *Beiträge zur Arabistik, Semitistik und Islamwissenschaft* (Leipzig 1944), 439–467.

39. On this see Immanuel Geiss, *Panafrikanismus: Zur Geschichte der Dekolonisation* (Frankfurt 1968).

40. On these problems see W. Montgomery Watt, *Islamic Political Thought* (Edinburgh 1968).

41. Huntington, *Political Order*, 239.

42. Ibid., 213.

43. Max Weber, "Der Beruf zur Politik," *in* Max Weber, *Soziologie, weltgeschichtliche Analysen, Politik* (Stuttgart 1964), 167ff.

44. Karl A. Wittfogel, *Die orientalische Despotie: Eine vergleichende Untersuchung totaler Macht* (Cologne 1962), 188.

45. See Peter C. Meyer-Tasch, *Thomas Hobbes und das Widerstandsrecht* (Tübingen 1965); also Bassam Tibi, "Widerstandsrecht in rechtlosen Gesellschaften," *Gegenwartskunde* 28, no. 3 (1979): 283–97.

46. Muhammad cited from Fritz Steppat, "Der Muslim und die Obrigkeit," *Zeitschrift für Politik* 12, (1965): 319–32, esp. 321.

47. Ibid., 330.

48. Abu Yusuf cited from ibid., 325.

49. Ibid.

50. Jacobs, *Sociology of Development*, 214.

51. See Erwin I. J. Rosenthal, *Islam in the Modern National State* (Cambridge 1965), 307ff.

52. Bahman Nirumand, *Persien: Modell eines Entwicklungslandes* (Reinbek-Hamburg 1967), 19.

53. Niklas Luhmann, *Funktion der Religion* (Frankfurt 1977), 120f.

54. Georges Balandier, *Politische Anthropologie* (Munich 1972), 135.

55. Rosenthal, *Islam*, 309.

56. A preliminary evaluation of these editions of *Iran Report* can be found in my Iran paper published in *Orient* 20, no. 3 (1979): 100–108.

57. *Iran Report* (September 1978), 18.

58. Jacobs, *Sociology of Development*, 234.

59. Emmerson, *Students and Politics*, 415.

Chapter 8. OIL PRODUCTION AND THE EMERGENCE OF A NEW SOCIAL STRATUM: THE OIL WORKERS. THE ISLAMIC SOCIAL SYSTEM AND TRADE UNION ORGANIZATION

1. See Bassam Tibi, "Das Selbstverständnis der OPEC," *Verfassung und Recht in Übersee* 12, no. 3 (1979): 259–66.

2. See chapter 7, section "Iranian Students Abroad as a Reservoir for Social Change and Their Place in the Political System"

3. See Fritz Steppat, "Der Muslim und die Obrigkeit," *Zeitschrift für Politik* 12 (1965): 319–33.

4. Jürgen Büse, *Gewerkschaften im Prozess des sozialen Wandels in Entwicklungsländern* (Bonn-Bad Godesberg 1974), 36.

5. Ibid., 102f.

6. Daniel Lerner, *The Passing of Traditional Society: Modernizing the Middle East* (New York 1966).

7. On this see Bernard Lewis, *The Middle East and the West*, 2d ed. (New York 1966).

8. George Lenczowski, *Oil and the State in the Middle East*, 2d ed. (Ithaca and London 1970), 253. See also the interesting case study by Ghazi Shanneik, "Ölreichtum und sozialer Wandel—Das Beispiel Kuwaits," *Orient* 20, no. 3 (1979): 25–48.

9. Moneir Nasr, *Mineralölwirtschaft im Nahen Osten* (Hannover 1967), 111f.

10. See "The Gulf-Expatriate Labor Creates Problems," *Arab Economist* 10, no. 108 (1978): 16–17; and "The Gulf: Foreign Workers Pose Social and Economic Problems," *Events* (August 26, 1977).

11. Nasr, *Mineralölwirtschaft*, 120.

12. Lenczowski, *Oil and the State*, 274.

13. Fred Halliday, *Iran: Analyse einer Gesellschaft im Entwicklungskrieg* (Berlin 1979), 169.

14. This section contains essential theses of the Islamic part of my article on trade unions in the Afro-Islamic countries. See Bassam Tibi, "Trade Unions as an Organizational Form of Political Opposition in Afro-Arab States," *Orient* 20, no. 4 (1979): 75–91, esp. 76ff.

15. Büse, *Gewerkschaften*, 267f.

16. Georges Balandier, *Politische Anthropologie* (Munich 1972), 122.

17. Shmuel N. Eisenstadt, *Tradition, Wandel und Modernität* (Frankfurt 1979), 206.

18. Ibid., 208f.

19. Ibid., 221. On Eisenstadt's theory see Bassam Tibi, "Unterentwicklung als kulturelle Traditionalität? Eisenstadts Beitrag zur makrosoziologischen Forschung," *Soziologische Revue* 3, no. 2 (1980): 121–31.

20. Steppat, *Muslim*, 325.

21. See Bassam Tibi, "Widerstandsrecht in rechtlosen Gesellschaften," *Gegenwartskunde* 28, no. 3 (1979): 283–97.

22. Steppat, *Muslim*, 332.

23. See Maxime Rodinson, *Islam und Kapitalismus* (Frankfurt 1971).

24. ʿAbd al-ʿAziz al-Duri, *Muqaddima fi al-taʾrikh al-iqtisadi al-ʿarabi* (Beirut 1969), 150.

25. Muhsin Shishakli, *Dirasat fi al-mujtamaʿ al-ʿarabi* (Aleppo 1965), vol. 2, 216.

26. Ibid., 218.

27. Ibid., 219.

28. See chapter 6.

29. See the discussion of this complex of questions in Bassam Tibi, *Internationale Politik und Entwicklungsländer-Forschung*, Edition Suhrkamp, no. 983 (Frankfurt 1979), chap. 1.

30. On Iran and Saudi Arabia see the two excellent contributions by Udo Steinbach and Thomas Koszinowski in *Politisches Lexikon Nahost*, Udo Steinbach et al., eds., Beck'sche Schwarze Reihe, vol. 199 (Munich 1979), 88ff., 245ff.

31. See Nikki R. Keddie, "Oil, Economic Policy and Social Conflict in Iran," *Race and Class* 21, no. 1 (1979): 13–29. On the structural changes caused by the production of oil see Robert Graham, *Iran: Die Illusion der Macht* (Frankfurt 1979), 25ff.

32. See Helen Lackner, *A House Built on Sand: A Political Economy of Saudi Arabia* (London 1978).

33. Halliday, *Iran*, 163ff.

34. Ibid., 169f. Halliday refers to Iran. On the relationship between oil and occupation in the Arab oil-producing countries see Kamal S. Sayegh, *Oil and Arab Regional Development* (New York 1968), 83ff.

35. Lenczowski, *Oil and the State*, 256f.

36. On the Tudeh party: Amad Farughy and Jean-Louis Reverier, *Persien: Aufbruch ins Chaos* (Munich 1979), 194ff.

37. Halliday, *Iran*, 187.

38. Lenczowski, *Oil and the State*, 259 and 268ff.

39. Lackner, *House Built on Sand*, 190.

40. Ibid., 98ff., 103ff.

41. Ibid., 165ff.

42. Arnold Hottinger, "Hintergründe der Moschee-Aktion in Mekka," *Neue Zürcher Zeitung*, Foreign Edition, 286 (December 9/10, 1979), 5.

43. See Lenczowski, *Oil and the State*, 261ff., and Halliday, *Iran*, 184ff.

44. Lackner, *House Built on Sand*, 191.

45. Hottinger, "Moschee-Aktion in Mekka," 42. On the future prospects of Saudi Arabia see Bassam Tibi, "A Typology of Arab Political Systems," *in* S. Farsoun, ed., *Arab Society* (London 1985), esp. 60ff.

46. On the Iranian revolution see Ahmad Naini, *Die Revolution in Iran: Hintergründe und Ereignisse* (Hamburg 1979). Naini discusses the role of the students as a political opposition (pages 82ff.), but completely overlooks the importance of the oil workers.

Conclusion. FUTURE PROSPECTS FOR ISLAM AS A PREINDUSTRIAL CULTURE IN THE SCIENTIFIC-TECHNOLOGICAL AGE: THE SECULARIZATION OF ISLAM

1. Carl Heinrich Becker, *Islamstudien: Vom Werden und Wesen der islamischen Welt* (Hildesheim 1967), vol. 1, 383.

2. Faruq ʿAbd al-Salam, *Al-ahzab al-siyasiyya wa al-fasl bayn al-din wa al-siyasa* (Cairo 1979), 122.

3. Ibid., 125.

4. ʿAli Garisha and Muhammad S. Zaybaq, *Asalib al-ghazu al-fikri li al-ʿalam al-islami*, 2d ed. (Medina 1978), 60.

5. Ibid.

6. Ibid., 61.

7. Sigmund Freud, "Die Zukunft einer Illusion," in Sigmund Freud, *Gesammelte Werke*, vol. 14 (London 1950), 323–80, esp. 359.

8. Herbert Marcuse, *Triebstruktur und Gesellschaft: Ein philosophischer Beitrag zu Sigmund Freud*, reprint (Frankfurt 1973), 74.

9. To be sure, Islam is known for its tolerance toward the members of other monotheistic religions (*ahl al-kitab*), but does not have a tradition of liberal tolerance since it did not have an Enlightenment. Albrecht Noth discusses in his study only tolerance vis-à-vis other religions, not toward dissidents, which Islam does not tolerate. See Albrecht Noth, "Möglichkeiten und Grenzen islamischer Toleranz," *Saeculum* 29, no. 2 (1978): 190–204. In practice, racism is not unknown in Islam, although this is not admitted by dogma. See Bernard Lewis, *Race and Color in Islam*, 2d ed. (New York 1977). The gap between dogma and reality has been central throughout all phases of Islamic history.

10. The secularly oriented Egyptian philosopher Mourad Wahba describes how warmly the Islamic philosopher Averroës was embraced by Europeans during the Enlightenment, and his simultaneous persecution in the Islamic world, as "the paradox of Averroës." This was the title of the paper he presented at the Islamic world conference in Cairo in November 1979 which appeared in *Archiv für Rechts- und Sozialphilosophie* 66, no. 2 (1980): 257–60. See also my conference report in *Entwicklung und Zusammenarbeit* 21, no. 2 (1980): 10–11.

11. Abu ʿAli Yasin, "Muharramayn: Al-din wa al-jins," *Dirasat ʿArabiyya* 7, no. 1 (Beirut 1970), 2–16, esp. 2.

12. Due to a delay of the publication of the conference proceedings related to an opposition to include my paper on "Islam and secularization," I published a slightly modified version of it in a European journal as "Islam and secularization: Religion and the functional differentiation of the social system," *Archiv für Rechts- und Sozialphilosophie* 66, no. 2 (1980): 207–22. The secularly oriented Lebanese, Anis Sayigh, who received his Ph.D. degree from Cambridge University and has achieved a high profile in the Arab Middle East through numerous books, has published in his Beirut journal an Arabic translation of my Cairo paper. See Bassam Tibi, "Al-Islam wa al-ʿalmana," *Qadaya ʿArabiyya* 7, no. 3 (1980): 13–23. Professor Wahba succeeded in publishing the papers, including my own, in Mourad Wahba, ed., *Islam and civilization*. Proceedings of the First Islamic International Islamic Philosophy Conference (Cairo: ʿAyn Shams University Press 1982), 65–79.

13. See Ernst Bloch, *Thomas Münzer als Theologe der Revolution*, reprint, (Frankfurt 1972).

14. On Luther's Reformation see Leo Kofler, *Zur Geschichte der bürgerlichen Gesellschaft* (Neuwied and Berlin 1966), 262ff.

15. Detlev Khalid, "Muslims and the Purport of Secularism," *Islam and the Modern Age* 5, no. 2 (1974): 28–40, esp. 36.

16. See Nikki R. Keddie, ed., *Scholars, Saints and Sufis: Muslim Religious Institutions in the Middle East since 1500* (Berkeley and Los Angeles 1972), esp. pt. 1, 17ff. See also the case study of Arnold H. Green, *The Tunisian Ulama, 1873–1915: Social Structure and Response to Ideological Currents* (Leiden 1978), esp. 25ff.

17. Niklas Luhmann, *Funktion der Religion* (Frankfurt 1977), 227.

18. Ibid., 227f.

19. Ibid., 229.

20. Ibid., 255.

21. Georges Balandier, *Politische Anthropologie* (Munich 1972), 122.

22. Shmuel N. Eisenstadt, *Tradition, Wandel und Modernität* (Frankfurt 1979), 206, 280f., 221. On Eisenstadt see Bassam Tibi, "Unterentwicklung als kulturelle Traditionalität?" *Soziologische Revue* 3, no. 2 (1980): 121–31.

23. For more on this distinction see Smith's Introduction in Donald E. Smith, ed., *Religion and Political Modernization* (New Haven and London 1974).

24. Ibid., 6.

25. Daniel Crecelius, "The Course of Secularization in Modern Egypt," *in* Smith, *Religion and Political Modernization*, 67–94, esp. 69.

26. Bruce M. Borthwick, "Religion and Politics in Israel and in Egypt," *The Middle East Journal* 33, no. 2 (1979): 145–63, esp. 154ff.

27. Johan Galtung, "Eine strukturelle Theorie des Imperialismus," *in* Dieter Senghaas, ed., *Imperialismus und strukturelle Gewalt* (Frankfurt 1978), 29ff, esp. 43.

28. On the economic history of this period see ʿAbd al-ʿAziz al-Duri, *Arabische Wirtschaftsgeschichte*, Jürgen Jacobi, trans. (Zurich and Munich 1979), 73ff.

29. Tayeb Tisini, *Mashruʿ ruʾya jadida li al-fikr al-ʿarabi fi al-ʿasr al-wasit* (Damascus, no year indicated), 406, 409.

30. See the article on Sufi Islam by Arthur J. Arberry *in* Peter M. Holt, Ann K. S. Lambton, and Bernard Lewis, eds., *The Cambridge History of Islam* (Cambridge 1970), vol. 2, 604ff.

31. Tisini, *Mashruʿ ruʾya jadida li al-fikr al-ʿarabi fi al-ʿasr al-wasit*, 410.

32. Amos Perlmutter, *Egypt: The Praetorian State* (New Brunswick 1974), viiif.

33. Eisenstadt, *Tradition, Wandel und Modernität*, 242f. See also Tibi, "Unterentwicklung als kulturelle Traditionalität?" esp. section 3, "Religion und sozialer Wandel."

34. Freud, "Zukunft einer Illusion," 360.

35. Sigmund Frued, "Der Mann Moses und die monotheistische Religion," *in* Sigmund Freud, *Gesammelte Werke*, vol. 16 (London 1950): 101–246, esp. 199. See also Bassam Tibi, "Religionsstiftung, Islam und Psychoanalyse," *Psyche* 33, no. 8 (1979): 773–83.

36. Freud, "Zukunft einer Illusion," 365.

37. Jamal al-Din al-Afghani, *Al-aʿmal al-kamila*, M. ʿAmmara, ed. (Cairo 1968), 238. See also the discussion of these problems in chapter 6.

38. Charles C. Adams, *Islam and Modernism in Egypt: A Study of the Modern Reform Movement Inaugurated by Muhammad 'Abduh*, 2d ed. (New York 1968), 127ff. The original edition dates from 1933.

39. See Arkoun's Introduction to Mohammed Arkoun, et al., *Pilgerfahrt nach Mekka* (Zurich 1978), esp. 34.

40. For this tradition in more detail see Bassam Tibi, *Arab Nationalism: A Critical Enquiry*, Marion Farouk-Sluglett and Peter Sluglett, eds. and trans. (London 1981), 61ff.; on Rida, see pages 67f.

41. Al-Afghani, *Al-a'mal al-kamila*, 327.

42. I am quoting here from the Arabic original: Shekib Arslan, *Limadha ta'akhara al-muslimun wa taqaddama ghayrahum*, reprint (Beirut 1965), 176. The English translation of this important book is *Our Decline and Its Causes*, 2d ed. (London 1952).

43. See my discussion of Luhmann's definition of religious dogmatism in chapter 6.

44. Muhammad 'Ali Yusuf, *Al-jafwa al-mufta'ala bayn al-din wa al-'ilm* (Beirut 1966), 6.

45. Sadiq Jalal al-'Azm, *Naqd al-fikr al-dini* (Beirut 1969), 22.

46. Ibid., 78.

47. The al-'Azm affair is documented in an instructive article by the Bonn Orientalist Stefan Wild, "Gott und Mensch im Libanon: Die Affäre Sadiq al-Azm," *Der Islam* 48 (1972): 206–53.

48. I am quoting from the original, 'Ali 'Abd al-Raziq, *Al-Islam wa usul al-hukm*, reprint (Beirut 1966). There is a French translation published in *Revue des Etudes Islamiques* 7 (1933), 8 (1934).

49. 'Abd al-Raziq, *Al-Islam*, 184. On the historical position of 'Abd al-Raziq see Tibi, *Arab Nationalism*, 148ff., and Rotraud Wielandt, *Offenbarung und Geschichte im Denken moderner Muslime* (Wiesbaden 1971), and my review of Wielandt in "Religion und sozialer Wandel: Bemerkungen zur modernen islamischen Apologetik," *in* Bassam Tibi, *Internationale Politik und Entwicklungsländer-Forschung: Materialien zu einer ideologiekritischen Entwicklungssoziologie* (Frankfurt 1979), 136ff.

50. Marshall G. S. Hodgson, *The Venture of Islam*, vol. 3, *The Gunpowder Empires and Modern Times* (Chicago 1974), 436.

51. Yusuf Qurdawi, *Al-hal al-islami, farida wa darura* (Beirut 1974).

52. I have coined the term "lawless societies" for such societies. See Bassam Tibi, "Widerstandsrecht in rechtlosen Gesellschaften," *Gegenwartskunde* 28, no. 3 (1979): 283–97.

53. See Werner Ende's review of Muhammad Arkoun and Louis Gardet's *L'Islam Hier-Demain* (Paris 1978) in *Der Islam* 56 (1979): 315f.

54. Arkoun, *Pilgerfahrt nach Mekka*, 26.

55. Fazlur Rahman, *Islam*, 2d ed. (Chicago 1979), 250f.

56. See Wielandt, *Denken moderner Muslime*, and my review article "Religion und sozialer Wandel." (Full citations in note 49.)

57. Gerd Zimmermann, *Sozialer Wandel und ökonomische Entwicklung* (Stuttgart 1969), 73.

58. Richard Mitchell is the author of the standard study *The Society of the Muslim Brothers* (London 1969). I cite him here from my conference notes on his Cairo paper.

59. Daniel Bell, *Die Zukunft der westlichen Welt: Kultur und Technologie im Widerstreit* (Frankfurt 1976), 275.

60. Ibid., 283.

61. Ibid., 39.

62. Arkoun, *Pilgerfahrt nach Mekka*, 34f.

63. Bryan S. Turner, *Weber and Islam* (London 1974), 151ff., esp. 158, 170.

64. Frank Rotter, *Verfassung und sozialer Wandel: Studien zur systemtheoretischen Rechtssoziologie* (Hamburg 1974), 59ff.

65. Sabir Tuʿayma, *Al-shariʿa al-islamiyya fi ʿasr al-ʿilm* (Beirut 1979), esp. 208ff.

66. Subhi al-Salih, *Maʿalim al-Shariʿa al-islamiyya* (Beirut 1975), 32ff.

67. Ibid., 157ff., 182ff.

68. On the problem of Islamic legal reform see the book by English legal scholar Norman Anderson, *Law Reform in the Muslim World*, University of London Legal Series, vol. 11 (London 1976).

69. See Muhammad Muslehuddin, *Philosophy of Islamic Law and the Orientalists: A Comparative Study of the Islamic Legal System* (Lahore, no year indicated), esp. the Introduction, xiff. Muslehuddin has a Ph.D. degree from the University of London and thus has a personal knowledge of Orientalism, contrary to most Islamic apologists.

SELECTED BIBLIOGRAPHY

The following bibligraphy contains a systematic selection of literature on the subject of this book. It is divided into three parts plus an addendum:
1. Religion, Culture, Underdevelopment, and Social Change
2. Arabic Sources on Modern Islam
3. Western Works on Islam

Since Arabic literature on Islam is not easily accessible I have kept the second part of the bibliography quite short although this literature has been exhaustively consulted in the course of completing this book.

Religion, Culture, Underdevelopment, and Social Change

Alatas, Syed M. *Intellectuals in Developing Societies.* London 1977.

Apter, David E. (ed.). *Ideology and Discontent.* London and New York 1964.

Balandier, Georges. *Politische Anthropologie.* Munich 1972.

Behrendt, R. F. *Soziale Strategie für Entwicklungsländer: Entwurf einer Entwicklungssoziologie.* Frankfurt 1965.

Bell, Daniel. *Die Zukunft der westlichen Welt: Kultur und Technologie im Widerstreit.* Frankfurt 1976.

——. *The End of Ideology.* Illinois 1960.

Bloch, Ernst. *Thomas Münzer als Theologe der Revolution.* Reprint. Frankfurt 1972.

Böhme, Helmut. *Europäische Wirtschafts- und Sozialgeschichte.* Vol. 1, *Morgenland und Abendland: Staatsbürokratie, Völkerwanderung und römisch-christliches Reich (300–750).* Frankfurt 1977.

Coleman, James S. (ed.). *Education and Political Development.* Princeton 1965.

Desroche, Henri. "Religion und gesellschaftliche Entwicklung," *in* Friedrich Fürstenberg (ed.). *Religionssoziologie,* 393ff. Neuwied 1964.

——. "Religionssoziologie und Entwicklungssoziologie." *Internationales Jahrbuch für Religionssoziologie* 5 (1969), 20–40.

Devereux, Georges. *Ethnopsychoanalyse.* Frankfurt 1978.

Eisenstadt, S. N. *Tradition, Wandel und Modernität.* Frankfurt 1979.

Elias, Norbert. *Über den Prozess der Zivilisation, Soziogenetische und psychogenetische Untersuchungen.* 2d ed. 2 vols. Bern and Munich 1969.

Emmerson, Donald K. (ed.). *Students and Politics in Developing Nations.* London 1968.

Fanon, Frantz. *Black Skin, White Masks: The Experience of a Black Man in a White World.* New York 1967.

Freud, Sigmund. "Der Mann Moses und die monotheistische Religion," *in* Sigmund Freud. *Gesammelte Werke,* vol. 16, 101–246. London 1950.

——. "Das Unbehagen in der Kultur," *in* Sigmund Freud. *Studienausgabe.* Vol. 9, *Fragen der Gesellschaft: Ursprünge der Religion,* 191ff. 2d. ed. Frankfurt 1974.

——. "Die Zukunft einer Illusion," *in* Sigmund Freud. *Gesammelte Werke,* vol. 14, 359. London 1950.

174   SELECTED BIBLIOGRAPHY

Galtung, Johan. *Strukturelle Gewalt: Beiträge zur Friedens- und Konfliktforschung.* Reinbek/
Hamburg 1975.
———. "Eine strukturelle Theorie des Imperialismus," *in* Dieter Senghaas (ed.). *Imperialismus und strukturelle Gewalt*, 29–103. 4th ed. Frankfurt 1978.
Gantzel, Klaus-Jürgen (ed.). *Herrschaft und Befreiung in der Weltgesellschaft.* Frankfurt 1975.
Hoffer, Eric. *The True Believer: Thoughts on the Nature of Mass Movements.* New York and
Evanston 1951.
Horkheimer, Max. *Kritische Theorie.* 2d ed. 2 vols. Frankfurt 1972.
———. "Ideologie und Handeln," *in* Max Horkheimer and Theodor W. Adorno. *Sociologica II*, 38ff. 3d ed. Frankfurt 1973.
Huntington, Samuel P. *Political Order in Changing Societies.* 2d ed. New Haven 1969.
Kodjo, Samuel. *Probleme der Akkulturation in Afrika.* Meisenheim/Glan 1973.
———. "Bildungsqualität als Schwerpunkt künftiger entwicklungstheoretischer Diskussion und Forschung." *Kölner Zeitschrift für Soziologie und Sozialpsychologie* 26 (1974):
287–300.
König, René. "Über einige offene Fragen und ungelöste Probleme der Entwicklungsforschung," *in* René König (ed.). *Aspekte der Entwicklungssoziologie.* Cologne and Opladen
1969.
Lane, Peter. *The Industrial Revolution: The Birth of the Modern Age.* London 1978.
Leclerc, Gérard. *Anthropologie und Kolonialismus.* Munich 1973.
Lerner, D. *The Passing of Traditional Society: Modernizing the Middle East.* New York 1966.
Ludz, Peter Christian. "Ideologieforschung: Eine Rückbesinnung und ein Neu-Beginn."
Kölner Zeitschrift für Soziologie und Sozialpsychologie 29 (1977): 1–31.
Luhmann, Niklas. *Funktion der Religion.* Frankfurt 1977.
Marx, Karl, and Friedrich Engels. *Über Religion.* East Berlin 1958.
Matus, Gustavo L. "Der Status der Nation und das internationale Schichtungssystem," *in*
Peter Heintz (ed.). *Soziologie der Entwicklungsländer.* Cologne and Berlin 1962.
Mies, Maria. "Kulturanomie als Folge westlicher Bildung." *Die Dritte Welt* 1, no. 1 (1972):
23–38.
Mirbach, Thomas. *Kritik der Herrschaft: Zum Verhältnis von Geschichtsphilosophie, Ideologiekritik
und Methodenreflexion in der Gesellschaftstheorie Adornos.* Frankfurt 1979.
Moore, Barrington, Jr. *Social Origins of Dictatorship and Democracy: Lord and Peasant in the
Making of the Modern World.* Boston 1966.
Mühlmann, Wilhelm E. *Chiliasmus und Nativismus.* Berlin 1961.
———. Rassen, Ethnien, Kulturen: Moderne Ethnologie. Neuwied 1964.
Parin, Paul. *Der Widerspruch im Subjekt: Ethnopsychoanalytische Studien.* Frankfurt 1978.
Ribeiro, Darcy. *Der zivilisatorische Prozess.* Frankfurt 1971.
Rotter, Frank. *Verfassung und sozialer Wandel: Studien zur systemtheoretischen Rechtssoziologie.*
Hamburg 1974.
Ryan, Bryce. "Die Bedeutung der Revitalisierungsbewegungen für den sozialen Wandel in
den Entwicklungsländern," *in* René König (ed.). *Aspekte der Entwicklungssoziologie.*
Cologne and Opladen 1969.
Service, Elman R. *Origins of the State and Civilization: The Process of Cultural Evolution.* New
York 1975.
Shils, Edward. "The Intellectuals in the Political Development of the New States," *in* John
H. Kautsky (ed.). *Political Change in Underdeveloped Countries*, 195–234. 7th ed. New
York 1967.
Sigmund, Paul S. *The Ideologies of Developing Nations.* 2d ed. New York 1967.
Simson, Uwe. *Auswärtige Kulturpolitik als Entwicklungspolitik: Probleme der kulturellen Kommunikation mit der Dritten Welt am Beispiel des arabischen Raums.* Meisenheim/Glan 1975.

Smith, Donald E. (ed.). *Religion and Political Modernization*. New Haven and London 1974.

Tibi, Bassam. *Arab Nationalism: A Critical Enquiry*, Marion Farouk-Sluglett and Peter Sluglett, eds. and trans. London 1981.

———. "Die feudalistische Weltordnung und die Neue Internationale Wirtschaftsordnung." *Die Neue Gesellschaft* 25, no. 9 (1978): 718–27.

———. *Internationale Politik und Entwicklungsländer-Forschung: Materialien zu einer ideologiekritischen Entwicklungssoziologie*. Frankfurt 1979.

———. *Militär und Sozialismus in der Dritten Welt: Allgemeine Theorien und Regionalstudien über arabische Länder*. Frankfurt 1973.

———. "Schwache Institutionalisierung als politische Dimension der Unterentwicklung." *Verfassung und Recht in Übersee* 13, no. 1 (1980): 3–26.

———. "Unterentwicklung als kulturelle Traditionalität? Eisenstadts Beitrag zur makrosoziologischen Forschung." *Soziologische Revue* 3, no. 2 (1980): 121–31.

———. "Widerstandsrecht in rechtlosen Gesellschaften: Friedensforschung und Dritte Welt." *Gegenwartskunde* 28, no. 3 (1979): 283–97.

———, and V. Brandes (eds.). *Unterentwicklung. Handbuch II, Politische Ökonomie*. Frankfurt and Cologne 1975.

Wallace, Anthony F. C. *Religion: An Anthropological View*. New York 1966.

Wittfogel, Karl A. *Die orientalische Despotie: Eine vergleichende Untersuchung totaler Macht*. Cologne 1962.

Zimmerman, Gerd. *Sozialer Wandel und ökonomische Entwicklung*. Stuttgart 1969.

Arabic Sources on Modern Islam

ʿAbd al-Raziq, ʿAli. *Al-Islam wa usul al-hukm* (Der Islam und die Regierungsformen). Reprint. Beirut 1966.

ʿAbd al-Salam, Faruq. *Al-ahzab al-siyasiyya wa al-fasl bayn al-din wa al-siyasa* (Die politischen Parteien und die Trennung zwischen Religion und Politik). Cairo 1979.

al-Afghani, Jamal al-Din. *Al-aʿmal al-kamila li Jamal al-Din al-Afghani*, M. ʿAmmara, ed. Cairo 1968.

Ali, Saʿid I. *Usul al-tarbiya al-islamiyya* (Grundzüge der islamischen Erziehung). Cairo 1978.

Arslan, Shekib. *Limadha taʾakhara al-muslimun wa taqaddama ghayrahum*. Reprint. Beirut 1965. English translation: *Our Decline and Its Causes*. 2d ed. London 1952.

al-ʿAzm, Sadiq Jalal. *Naqd al-fikr al-dini* (Kritik des religiösen Denkens). Beirut 1969.

al-Duri, ʿAbd al-ʿAziz. *Al-gudhur al-taʾrikhiyya li al-qawmiyya al-ʿarabiyya* (Die historischen Wurzeln des arabischen Nationalismus). Beirut 1960.

———. *Muqaddima fi al-taʾrikh al-iqtisadi al-ʿarabi* (Einführung in die arabische Wirtschaftsgeschichte). Beirut 1969.

El-Bahey, Muhammed. *Al-din wa al-hadara al-insaniyya* (Die Religion und die Kultur der Menschheit). Cairo n.d.

———. *Al-fikr al-islami al-hadith wa silatuhu bi al-istiʿmar al-gharbi* (Das moderne islamische Denken und seine Beziehung zum westlichen Imperialismus). 4th ed. Cairo 1964.

Fakiki, ʿAbd al-hadi. *Al-shuʿubiyya wa al-qawmiyya al-ʿarabiyya* (Die Ausländerei und der arabische Nationalismus). Beirut 1963?

Garisha, ʿAli M., and Muhammed S. Zaybaq. *Asalib al-ghazu al-fikri li al-ʿalam al-islami* (Methoden der intellektuellen Invasion der islamischen Welt). 2d ed. Medina 1978.

Khashab, Ahmad. *Al-ijtima' al-dini* (Religionssoziologie). 2d ed. Cairo 1964 (1st ed. 1959).

Mahmud, ʿAbd al-Halim. *Al-jihad wa al-nasr* (Der heilige Kampf und der Sieg). Cairo 1968.

al-Qurdawi, Yusuf. *Al-hal al-islami, farida wa darura* (Die islamische Lösung ist eine Pflicht und eine Notwendigkeit). Beirut 1974.

al-Salih, Subhi. *Maʿalim al-shariʿa al-islamiyya* (Grundzüge des islamischen Rechts). Beirut 1975.

Shishakli, Muhsin. *Dirasat fi al-mujtamaʿ al-ʿarabi* (Studien über die arabische Gesellschaft). 2 vols. Aleppo 1965.

Tisini, Tayeb. *Mashruʿ ru'ya jadida li al-fikr al-ʿarabi fi al-ʿasr al-wasit* (Entwurf für eine neue Sicht des arabischen Denkens im Mittelalter). Damascus n.d.

Tuʿayma, Sabir. *Al-Shariʿa al-islamiyya fi ʿasr al-ʿilm* (Das islamische Recht im Zeitalter der Wissenschaft). Beirut 1979.

Tuffaha, Ahmad Z. *Al-mar'a wa al-Islam* (Die Frau und der Islam). Cairo and Beirut 1979.

Yasin, Abu ʿAli. "Muharramayn: Al-din wa al-jins" (Zwei Tabus: Die Religion und die Sexualität). *Dirasat ʿarabiyya* (Beirut) 7, no. 1 (1970): 2–16.

Yusuf, Mohammed ʿAli. *Al-jafwa al-mufta'ala bayn al-din wa al-ʿilm* (Die unterstellte Kluft zwischen Wissenschaft und Religion). Beirut 1966.

Western Works on Islam

Adams, Charles C. *Islam and Modernism in Egypt: A Study of the Modern Reform Movement, Inaugurated by Muhammad ʿAbduh.* 2d ed. New York 1968 (1st ed. 1933).

Anderson, J. N. D. *Islamic Law in Africa.* 3d ed. London 1978.

Anderson, Norman. *Law Reform in the Muslim World.* London 1976.

Arkoun, Mohammed. *Essais sur la pensée Islamique.* Paris 1977.

———, and L. Gardet. *L'Islam Hier-Demain.* Paris 1978.

———, et al. *Pilgerfahrt nach Mekka* (Bildband). Zurich 1978.

Arnold, Sir Thomas W. *The Caliphate.* 2d ed. London 1965.

Becker, C. H. *Islamstudien: Vom Werden und Wesen der islamischen Welt.* 2d ed. 2 vols. Hildesheim 1967 (1st ed. Leipzig 1924 and 1932).

Behrman, Lucy C. *Muslim Brotherhoods and Politics in Senegal.* Cambridge, Mass. 1970.

Bell, Richard. *The Origins of Islam in its Christian Environment.* 2d ed. London 1968 (1st ed. 1926).

———, and W. M. Watt. *Introduction to the Qur'an.* 2d ed. Edinburgh 1977.

Bloch, Ernst. *Avicenna und die Aristotelische Linke.* Frankfurt 1963.

Borthwick, Bruce M. "Religion and Politics in Israel and in Egypt." *The Middle East Journal* 33, no. 2 (1979): 145–63.

Carré, Olivier. *La légitimation islamique des socialismes arabes.* Paris 1979.

Coulsen, N. J. *A History of Islamic Law.* 3d ed. Edinburgh 1978.

Crecelius, Daniel. "The Course of Secularization in Modern Egypt," *in* Donald E. Smith (ed.). *Religion and Political Modernization,* 67–94. New Haven and London 1974.

Crone, Patricia, and Michael Cook. *Hagarism: The Making of the Islamic World.* Cambridge 1977.

Ende, Werner. *Arabische Nation und islamische Geschichte.* Beirut 1977.

———. "The Flagellations of Muharram and the Shiʿite Ulema." *Der Islam* 55 (1978): 19–36.

Gibb, H. A. R. *Islam*. 3d ed. Oxford 1978.

Green, Arnold H. *The Tunisian Ulama, 1873–1951: Social Structure and Response to Ideological Currents*. Leiden 1978.

Grunebaum, Gustav E. von. *Studien zum Kulturbild und Selbstverständnis des Islam*. Zurich and Stuttgart 1969.

Habib, John S. *Ibn Saʿud's Warriors of Islam: The Ikhwan of Nagd and Their Role in the Creation of the Saʿudi Kingdom 1910–1930*. Leiden 1978.

al-Hallaj, Husayn Ibn Mansur. *Märtyrer der Gottesliebe*, Annemarie Schimmel, trans. and ed. Cologne 1968.

Hartmann, Richard. "Die Wahhabiten." *Zeitschrift der Deutschen Morgenländischen Gesellschaft* 78, no. 2 (1924): 176–213.

Hiskett, Mervyn. "The Development of Islam in Hausaland," *in* Michael Brett (ed.). *Northern Africa: Islam and Modernization*, 57–64. London 1973.

Hodgson, Marshall G. S. *The Venture of Islam*. 3 vols. Chicago 1974.

Holt, P. M., A. K. S. Lambton, and B. Lewis (eds.). *The Cambridge History of Islam*. 2 vols. Cambridge 1970.

Hourani, Albert. *Arabic Thought in the Liberal Age, 1798–1939*. London 1962.

Jafri, S. Husain M. *The Origins and Early Development of Shiʿa Islam*. London 1979.

Keddie, Nikki (ed.). *An Islamic Response to Imperialism*. Berkeley and Los Angeles 1968.

———. *Sayyid Jamal ad-Din "al-Afghani"*. Berkeley and Los Angeles 1972.

——— (ed.). *Scholars, Saints and Sufis: Muslim Religious Institutions in the Middle East since 1500*. Berkeley and Los Angeles 1972.

Kedouri, Elie. *Afghani and Abduh*. London 1966.

Khalid, Detlev. "Muslims and the Purport of Secularism." *Islam and the Modern Age*. 5, no. 2 (1974): 28–40.

———. "Das Phänomen der Re-Islamisierung." *Aussenpolitik* 29 (1978): 430–51.

———. "Das Wiedererstarken des Islam als Faktor sozialer Umwälzung." *Aus Politik und Zeitgeschichte* 10 (March 1979): 3–17.

Klein, Martin A. *Islam and Imperialism in Senegal*. Stanford 1968.

Laban, Abdel Moneim. *Einige Aspekte der Akkulturation und des sozialen Wandels in Ägypten von 1900 bis 1952*. Frankfurt 1977.

Laroui, Abdallah. *The Crisis of the Arab Intellectual: Traditionalism or Historism*. Berkeley and Los Angeles 1976.

Lewis, Bernard. *The Middle East and the West*. 2d ed. New York 1966.

———. *Race and Color in Islam*. 2d ed. New York 1977.

——— (ed.). *Islam*. 2 vols. New York 1974.

Mitchell, Richard P. *The Society of the Muslim Brothers*. London 1969.

Muslehuddin, Muhammad. *Philosophy of Islamic Law and the Orientalists: A Comparative Study of the Islamic Legal Systems*. Lahore n.d.

Nasr, Seyyed H. *Islam and the Plight of Modern Man*. London 1975.

Noth, Albrecht. "Möglichkeiten und Grenzen islamischer Toleranz." *Saeculum* 29, no. 2 (1978): 190–204.

O'Brien, Donal B. C. *The Mourides of Senegal: The Political and Economic Organization of an Islamic Brotherhood*. London 1971.

Paret, Rudi. *Der Koran: Kommentar und Konkordanz*. 2d ed. Stuttgart 1977.

———. *Mohammed und der Koran: Geschichte und Verkündigung des arabischen Propheten*. 4th ed. Stuttgart 1976.

——— (ed.). *Der Koran, Deutsche Übersetzung*. Stuttgart 1979.

Rahman, Fazlur. *Islam*. 2d ed. Chicago 1979.

Rodinson, Maxime. *Islam und Kapitalismus*. Frankfurt 1971.

————. *Mohammed*, Anne Carter, trans. New York 1971.

Rondot, Pierre. *Der Islam und die Mohammedaner von heute*. Stuttgart 1963.

Rosenthal, Erwin I. J. *Islam in the Modern National State*. Cambridge 1965.

Said, Edward W. *Orientalism*. London 1978.

Schacht, Joseph. *An Introduction to Islamic Law*. 5th ed. London 1979.

————, and C. E. Bosworth (eds.). *The Legacy of Islam*. London 1974.

Spittler, Gert. *Herrschaft über Bauern: Die Ausbreitung staatlicher Herrschaft und einer islamisch-urbanen Kultur in Gobir (Niger)*. Frankfurt 1978.

Srour, Hani. *Die Staats- und Gesellschaftstheorie bei S. G. "Al-Afghani"*. Freiburg/Breisgau 1977.

Stoddart, William. *Sufism: The Mystical Doctrines and Methods of Islam*. Wellingborough, Northhamptonshire 1976.

Tabataba'i, Allamah Sayyid M. H. *Shi'ite Islam* (translated from the Persian by Sayyed H. Nasr). London 1975.

Tibi, Bassam. "Akkulturationsprozesse im modernen Orient." *Neue politische Literatur* 15, no. 1 (1970): 77–84.

————. "Islam and Secularization: Religion and the Functional Differentiation of the Social System." *Archiv für Rechts- und Sozialphilosophie* 66, no. 2 (1980): 207–22.

————. "Religion und sozialer Wandel: Bemerkungen zur modernen islamischen Apologetik," *in* Bassam Tibi. *Internationale Politik und Entwicklungsländer-Forschung*, 136–41. Frankfurt 1979.

————. "Religionsstiftung, Islam und Psychoanalyse." *Psyche: Zeitschrift für Psychoanalyse und ihre Anwendungen* 33, no. 8 (1979): 773–83.

————. "Trade Unions as an Organizational Form of Political Opposition in Afro-Arab States." *Orient* 20, no. 4 (1979): 75–91.

————. "Zum Verhältnis von Religion, Politik und Staat in islamisch legitimierten Monarchien." *Orient* 21, no. 2 (1980): 158–74.

Tisini, Tayeb. *Die Materieauffassung in der islamisch- arabischen Philosophie des Mittelalters*. East Berlin 1972.

Trimingham, J. S. *A History of Islam in West Africa*. 5th ed. Oxford 1978.

————. *The Influence of Islam upon Africa*. 2d ed. London and Beirut 1980 (1st ed. 1968).

Turner, Bryan S. *Weber and Islam*. London 1974.

Watt, W. M. *The Formative Period of Islamic Thought*. Edinburgh 1973.

————. *Islamic Philosophy and Theology*. 5th ed. Edinburgh 1979.

————. *Islamic Political Thought: The Basic Concepts*. Edinburgh 1968.

————. *Islamic Revelation in the Modern World*. Edinburgh 1969.

————. *Muhammad: Prophet and Statesman*. 4th ed. Oxford 1978.

————. *Muhammad at Medina*. 6th ed. London 1977.

————. *What Is Islam?* London and New York 1979 (1st ed. 1968).

Wielandt, Rotraud. *Offenbarung und Geschichte im Denken moderner Muslime*. Wiesbaden 1971.

Wild, Stefan. "Gott und Mensch im Libanon: Die Affäre Sadiq al-Azm." *Der Islam* 48 (1972): 206–53.

Addendum

Baljon, J. M. S. *Modern Muslim Koran Interpretation (1880–1960)*. Leiden 1968.

Braukämper, Ulrich. *Der Einfluss des Islam auf die Geschichte und Kulturentwicklung Adamaus*. Wiesbaden 1970.

Fitzgerald, M., et al. (eds.). *Islam und Westliche Welt*. Vol. 1, *Moslems und Christen*; vol. 2, *Mensch, Welt, Staat im Islam*. Graz and Vienna 1976–77.

Geertz, Clifford. *Islam Observed: Religious Development in Morocco and Indonesia*. New Haven 1968.

Hodgkin, Thomas. "The Revolutionary Tradition in Islam." *Race and Class* 21, no. 3 (1980): 221–37.

Klein, F. A. *The Religion of Islam*. 3d ed. London and New York 1979 (1st ed. 1906).

Jansen, J. J. G. *The Interpretation of the Koran in Modern Egypt*. Leiden 1974.

Le Gassick, Trevor J. *Major Themes in Modern Arabic Thought: An Anthology*. Ann Arbor 1979.

Mörth, Ingo. *Die gesellschaftliche Wirklichkeit von Religion: Grundlegung einer allgemeinen Religionstheorie*. Stuttgart 1978.

Sivan, Emmanuel. *Radical Islam*. New Haven 1986.

Sivers, Peter von. "National Integration and Traditional Rural Organization in Algeria 1970–1980: Background for Islamic Traditionalism?" *in* S. Arjomand (ed.). *From Nationalism to Revolutionary Islam*. Albany and New York 1984.

Tibi, Bassam. "The Interplay between Cultural and Socio-Economic Change," *in* Klaus Gottstein (ed.). *Islamic Cultural Identity and Scientific-Technological Development*. Baden Baden 1987.

———. "The Iranian Revolution and the Arabs: The Quest for Islamic Identity and the Search for an Islamic System of Government," *Arab Studies Quarterly* 8, no. 1 (1986): 29–44.

———. "Islam and Arab Nationalism," *in* Barbara Stowasser (ed.). *The Islamic Impulse*. London 1987.

———. "Islam and Modern European Ideologies," *International Journal of Middle Eastern Studies* 18, no. 1 (1986): 15–29.

———. *Der Islam und das Problem der kulturellen Bewältigung sozialen Wandels*. Frankfurt 1985.

———. "The Renewed Role of Islam in the Political and Social Development of the Middle East," *The Middle East Journal* 37, no. 1 (1983): 3–13.

———. *Vom Gottesreich zum Nationalstaat: Islam und panarabischer Nationalismus*. Frankfurt 1987.

Trimingham, J. Spencer. *The Sufi Orders in Islam*. Oxford 1971.

INDEX